PLATINUM EDITION

2

Series Director: Diane Larsen-Freeman

GRAMMAR DIMENSIONS

FORM, MEANING, and USE

Heidi Riggenbach
University of Washington

Virginia Samuda

THOMSON

HEINLE

Australia Canada Mexico Singapore Spain United Kingdom United States

Acquisitions Editor: Eric Bredenberg
Senior Developmental Editor: Amy Lawler
Production Editor: Michael Burggren
Senior Marketing Manager: Charlotte Sturdy
Manufacturing Coordinator: Mary Beth Hennebury
Composition/Project Management: The PRD Group, Inc.
Text Design: Sue Gerould, Perspectives
Cover Design: Hannus Design Associates

For permission to use material from this text, contact us:
web   www.thomsonrights.com
fax   1-800-730-2215
phone   1-800-730-2214

Heinle
25 Thomson Place
Boston, MA 02210

AUSTRALIA/NEW ZEALAND:
Nelson/Thomson Learning
102 Dodds Street
South Melbourne
Victoria 3205 Australia

CANADA:
Nelson/Thomson Learning
1120 Birchmount Road
Scarborough, Ontario
Canada M1K 5G4

UK/EUROPE/MIDDLE EAST:
Thomson Learning
Berkshire House
168-173 High Holborn
London, WC1V 7AA, United Kingdom

LATIN AMERICA:
Thomson Learning
Seneca, 53
Colonia Polanco
11560 México D.F. México

SPAIN:
Thomson Learning
Calle Magallanes, 25
28015-Madrid
Espana

ASIA (excluding Japan):
Thomson Learning
5 Shenton Way #01-01
UIC Building
Singapore 068808

JAPAN:
Thomson Learning
Nihonjisyo Brooks Bldg. 3-F
1-4-1 Kudankita
Chiyoda-ku
Tokyo 102-0073, Japan

ISBN: 0-8384-0268-2

 This book is printed on acid-free recycled paper.

Printed in the United States of America
6 7 8 9   04 03

TOEFL® is a registered trademark of Educational Testing Service (ETS). This product is not endorsed or approved by ETS.

A Special Thanks

The series director, authors, and publisher would like to thank the following individuals who offered many helpful insights and suggestions for change throughout the development of *Grammar Dimensions*.

Jane Berger
Solano Community College, California
Mary Bottega
San Jose State University
Mary Brooks
Eastern Washington University
Christina Broucqsault
California State Polytechnic University
José Carmona
Hudson Community College
Susan Carnell
University of Texas at Arlington
Susana Christie
San Diego State University
Diana Christopher
Georgetown University
Gwendolyn Cooper
Rutgers University
Sue Cozzarelli
EF International, San Diego
Catherine Crystal
Laney College, California
Kevin Cross
University of San Francisco
Julie Damron
Interlink at Valparaiso University, Indiana
Glen Deckert
Eastern Michigan University
Eric Dwyer
University of Texas at Austin
Ann Eubank
Jefferson Community College
Alice Fine
UCLA Extension
Alicia Going
The English Language Study Center, Oregon
Molly Gould
University of Delaware
Maren M. Hargis
San Diego Mesa College
Mary Herbert
University of California, Davis Extension

Jane Hilbert
ELS Language Center, Florida International University
Eli Hinkel
Xavier University
Kathy Hitchcox
International English Institute, Fresno
Joyce Hutchings
Georgetown University
Heather Jeddy
Northern Virginia Community College
Judi Keen
University of California, Davis, and Sacramento City College
Karli Kelber
American Language Institute, New York University
Anne Kornfeld
LaGuardia Community College
Kay Longmire
Interlink at Valparaiso University, Indiana
Robin Longshaw
Rhode Island School of Design
Bernadette McGlynn
ELS Language Center, St. Joseph's University
Billy McGowan
Aspect International, Boston
Margaret Mehran
Queens College
Richard Moore
University of Washington
Karen Moreno
Teikyo Post University, Connecticut
Gino Muzzetti
Santa Rosa Junior College, California
Mary Nance-Tager
LaGuardia Community College, City University of New York
Karen O'Neill
San Jose State University
Mary O'Neal
Northern Virginia Community College

Nancy Pagliara
Northern Virginia Community College
Keith Pharis
Southern Illinois University
Amy Parker
ELS Language Center, San Francisco
Margene Petersen
ELS Language Center, Philadelphia
Nancy Pfingstag
University of North Carolina, Charlotte
Sally Prieto
Grand Rapids Community College
India Plough
Michigan State University
Mostafa Rahbar
University of Tennessee at Knoxville
Dudley Reynolds
Indiana University
Ann Salzman
University of Illinois at Urbana-Champaign
Jennifer Schmidt
San Francisco State University
Cynthia Schuemann
Miami-Dade Community College
Jennifer Schultz
Golden Gate University, California
Mary Beth Selbo
Wright College, City Colleges of Chicago
Stephen Sheeran
Bishop's University, Lenoxville, Quebec
Kathy Sherak
San Francisco State University
Keith Smith
ELS Language Center, San Francisco
Helen Solorzano
Northeastern University

Contents

Unit 11 Modals of Necessity and Prohibition   166

Unit 12 Expressing Likes and Dislikes   184

A Word from Diane Larsen-Freeman, Series Director

Before **Grammar Dimensions** was published, teachers would always ask me, "What is the role of grammar in a communicative approach?" These teachers recognized the importance of teaching grammar, but they associated grammar with form and communication with meaning, and thus could not see how the two easily fit together. **Grammar Dimensions** was created to help teachers and students appreciate the fact that grammar is not just about form. While grammar does indeed involve form, in order to communicate, language users also need to know the meaning of the forms and when to use them appropriately. In fact, it is sometimes not the form, but the *meaning* or *appropriate use* of a grammatical structure that represents the greatest long-term learning challenge for students. For instance, learning when it is appropriate to use the present perfect tense instead of the past tense, or being able to use two-word or phrasal verbs meaningfully, represent formidable challenges for ESL students.

The three dimensions of form, meaning, and use can be depicted in a pie chart with their interrelationship illustrated by the three arrows:

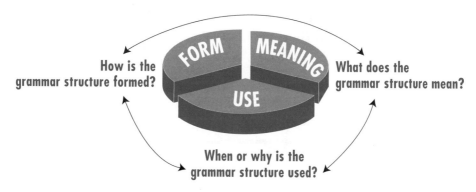

Helping students learn to use grammatical structures accurately, meaningfully, and appropriately is the fundamental goal of **Grammar Dimensions.** It is consistent with the goal of helping students to communicate meaningfully in English, and one that recognizes the undeniable interdependence of grammar and communication.

Enjoy the Platinum Edition!

To learn more about form, meaning, and use, read **The Grammar Book: An ESL/EFL Teacher's Course,** Second Edition, by Marianne Celce-Murcia and Diane Larsen-Freeman, also from Heinle & Heinle. It helps both prospective and practicing teachers of ESL/EFL enhance their understanding of English grammar, expand their skills in linguistic analysis, and develop a pedagogical approach to teaching English grammar that builds on the three dimensions. ISBN: 0-8384-4725-2.

Welcome to Grammar Dimensions, Platinum Edition!
The most comprehensive communicative grammar series available.

Updated and revised, *Grammar Dimensions, Platinum Edition,* makes teaching grammar easy and more effective than ever. Clear grammar explanations, a wealth of exercises, lively communicative activities, and fully annotated Teacher's Editions help both beginning and experienced teachers give their students the practice and skills they need to communicate accurately, meaningfully, and appropriately.

Grammar Dimensions, Platinum Edition, is:

Communicative	• Students practice the **form, meaning,** and **use** of each grammar structure.
	• **Improved! A variety of communicative activities** helps students practice grammar and communication in tandem, eliciting self-expression and personalized practice.
	• Students learn to communicate accurately, meaningfully, and appropriately.
Comprehensive	• **Improved!** Grammar is presented in **clear charts.**
	• **A wealth of exercises** helps students practice and master their new language.
	• **The Workbook** provides extra practice and helps students prepare for the TOEFL® Test.
	• **Engaging listening activities** on audiocassette further reinforce the target structure.
Clear	• **Improved! Simplified grammar explanations** help both students and teachers easily understand and comprehend each language structure.
	• **Improved! A fresh new design** makes each activity engaging.
	• **New! Communicative activities** ("the Purple Pages") are now labeled with the skill being practiced.
	• **New!** The Teacher's Edition has **page references** for the Student Book and Workbook, minimizing extra preparation time.

User-Friendly for Students	• **Contextualized grammar explanations and examples** help students understand the target language.
	• **New! Goals** at the beginning of each unit focus students' attention on the learning they will do.
	• **Sample phrases and sentences** model the appropriate use of the structure.
User-Friendly for Teachers	• **New!** Teacher's Edition now contains answers, tests, tape scripts, and complete, **step-by-step teaching suggestions** for every activity.
	• **New!** "Purple Page" activities are now labeled with the skill.
	• **Improved! A tight integration** among the Student Book, the Workbook and the Teacher's Edition make extension activities easy to do.
Flexible	• Instructors can use the units in order or as set by their curriculum.
	• Exercises can be used in order or as needed by the students.
	• "Purple Page" activities can be used at the end of the unit or interspersed throughout the unit.
Effective	Students who learn the form, meaning, and use of each grammar structure will be able to communicate more accurately, meaningfully, and appropriately.

Grammar Dimensions, Platinum Edition

With *Grammar Dimensions, Platinum Edition,* students progress from the sentence level to the discourse level, and learn to communicate appropriately at all levels.

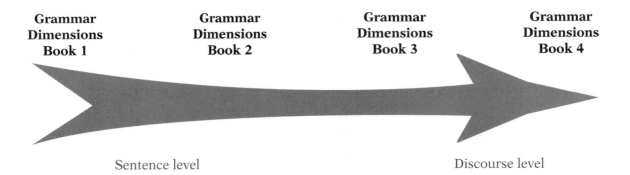

Grammar Dimensions Book 1   Grammar Dimensions Book 2   Grammar Dimensions Book 3   Grammar Dimensions Book 4

Sentence level   Discourse level

	Grammar Dimensions, Book 1	**Grammar Dimensions, Book 2**	**Grammar Dimensions, Book 3**	**Grammar Dimensions, Book 4**
Level	High beginning	Intermediate	High intermediate	Advanced
Grammar level	Sentence and subsentence level	Sentence and subsentence level	Discourse level	Discourse level
Primary language and communication focus	Semantic notions such as *time* and *place*	Social functions, such as *making requests* and *seeking permission*	Cohesion and coherence at the discourse level	Academic and technical discourse
Major skill focus	Listening and speaking	Listening and speaking	Reading and writing	Reading and writing
Outcome	Students form accurate, meaningful, and appropriate structures at the sentence level.	Students form accurate, meaningful, and appropriate structures at the sentence level.	Students learn how accurate, meaningful, and appropriate grammatical structures contribute to the organization of language above the simple sentence.	Students learn how accurate, meaningful, and appropriate grammatical structures contribute to the organization of language above the simple sentence.

Unit Organization

Used with or without the Workbook and the *Grammar 3D* CD-ROM, *Grammar Dimensions* Student Book units are designed to be clear, comprehensive, flexible, and communicative.

Goals	• **Focus students' attention** on the learning they will do in each unit.
Opening Task	• **Contextualizes** the target grammatical structure. • **Enables teachers to diagnose** their students' performance and identify the aspect of the structure with which their students have the most difficulty. • **Provides a roadmap** for the grammar points students need to work on in that chapter.
Focus Boxes	• **Present the form, meaning,** or **use** of a particular grammatical structure. • **Focus students' attention** to a particular feature of the target structure. Each rule or explanation is preceded by examples, so teachers can have students work inductively to try to discover the rule on their own.
Exercises	• Provide a wealth of opportunity to **practice** the form and meaning of the grammar structures. • Help students develop the skill of **"grammaring"**—the ability to use structures accurately, meaningfully, and appropriately. • Are varied, thematically coherent, but purposeful. • Give students many opportunities to personalize and own the language.
Communicative Activities ("The Purple Pages")	• Help students practice **grammar and communication in tandem.** • **Are engaging!** • Encourage students to **use their new language** both inside and outside the classroom. • Provide an opportunity to **practice reading, writing, listening, and speaking skills,** helping students realize the communicative value of the grammar they are learning.

Student Book Supplements

Audiocassettes	• **Provide listening activities for** each unit so students can practice listening to **grammar structures in context.**
Workbooks	• **Provide additional exercises** for each grammar point presented in the student text.
	• Offer question types found on the TOEFL® Test.
Teacher's Editions	• **Facilitate teaching** by providing in one place notes and examples, answer keys to the Student Book and Workbook, page references to all of the components, the tapescript for the audiocassette activities, and tests with answer keys for each unit.
	• **Minimize teacher preparation time** by providing step-by-step teaching suggestions for every focus box and activity in the Student Book.

The *Grammar Dimensions, Platinum Edition* Student Books and the additional components help teachers teach and students learn to use English grammar structures in communication accurately, meaningfully, and appropriately.

Acknowledgments

Series Director Acknowledgments

This edition would not have come about if it had not been for the enthusiastic response of teachers and students using the previous editions. I am very grateful for the reception **Grammar Dimensions** has been given.

I am also grateful for all the authors' efforts. To be a teacher, and at the same time a writer, is a difficult balance to achieve . . . so is being an innovative creator of materials, and yet, a team player. They have met these challenges exceedingly well in my opinion. Then, too, the Heinle & Heinle team has been impressive. I am grateful for the leadership exercised by Erik Gundersen, formerly of Heinle & Heinle. I also appreciate all the support from Charlotte Sturdy, Eric Bredenberg, Mike Burggren, Mary Beth Hennebury, and Marianne Bartow. Deserving special mention are Amy Lawler and Nancy Jordan, who never lost the vision while they attended to the detail with good humor and professionalism.

I have also benefited from the counsel of Marianne Celce-Murcia, consultant for the first edition this project, and my friend. Finally, I wish to thank my family members, Elliott, Brent, and Gavin, for not once asking the (negative yes–no) question that must have occurred to them countless times: "Haven't you finished yet?"

Author Acknowledgments

We'd like to give very special thanks to our families, to our friends and above all, to each other, for hanging in through this.

UNIT 1

SIMPLE PRESENT

Habits, Routines, and Facts

UNIT GOALS:

- To know when to use simple present tense
- To form simple present tense correctly
- To understand the meanings of various adverbs of frequency
- To place adverbs of frequency in correct sentence position

▶ OPENING TASK
How Do You Learn Grammar?

STEP 1 Read each statement about learning English grammar.
Circle the number that describes you best.

1 = never   2 = rarely   3 = sometimes   4 = often   5 = always

1.	I study grammar books and memorize the rules.	1 2 3 4 5
2.	I read newspapers, watch TV and movies, and listen to songs.	1 2 3 4 5
3.	I use English as much as possible to practice the grammar I know.	1 2 3 4 5
4.	I observe native speakers in different situations and notice what they say and do.	1 2 3 4 5
5.	When I don't know how to say something perfectly, I don't say anything at all.	1 2 3 4 5
6.	I don't worry about making mistakes because I learn from them.	1 2 3 4 5
7.	I learn better when I work in groups with my classmates.	1 2 3 4 5
8.	When a teacher uses words I don't understand, I ask for help.	1 2 3 4 5
9.	When I don't know how to say something, I try to say it another way.	1 2 3 4 5
10.	I think of grammar rules when I speak.	1 2 3 4 5

STEP 2 Compare your answers with another student. Do you like to learn English grammar in the same ways? In what ways are you similar and in what ways are you different? Use the chart below to write down your similarities and differences.

SIMILARITIES	DIFFERENCES

STEP 3 Use the chart to tell the rest of the class how you and your partner learn English grammar.

FOCUS **1**

▶ **Verbs in the Simple Present Tense**

Habits and Routines

EXAMPLES	EXPLANATIONS
(a) I **ask** questions when I **do not understand.**	*Ask, do not understand*, and *uses* are simple present verbs.
(b) Elzbieta **uses** English as much as possible.	Use the simple present to talk about habits (things you do again and again).
(c) Our classes **start** at 9:00 A.M.	Use the simple present to talk about everyday routines (things you do regularly).
(d) Daniela **goes** to school five days aweek.	

EXERCISE 1

Go back to Step 1 of the Opening Task on page 1. Underline all the simple present verbs you can find. Compare your answers with a partner's.

FOCUS **2**

▶ **Simple Present Tense**

STATEMENT	NEGATIVE	QUESTION	SHORT ANSWER
I You We They } work.	I You We They } do not/don't work.	Do, { I you we they } work?	Yes, { I you we they } do.
He She It } works.	He She It } does not/doesn't work.	Does { he she it } work?	Yes, { he she it } does.
			No, { I you we they } don't.
			No, { he she it } doesn't.

EXERCISE 2

Look at what you wrote in Step 2 of the Opening Task on page 1. Underline all the simple present verbs that you used. Did you use them correctly? Check your answers with a partner and then with your teacher.

EXERCISE 3

STEP 1 What are some of the *other* things you do and do not do to learn English grammar? Complete the following, using full sentences.

Some things I do:

1. I_____

2. I_____

3. I_____

Some things I don't do:

1. I_____

2. I_____

3. I_____

STEP 2 Get together with a partner and tell each other about things you do and do not do to learn English grammar. Then, without showing your answers to each other, write about your partner here.

My partner, (name) _____

does several different things to learn English grammar. She or he ____

_____

_____

_____

STEP 3 Now get together with a different partner. Ask each other what you do to learn English grammar (*Do you . . . ?*). Together with your new partner, decide on the three most useful ways to learn English grammar. Share your ideas with the rest of the class. Write them here:

1. We _____

2. We _____

3. We _____

▶ **S**howing How Often Something Happens

Adverbs of Frequency

EXAMPLES	EXPLANATIONS

(a) Kazue **often** uses a dictionary, but Florian **never** uses one.
 	
Most Often (100%)
   ↑ always
      usually
      often
      sometimes
      seldom
      rarely
      hardly ever
   ↓ never
Least Often (0%)
	Often and *never* are adverbs of frequency. They show how often something happens.
	
	For more information on adverbs of frequency, see Unit 18, Focus 5.

(b) I **usually** get up early. **(c)** He **never** calls me.	Where to put adverbs of frequency: **before** the main verb (b and c)
(d) She is **always** happy. **(e)** They are **rarely** late.	**after** the verb *be* (d and e)

EXERCISE 4

1

2

3

4

We asked several students to describe their English classes. Read the descriptions on the next page and match each description to a picture. Write the number of the picture beside each description. Compare your answers with a partner's.

A We sit in rows and the teacher stands at the front. The teacher explains grammar rules and the students listen and take notes. Students sometimes practice their writing in class.

B Our English classes are always very relaxed. We usually work in pairs or small groups and often play games in class to practice our English. These games are a lot of fun and we sometimes laugh a lot. We don't feel nervous about speaking English when we play games.

C We often work on special projects in our English class. We use computers to find information about a topic or we interview people to see what they think. Then we make a presentation about our topic to the rest of the class.

D The students in my English class are very enthusiastic. Every time the teacher asks a question, everybody wants to answer it. We always raise our hands and hope that the teacher will choose us.

How are the classes in the photographs like (or unlike) classes in your country? First, discuss this question with your partner and then be ready to tell the rest of the class.

EXERCISE 5

STEP 1 Complete the chart about students and teachers in your country and in this country. The first one has been done for you as an example. If you do not have enough room to write your answers on the chart, copy the chart into your notebook.

	TEACHERS IN MY COUNTRY	STUDENTS IN MY COUNTRY	TEACHERS IN THIS COUNTRY	STUDENTS IN THIS COUNTRY
Usually	stand in front of the class			
Sometimes				
Hardly ever				
Never				

STEP 2   Get together with a student from another country, if possible. Ask him or her questions about teachers and students in his or her country. For example: *Tell me about teachers in your country. Do they usually give a lot of homework? Do they tell jokes in class?*

STEP 3   Look at the information from your chart and from your partner's. Use this information to make as many true sentences as you can. For example: *Students in this country never stand up when the teacher comes into the room.*

EXERCISE 6

STEP 1   Get together with a partner. Quickly look at the occupations in the box below.

OCCUPATIONS

a student	a police officer	a businessperson
secretaries	a flight attendant	a bartender
mechanics	teachers	a nurse
an architect	a bus driver	a waitress

STEP 2 Read the job descriptions below. Can you match them with the occupations in the box? Write the occupation on the line next to each description.

1. He wears a uniform and usually travels many miles a day. He serves food or drink, but he hardly ever prepares them himself. _____

2. She works in an office, but she often takes work home with her. She generally earns a high salary, but often feels a lot of stress. She sometimes entertains clients in the evening. _____

3. He usually wears a uniform and always carries a gun. He leads a dangerous life, so his job rarely gets boring. _____

4. He often works at night and meets many different people. He serves drinks and gets tips when people like his service. _____

5. She wears a uniform and drives many miles a day. She never serves food drinks. _____

6. He spends many hours in the classroom and asks questions. He always has a lot of work to do and sometimes writes on the board. _____

7. She often wears a uniform and walks many miles a day. She works very hard and does not earn very much money, although she sometimes gets generous tips. _____

8. They spend a lot of time in the classroom and like to ask questions. They often write on the board. _____

STEP 3 Now write similar descriptions for the jobs in the box that are not described above. What do these workers do?

9. _____
   _____

10. _____
   _____

11. _____
   _____

12. _____
   _____

STEP 4 On your own, think of two more jobs and write a short job description for each one.

13. _____

_____

14. _____

_____

STEP 5 Get together with another student and read your descriptions to each other. Ask and answer questions until you guess the jobs your partner has described. For example: *Does she or he . . . ? Is he or she a . . . ?*

EXERCISE 7

Sam is looking for a roommate to share his apartment, and Dave is looking for a place to live. They are trying to find out if they will get along as roommates. Complete their conversation, using verbs that fit the meaning of the sentences. Sometimes more than one answer is possible.

Sam: What do you usually do on weekends?

Dave: Well, I usually (1) ___wake up___ early, about 5:30, and then I

(2) _____ by the river for an hour or so before breakfast.

Sam: Yeah? And what (3) _____ you _____ next?

Dave: After breakfast, I (4) _____ a cold shower, and

then I usually (5) _____ my bike or I sometimes

(6) _____ tennis for a couple of hours. What (7) _____

you _____ on Saturday mornings?

Sam: I like to relax on weekends; I (8) _____ home and

(9) _____ the newspaper and (10) _____ TV.

Dave: All weekend?

Sam: No. On Sundays, I often get in my sports car and (11) _____

to the beach.

Dave: Great! I like swimming too. It's a habit that I learned from my

brother. He (12) _____ in the ocean every day of the year, even in

the winter.

Sam: Well, I rarely (13) _____ in the ocean. I usually

(14) _____ on the beach and try to get a good sun tan. Then I

(15) _____ some of my friends and we go to a nightclub and dance.

Dave: Don't you ever exercise?

Sam: Well, I (16) (not) _____ to a health club or gym, but every

Saturday night, I go to a disco and I (17) _____ for hours. That's

my idea of exercise.

Dave: Look, here's the phone number of a friend of mine. He

(18) _____ dancing and night clubs, just like you. Why don't you

give him a call and see if he wants to be your roommate?

FOCUS **4**

▶ **Talking About Facts**

EXAMPLES	EXPLANATION
(a) The sun **rises** in the east and **sets** in the west. **(b)** Brazilians **speak** Portuguese. **(c)** Water **boils** at 100° C.	Use the simple present to talk about facts (things that are true).

EXERCISE 8

STEP 1 Match the pictures to the animal names.

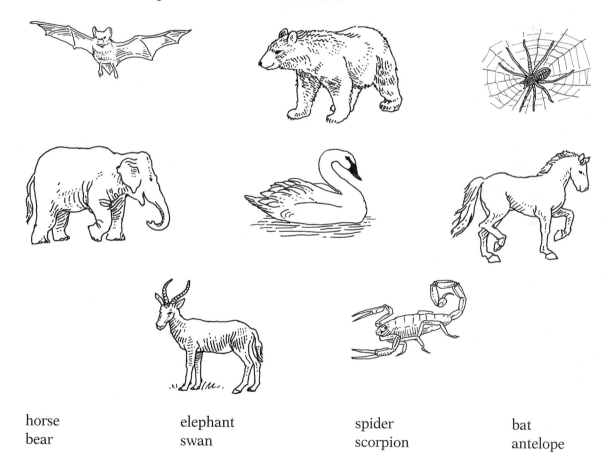

horse	elephant	spider	bat
bear	swan	scorpion	antelope

What do you know about these animals? Be ready to tell the rest of the class anything that you know.

STEP 2   Get together with a partner and draw lines connecting the animals in Column A with appropriate information about them in Column B. Don't worry if you are not sure of all the answers. With your partner, decide what you think is **probably** the best match for each piece of information.

A	B
Horses	live for about two years.
Bats	sometimes go for four days without water.
Scorpions	stay with the same mates all their lives.
Elephants	use their ears to "see."
Swans	have twelve eyes.
Antelopes	sleep during the winter months.
Bears	sleep standing up.
Spiders	run at 70 miles per hour.

STEP 3   Get together with another pair and compare your answers. When you are ready, compare your answers with the rest of the class. As a class, decide on what you think are **probably** the best answers. Then check your answers on page A-14.

STEP 4   Do you know any other unusual facts about these animals or any other animals? Tell the rest of the class about them.

Use Your English

ACTIVITY 1: SPEAKING/LISTENING

The purpose of this activity is to prove or disprove the following statements about your classmates. Stand up, walk around the room, and ask your classmates questions to see if the following are true (T) or false (F).

1.	Most of the people in this room do not eat breakfast.	T	F
2.	Women drink more coffee than men.	T	F
3.	Fifty percent of the people in this room watch TV at night.	T	F
4.	Somebody in this room wears contact lenses.	T	F
5.	More than three people read a newspaper in English every day.	T	F
6.	More than 50% of the people in this room drive a car.	T	F
7.	Nobody likes opera.	T	F
8.	More than two people here come to school by bike.	T	F
9.	Everybody gets more than six hours of sleep a night.	T	F
10.	Most of the people in this room have a sister.	T	F

ACTIVITY 2: SPEAKING/LISTENING

The purpose of this activity is to find out what North Americans usually do on certain special days.

STEP 1 Form a team with one or two other students and choose one of the special days from the chart below.

STEP 2 Tell the rest of the class which special day your team has chosen. Make sure that there is at least one team for each special day.

STEP 3 With your team, interview three different people (native speakers of English if possible) and find out what usually happens on this special day. Make notes on the chart below or in your notebook. If possible, tape-record your interviews.

STEP 4 After doing your interviews, use your notes to tell the rest of the class what your team found.

ST. PATRICK'S DAY
VALENTINE'S DAY
THANKSGIVING DAY
HALLOWEEN

STEP 5 Listen to your tape-recorded interview or use your notes to identify and write down any sentences that contain the simple present tense or adverbs of frequency.

ACTIVITY 3: LISTENING

STEP 1 Listen to the tape of people describing what they do on certain special days. Which special days do you think each speaker is talking about? Write your answers under "Special Day" in the chart below.

Speaker	Special Day	Verbs in the Simple Present Tense
Speaker 1		
Speaker 2		
Speaker 3		

STEP 2 Listen to the tape again. On the right side of the chart, write down as many examples of verbs in the simple present tense as you can.

ACTIVITY 4: SPEAKING/LISTENING/WRITING

STEP 1 Complete the following with information that is true about yourself. Write complete sentences.

Something I usually do in summer	
Something I often do on weekends	
Something I rarely do in this country	
Something I sometimes do on Fridays	

STEP 2 Memorize these four sentences about yourself.

STEP 3 Walk around the room. When your teacher tells you to stop, find the nearest person. Tell the person your four sentences and listen to that person's sentences. Then memorize each other's sentences.

STEP 4 Walk around the room. When your teacher tells you to stop, find a different person. Tell this new person about **the last person you spoke to.** Then listen to that person's sentences. Do not talk about yourself. Memorize what he or she tells you.

STEP 5 Find someone different. Tell him or her the information the last person told you. Listen to the new person's sentences. Memorize what he or she tells you.

STEP 6 Now find someone new. Continue the process for as long as possible. Remember, you always pass along the information the last person tells you. Try to speak to as many different people as possible.

STEP 7 At the end, tell the rest of the class the information you heard from the last person. Is all the information true?

ACTIVITY 5: SPEAKING/LISTENING

STEP 1 Prepare a short talk for your classmates, describing a special day or holiday that people celebrate in your country, city, or region. Talk about what people usually do on this day and how they celebrate. Don't forget to include an introduction to your talk. For example: *I am going to tell you about a very special holiday in my country. The name of the holiday is. . . .* If possible, tape your talk.

STEP 2 After you give your talk, listen to your tape. Did you use any verbs in the simple present tense? Did you use any adverbs of frequency?

ACTIVITY 6: WRITING

STEP 1 Write a description of a typical high school classroom in your country. For example, what does the room look like? Where do the students sit? Where does the teacher sit? Is there any special equipment in the room? What is on the walls? What do teachers and students usually do when they are in the classroom? In your opinion, what are the strengths (best parts) of this kind of class-room and what are the weaknesses (worst parts)?

STEP 2 When you finish, read your work carefully. Did you use any simple present verbs or adverbs of frequency?

UNIT 2

PRESENT PROGRESSIVE AND SIMPLE PRESENT

Actions and States

UNIT GOALS:
- To know when to use present progressive
- To form present progressive correctly
- To choose between simple present and present progressive
- To know which verbs are not usually used in the present progressive

▶ OPENING TASK
What's Happening?

STEP 1 Many parts of the picture on the next page are missing. Get together with a partner and decide what the whole picture is about. For example, where is this? Who are the people? What are they doing? Write your ideas in the chart below.

Where is this?	Who are the people?	What are they doing?

STEP 2 Describe what you think is happening in the picture to the rest of the class. Decide who has the most interesting explanation.

▶ **P**resent Progressive:
Actions in Progress

EXAMPLES	EXPLANATIONS
(a) Right now, I **am sitting** on the couch and my brothers **are cooking** dinner. **(b)** It **is raining** and Oscar **is waiting** for the bus.	*Am sitting* and *are cooking* are present progressive forms. Use the present progressive to describe an action that is in progress and happening at the time of speaking.
(c) This semester, I **am taking** three math classes. **(d)** Their baby **is waking up** very early these days.	Use the present progressive for an action that is happening **around** the time of speaking, but not happening **exactly** at that time.
At time of speaking: *right now* *at the moment* *today* *at present* Around time time of speaking: *this year* *this semester* *this week* *these days*	These time expressions are often used with the present progressive.

EXERCISE 1

Read the following statements about the picture in the Opening Task and decide which ones are probably true (T) and which ones are probably false (F).

  1. Somebody is eating.   **T**   **F**

  2. A customer in a restaurant is ordering a meal.   **T**   **F**

  3. Somebody is playing the piano.   **T**   **F**

  4. Somebody is reading a newspaper.   **T**   **F**

  5. Somebody is writing a letter.   **T**   **F**

  6. Somebody is talking on the telephone.   **T**   **F**

Now look at the complete picture on page A-15 at the back of this book. How many of your guesses were correct?

FOCUS 2

▶ Present Progressive

To form the present progressive, use *be* + present participle (*-ing*) of the main verb:

STATEMENT	NEGATIVE	QUESTION	SHORT ANSWER
I am (I'm) working.	I am not (I'm not) working.	Am I working?	Yes, I am. No, I'm not.
You are (you're) working.	You are not (aren't) working.	Are you working?	Yes, you are. No, you aren't. (No, you're not.)
She/He/It is (She's/He's/It's) working.	She/He/It is not (isn't) working.	Is she/he/it working?	Yes, she/he/it is. No, she/he/it isn't. (No, she's/he's/it's not.)
We are (We're) working.	We are not (aren't) working.	Are we working?	Yes, we are. No, we aren't. (No, we're not.)
They are (They're) working	They are not (aren't) working.	Are they working?	Yes, they are. No, they aren't. (No, they're not.)

EXERCISE 2

STEP 1 Study the complete picture on page A-15 for one minute. Close your book and, from memory, write as many sentences as possible to describe what is happening in the picture. Compare your sentences with those of the rest of the class. Who can remember the most?

STEP 2 Look back at the sentences you wrote in Step 1. Did you use the present progressive correctly? If not, go back and rewrite the sentences.

▶ **Simple Present or Present Progressive?**

EXAMPLES	EXPLANATIONS	
	Simple Present	Present Progressive
(a) Philippe **watches** six TV programs a day.	For an action that happens regularly, again and again. (See Unit 1.)	
(b) A: Where's Philippe? B: In his room. He's **watching** TV. **(c)** Leanne can't come to the phone right now because she's **taking** a shower.		For an action that is in progress **at** the time of speaking.
(d) Philippe **is watching** more TV than usual these days because he'd rather do that than study for his final exams. **(e)** Audrey **is learning** Greek this semester.		For an action in progress **around** the time of speaking.
(f) Carmina **lives** in Mexico City. **(g)** The sun **rises** in the east. **(h)** Mark always **reads** the sports section of the newspaper first.	For facts, situations, and states that we do not expect to change.	
(i) Angela **is living** with her mother for the time being. (Someday she will move into a house of her own.) **(j)** Matt will start college next year. Until then, he **is working** at Fat Burger.		For situations and actions that are temporary and that we expect to change.

EXERCISE 3

Check (✔) the sentence (*a* or *b*) that is closest in meaning to the first statement(s). Compare your answers with a partner.

1. Kristen's getting really good grades this semester.
(**a**) Her grades are always good.
(**b**) Her grades are better than they were last semester.

2. Look! Terry's wearing a dress today.
(**a**) Terry seldom wears dresses.
(**b**) Terry probably wore a dress yesterday, too.

3. Vince and Irene live in New Jersey.
(**a**) They expect to move very soon.
(**b**) New Jersey is their home.

4. I'm taking the train to work this week.
(**a**) I'm sitting on the train right now.
(**b**) I don't usually take the train.

5. A: Where's Eddie?
B: He's asleep on the couch.
(**a**) He's sleeping on the couch.
(**b**) He sleeps on the couch.

6. A: How's Nina these days?
B: Busy. She's learning how to dance the tango.
(**a**) Nina has a new hobby.
(**b**) She's dancing right now.

EXERCISE 4

Complete the following sentences using either the simple present or the present progressive. Use a form of the verb in parentheses. The first one has been done for you.

1. A: Ray! The phone __is ringing__ (ring).

B: I can't get it. I _____ (wash) my hair.

2. A: Hey, Pam! What a surprise! What _____ you
_____ (do) on campus?

B: I _____ (take) an art class this semester. It's great!
I _____ (learn) a lot.

3. A: Please be quiet, we _____ (study) for a test!

B: What kind of test?

A: Math. We _____ (have + always) a math test on
Mondays.

4. (The phone rings.)

A: Hi, honey. How _____ you _____ (do)?

B: Mom! What a coincidence! I was about to write you a letter.

A: Really? You _____ (write + hardly ever) me letters. Is something wrong?

5. A: What's the matter?

B: It _____ (rain) and I want to go on a picnic today.

A: Why _____ it _____ (rain + always) on the weekends? It _____ (rain + never) during the week.

6. A: Why _____ Brian _____ (wear) a suit today?

B: It's Tuesday. He _____ (go + generally) to lunch with his boss on Tuesdays.

7. A: I just can't go on like this with my roommate.

B: Why? What's wrong?

A: The main problem is that she's a morning person and, as you know, I'm a night person. This means that almost every morning she _____ (get up) before 6:00, _____ (play) really loud music, and _____ (do) aerobics in the living room. She _____ (make) an incredible amount of noise, which _____ (make) me really mad because I usually _____ (get + not) home until after 2:00 A.M. and _____ (like) to sleep late. But these days, thanks to my roommate, I _____ (wake up) at 6:00.

B: Do you want me to talk to her about this? What _____ she _____ (do) at the moment?

A: Thanks for the offer, but she _____ (sleep). She always _____ (go) to bed around 8:00.

EXERCISE 5

Can you translate the following into written English? Write your answers below. After that, underline the verbs in each sentence and write each verb in the appropriate box. The first one has been done for you.

1. 👁 ❤ U.   _I love you._

2. 👁 CU. _____

3. 👁 H+8 U. _____

4. 👁 H+🤔 U. _____

5. He 🦅 U. _____

6. RU 21 ? _____

7. 👁 CUR YY 4 me! _____

8. 👁 TH+🫙 UR GR+8. _____

You can find the answers to this puzzle on page A-16.

Now underline all the verbs in your sentences and write them in the appropriate boxes below. The first one has been done for you.

Verbs that express emotions and feelings	Verbs that express senses and perceptions	Verbs that express cognition: knowledge thoughts, and beliefs
love		

Which verb does not fit these categories? _____

▶ **V**erbs Not Usually Used in the Progressive

EXAMPLES	EXPLANATIONS
(a) He **loves** me, but he **hates** my cat. **(b)** NOT: He is loving me, but he is hating my cat. **(c)** I **know** your sister. **(d)** NOT: I am knowing your sister.	Some verbs are not usually used in the progressive. The reason is that they describe states or situations that we do not expect to change. They do not describe actions.
(e) Hugo **likes** opera, but his girlfriend **prefers** ballet. **(f)** Those flowers **smell** wonderful! **(g)** I **think** the President has some interesting ideas about health care, but many people **believe** he is wrong. **(h)** Please be careful with that vase. It **belongs** to my aunt. **(i)** A: Are you going to buy that radio? B: No, it **costs** too much.	Common nonprogressive (stative) verbs: • Verbs that express feelings and emotions: *love prefer hate like appreciate want dislike* • Verbs that describe the senses: *see hear taste smell* • Verbs that express knowledge, opinions, and beliefs: *think believe know understand* • Verbs that express possession: *have belong own possess* • Other common nonprogressive verbs: *be seem owe exist need appear cost weigh*

EXERCISE 6

Complete the following with the simple present or the present progressive, using the verbs in parentheses.

Today, more and more people (1) _____ (discover) the joys of riding a bicycle. In fact, mountain biking (2) _____ (become) one of America's most popular recreational activities. The bicycle business (3) _____ (grow) fast, and every year it (4) _____ (produce) hundreds of new-model bikes. In general, bike shops (5) _____ (sell) not only bicycles but also a full range of accessories and equipment.

Paul Brownstein (6) _____ (manage) a popular bike shop in Boston. Many of his customers (7) _____ (be) enthusiastic cyclists, and several of them (8) _____ (own) more than one bicycle. These people usually (9) _____ (ride) several times a week for pleasure, although according to Paul, more and more people these days (10) _____ (ride) their bicycles to work too. They (11) _____ (believe) that bicycles (12) _____ (provide) an alternative to the automobile.

Paul (13) _____ (sell) all kinds of bikes, but these days he (14) _____ (sell) a lot of bicycle clothing as well. In fact, one of his customers regularly (15) _____ (come) into the shop and (16) _____ (buy) clothes, even though she (17) _____ (not + own) a bicycle. She (18) _____ (like) the clothes, but (19) _____ (hate) the sport! Unfortunately, this attitude (20) _____ (not + be) unusual these days, because as everybody (21) _____ (know), some people (22) _____ (think) style and appearance (23) _____ (be) more important than anything else in life.

▶ **States and Actions**

EXAMPLES	EXPLANATIONS
(a) I **love** you. **(b)** I **hate** my job. **(c)** She **knows** a lot about the history of her country.	Nonprogressive verbs usually describe a state or quality that we do not expect to change. They do not describe actions.
State — Action **(d)** I **weigh** 120 pounds. — I **am weighing** myself (to see if I've gained weight). **(e)** Mmm! Dinner **smells** great! — I'**m smelling** the milk (to see if it smells fresh). **(f)** This soup **tastes** good. — He **is tasting** the soup (to see if it needs salt).	Some verbs describe both a state **and** an action. If the verb describes a state, use the simple present. If the verb describes an action, use the present progressive.
(g) David **is** very polite. **(h)** Tanya **is** a little shy.	Do not use *be* in the progressive when it describes a state or quality you do not expect to change.
(i) We **have** two cars. **(j)** NOT: We are having two cars. **(k)** We **are having fun**. **(l)** We always **have fun** on vacation.	Do not use *have* in the progressive to describe possession. However, you can use *have* in the progressive to describe an experience. Use the progressive if the experience is in progress at or around the time of speaking (k). Use the simple present if the experience happens again and again (l). Common expressions using *have* to describe an experience: *have fun — have a good time* *have problems — have trouble with* *have difficulty with*
(m) I can't talk to you right now because I **have** a really sore throat. **(n)** NOT: I am having a sore throat. **(o)** Sandy **has** a headache and a high fever today; maybe she **has** the flu. **(p)** NOT: Sandy is having a headache and a high fever today; maybe she is having the flu.	Do not use *have* in the progressive to describe a medical problem or physical discomfort.

EXERCISE 7

Work with a partner or in a small group. You need a die and a small object (like a coin) to represent each person.

STEP 1 Take turns throwing the die. The person who throws the highest number starts.

STEP 2 Put your coins (or objects) on the square marked "Start" on the following page.

STEP 3 Throw the die and move your coin that number of squares.

STEP 4 Complete the sentence in the square on page 30 and say it out loud. If everyone agrees with your answer, you may write it in the square and take another turn. If the class is not sure, the teacher will be the referee. If you make a mistake or do not know the answer, the next person gets a turn. The winner is the first person to reach the final square.

I _____ (love) grammar! 〔25〕	A: The Chef _____ (taste) the food right now. B: Is it good? A: Yes! It _____ (taste) wonderful! 〔26〕	MISS A TURN 〔27〕	Did you cut your hand? It _____ (bleed). 〔28〕
She _____ (write) a letter now, but she rarely _____ (write) letters. 〔24〕	MISS A TURN 〔23〕	The students _____ (have) some trouble with verbs today. 〔22〕	She _____ (take) three classes this semester, but she usually _____ (take) more. 〔21〕
MISS A TURN 〔17〕	How many pairs of shoes _____ she _____ (own) now? 〔18〕	This suitcase _____ (weigh) too much. I can't carry it. 〔19〕	A: What's wrong? B: I _____ (have) problems with my boyfriend at the moment. 〔20〕
A: Look! There's the President. B: Where? I _____ (not + see) him. 〔16〕	A: _____ you _____ (like) your job? B. No, I _____ (hate) it. 〔15〕	A: _____ you always _____ (take) the bus? B: No, I usually ___ (walk) to work. 〔14〕	A: Where's Tim? B: I _____ (think) he _____ (take) a nap. 〔13〕
A: How are the kids? B: They both _____ (have) sore throats today. 〔9〕	A: Shhh! We _____ (study) for a test. 〔10〕	A: _____ you _____ (like) Mexican food? B: Yes, I _____ (love) it! 〔11〕	A: How's Joe? B: Great. He _____ (have) fun because he _____ (have) a new car. 〔12〕
MISS A TURN 〔8〕	Mmm! Is that a new perfume? You _____ (smell) great. 〔7〕	What _____ you _____ (think) Henry _____ (think) about right now? 〔6〕	People _____ (spend) less money on entertainment these days. 〔5〕
START 〔1〕	Moya always _____ (sit) at the back of the class, but today she _____ (sit) at the front. 〔2〕	Rose _____ (not + know) that it is my birthday today. 〔3〕	MISS A TURN 〔4〕

Use Your English

ACTIVITY 1: LISTENING/WRITING

In this activity, you will hear a radio correspondent describing her visit to a country fair. Listen to how she describes what is going on at the fair.

STEP 1 Write down three things that are happening at the fair.

STEP 2 Listen to the tape again. Write down examples of simple present and present progressive verbs in the chart below.

Simple Present	Present Progressive

ACTIVITY 2: WRITING/LISTENING

Go to a crowded place where you can sit, watch, and listen to what is happening around you. Look carefully at everything that is happening. Pretend you are a journalist or radio or television reporter. Describe in writing everything that you see. Do not forget to include everything you hear as well.

ACTIVITY 3: SPEAKING/LISTENING

Do you know how to play tic-tac-toe? In this activity, you will be playing a version of this well-known game. Work with a partner or in teams.

STEP 1 Copy each of the following onto separate cards or different pieces of paper.

she/speak	she/dance (?)*	you/live
we/hear	we/sing	I/see
I/understand	they/work (?)*	
they/eat	he/believe	(?)* = make a question
they/think about	you/write (?)*	

STEP 2 Place the cards face down on the table in front of you.

STEP 3 Player or Team X chooses a square from the box below and picks up a card from the pile. The player must make a meaningful statement that includes the word(s) in the square and the word(s) on the card. If the card has a "?" on it, the player must ask a question. Each statement or question must contain at least four words, not including the words in the square. Use the simple present or present progressive.

STEP 4 If everyone accepts the statement, Player or Team X marks the square with an X.

STEP 5 Player or Team O then chooses a different square and takes a new card. The Player or Team O makes a statement. If the statement is correct, Player or Team O marks the square with an O.

STEP 6 The first person or team to have three Xs or three Os in a straight line wins.

You can play this game again and again by erasing the Xs and Os at the end of each round, or by writing them on small pieces of paper and covering the squares with these. Good luck!

every day	**today**	**usually**
this week	**occasionally**	**right now**
often	**at the moment**	**sometimes**

ACTIVITY 4: SPEAKING/LISTENING/WRITING

STEP 1 Go around the classroom and try to find a different person for each of the situations in the chart below. Write the person's name in the box marked *Name* and add more information in the box marked *Information*. We have given some suggestions here, but you probably have more ideas of your own.

Situation	Name	Information
. . . is reading a book in English		*Title? His/her opinion?*
. . . regularly reads a newspaper from his/her country		*Why?*
. . . has more than $10.00 in cash with him/her right now		*Any coins as well as bills?*
. . . reads more than one book a month (in any language)		*Favorite books?*
. . . is living with an American host family		*Who? Where?*
. . . usually goes to the movies several times a month		*How often? Favorite movie?*
. . . is wearing an article of clothing made in the U.S.A.		*Describe it.*
. . . regularly plays a musical instrument		*What kind? How often?*
. . . is wearing perfume or cologne at the moment		*What kind? Describe it.*
. . . has a pet		*What kind? How old?*

STEP 2 Look at all the information that you collected. Choose three or four of the most interesting or surprising things that you learned about your classmates and write about this information. Remember to include an introduction. For example: *I interviewed some of my classmates and I learned several new things about them. First, I learned that Maria likes to read; in fact, she is reading a book in English that she is enjoying very much. . . .*

Read your report to a partner. Ask your partner to listen first to count the examples of the **simple present** and then listen again, doing the same for the **present progressive**.

TALKING ABOUT THE FUTURE

Be Going To and Will

UNIT GOALS:

- To correctly form statements and questions about the future using *be going to* and *will*
- To know the uses of *be going to* and *will*
- To choose between *be going to* and *will*

▶ OPENING TASK

Fortune Cookie

In North America, Chinese restaurants traditionally give customers a fortune cookie at the end of the meal. This cookie is small and hollow. Inside you find a piece of paper that predicts something about your future.

1 You will help
2 Your boss is going to
3 You will be lucky
4 You are going to take
5 Your friends and family
6 You are going to get
7 You will
8 You are going
9 Your life
10 An interesting stranger is

A a trip around the world.
B an "A" in this class.
C to have a large and happy family.
D and win a lot of money.
E are going to throw a big party in your honor.
F give you a big raise.
G make an important contribution to the world
H is going to change dramatically.
I a friend in need.
J going to enter your life.

STEP 1   Match the two parts of these fortunes on page 34.

STEP 2   The writer of these fortunes has run out of ideas and needs some help.
What kinds of fortunes do **you** like to receive? Write some examples in
the spaces below.

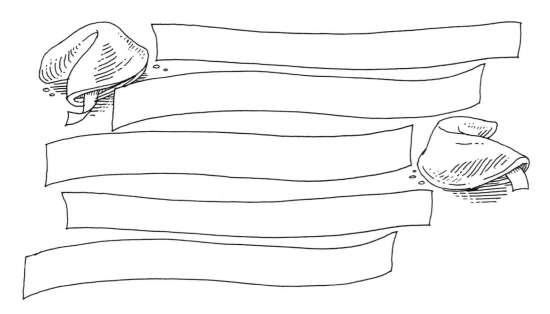

▶ **T**alking About the Future with **Will** and **Be Going To**

EXAMPLES	EXPLANATION
(a) An interesting stranger **is going to** enter your life. OR **(b)** An interesting stranger **will** enter your life. **(c)** You **are going to** take a trip around the world. OR **(d)** You **will** take a trip around the world.	Use either *be going to* or *will* to make a prediction or talk about the future

EXERCISE 1

Write the complete predictions about the future from the fortune cookies in the Opening Task on page 34.

1. _____

2. _____

3. _____

4. _____

5. _____

6. _____

7. _____

8. _____

9. _____

10. _____

Look at the fortunes you wrote in Step 2 of the Opening Task. Did you use *will* and *be going to*? If you did not, rewrite the fortunes to include *will* and *be going to*.

▶ *Will* and *Be Going To*

Will does not change to agree with the subject:

STATEMENT	NEGATIVE	QUESTION
I You We They She He It } **will** leave. **'ll**	I You We They She He It } **will not/won't** leave.	**Will** { I you we they she he it } leave?

Be going to changes to agree with the subject:

STATEMENT	NEGATIVE	QUESTION
I } **am going to** leave. **'m**	I } **am not** **'m not going to** leave.	**Am** I **going to** leave?
She He It } **is going to** leave. **'s**	She } **is not** He } **isn't going to** leave. It } **'s not**	**Is** { he she it } **going to** leave?
You We They } **are going to** leave. **'re**	You } **are not** We } **aren't going to** leave. They } **'re not**	**Are** { you we they } **going to** leave?

EXERCISE 2

STEP 1   Write predictions about the future for five of your classmates. Be sure to include some predictions that use negative forms. Do not use your classmates' names.

▶ **EXAMPLES:**   *He will go to China.*

She will not live at home.

He is going to get an A *in this class.*

1. _____

2. _____

3. _____

4. _____

5. _____

STEP 2 Read each of your predictions aloud. If one of your classmates thinks a prediction is about him or her, invite this person to ask a question to find out if this is true.

▶ **EXAMPLES:** _Will I go to China?_

Yes, you will.

Am I going to get an A?

Yes, you are.

FOCUS **3**

▶ # Making Predictions: _Will_ or _Be Going To?_

EXAMPLES	EXPLANATIONS
(a) Be careful! That chair **is going to** break. **(b)** NOT: Be careful! That chair will break! **(c)** Oh no!! That little boy **is going to** fall off the bridge. **(d)** NOT: Oh no!! That little boy will fall off the bridge.	It is better to use _be going to_ for actions or events that you think will happen very soon or immediately.
(e) _Babysitter to child:_ Your mommy's **going to** be very angry about this. **(f)** _Student to professor:_ **Will** the test be difficult? _Professor:_ It **will** be tough, but I don't think you **will** have too many problems with it.	When the future event or action will not happen immediately: It is better to use _be going to_ in informal situations (relaxed and friendly situations, with family or friends). In informal speech, _going to_ is usually pronounced _gonna._ It is better to use _will_ in more formal situations.

EXERCISE 3

For each of the following, decide on the best form to use: *be going to* or *will*. In some sentences, it is possible to use both. The first one has been done for you.

1. Quick! Catch the baby! I think he <u>is going to</u> roll off the bed.

2. Excuse me, Mr. President. Do you think unemployment _____ decrease in the foreseeable future?

3. Uh-oh. Look at those clouds. It _____ rain.

4. I predict that you _____ meet a tall, dark, and handsome stranger, and you _____ fall in love and get married.

5. One day we _____ look back at all this and laugh.

6. I don't believe it. Look at Paula! I think she _____ ask that guy to dance with her.

7. A: What do you think about my son's chances of getting into Harvard, Dr. Heath?

   B: I don't think he _____ have any problems at all, Mrs. Lee.

8. Meteorologists predict that the drought _____ end sometime this fall.

FOCUS **4**

▶ **Future Plans and Intentions: Be Going To**

EXAMPLES	EXPLANATION
(a) We**'re going to** spend the month of August in Italy. We bought the tickets last week, and we**'re going to** leave on August 2nd. (b) Tasha, age 9: When I grow up, I**'m going to** be the president of the United States.	It is better to use *be going to* to talk about a future plan or intention (something you want to do in the future). This shows that you made the decision to do this **before** speaking.

EXERCISE 4

In this exercise, you need to get information from one of your classmates. Use *be going to* or *will* in your answers, as appropriate.

1. Get together with a partner and find out three things she or he intends to do after class:

   My partner _____

   _____ .

2. Now find out three things she or he does not intend to do after class:

   My partner _____

   _____ .

3. Now make three predictions about your partner's future:

   My partner _____

   _____ .

Finally, look back at what you have written in this exercise. Where did you choose *be going to* and where did you choose *will*? Why did you make these choices?

EXERCISE 5

Read the following carefully and decide if the use of *be going to* or *will* is more appropriate. Check (✔) the sentences you think are acceptable. Correct the sentences you think are unacceptable.

1. A: Do you have any plans for tonight?
   B: Yes. We will go to the baseball game. Do you want to come with us?

2. A: Your nephew is a very talented artist, isn't he?
   B: Yes. We believe he'll be very famous one of these days.

3. A: Who do you think will win the next World Cup?
   B: I think Brazil is going to win next time.
   A: Really?

4. A: Where's Freddie?
   B: He will spend the night at his friend's house.

5. A: Have you heard the news? Heidi's going to get married.
   B: That's great!

FOCUS **5**

USE

▶ **T**wo More Uses of *Will*:
Making Quick Decisions and
Serious Promises

EXAMPLES	EXPLANATIONS
(a) A: I think there's someone at the front door. B: I**'ll** go and check.	Use *will* to show you have decided to do something at that moment. You decide to do this as you speak.
(b) A: Telephone! B: OK. I**'ll** get it.	The contracted *'ll* is usually used in these situations.
(c) A: I need someone to help out at the recycling center. B: Oh, I **will**!	Do not use *'ll* in short answers.
(d) I **will** always love you.	
(e) I**'ll** give you my homework tomorrow, I promise!	Use *will* to make a serious promise.
(f) A: Remember, this is top secret. B: I **won't** tell anybody. You can count on me.	

EXERCISE 6

Complete the following, using *be going to, 'll* or *will* as appropriate.

1. A: What are your plans for the weekend?

B: We _____ take the boat and go fishing.

A: Sounds great. Can I join you?

2. A: Excuse me, but I can't reach those books on the top shelf.

B: Move over. I _____ get them down for you.

3. A: You've bought a lot of groceries today.

B: Yes. I _____ cook dinner for the people who work in my office.

4. A: Here's $20.

B: Thank you. I promise I _____ pay you back next week.

5. A: Oops! I've just spilled my drink all over everything.

B: Don't panic. I _____ get a cloth.

6. A: What (you) _____ wear to Aki's party?

B: Kuniko and I _____ wear jeans. What about you?

7. A: Now, kids, I want you to be very good this afternoon because I'm not feeling well.

B: It's O.K., Mrs. Swanson. We promise we _____ behave.

8. A: What's up?

B: I'm late for work and my car won't start.

A: Don't worry. I _____ give you a ride.

9. A: What (you) _____ do with your brother when he comes to visit next weekend?

B: First, Jody and I _____ take him out to brunch down by the beach, and after that Kate _____ show him the sights.

EXERCISE 7

With a partner, look at these situations and decide on ways to respond using *will* or *be going to*.

1. You look out of the window and notice there are a lot of stormy, black clouds in the sky. What do you say?

_____

_____

2. Your friend Oscar is interested in music and in physics, but he can't decide which one to major in next year. After a lot of thought and discussion, he has finally decided to major in music. What does he say to his family?

_____

_____

3. Your friend is organizing an international potluck. She needs people to bring food from different countries. You want to help. What do you say?

_____

_____

4. It's 6:30 A.M. You have to drive to the airport to pick up your uncle at 7:30 A.M., but your car won't start. Your roommate offers to lend you hers, but she needs to have it back by 9:00 A.M. to get to work. What do you tell her?

_____

_____

5. You are standing in line in the campus cafeteria. You notice that the back-pack of the student in front of you is open and all her books are about to fall out. What do you tell her?

_____

_____

6. One of your classmates is sick and has to go to the doctor's office. He is very worried about missing his history class. You are also in that class. What can you say to reassure him?

_____

_____

7. Your friend is giving you a ride home. Suddenly you notice a little boy who is about to run into the road. Your friend hasn't seen him. What do you say?

_____

_____

8. Your friend Frank loves ballet. He has just bought the last ticket for a special gala performance of "Swan Lake" next Saturday night. You ask him about his plans for the weekend. What does he say?

_____

_____

9. You have promised to do the dishes and clean up the kitchen after dinner. Just before you get started, you receive an unexpected phone call from a friend whose car has broken down and he urgently needs your help. As you are leaving, your roommate comes into the room and asks, "What about the dishes?" What do you say?

_____

_____

10. Madame Cassandra is a fortune-teller who makes exciting predictions about the future. Your teacher is consulting Madame Cassandra. What does Madame Cassandra tell your teacher?

_____

_____

Use Your English

ACTIVITY 1: SPEAKING/LISTENING/WRITING

The purpose of this activity is to collect as much information as possible about the future plans and intentions of your classmates. Look at the chart below. Complete as many squares as you can by finding the required information. *Maybe* and *I don't know* are not acceptable answers! Write the information in the appropriate square and also the name or names of the people who gave you the information. The first person to get information for three squares in a row in any direction is the winner. Good luck!

Find someone who is going to take the TOEFL soon. When is she or he going to take it?	Find three people who are going to cook dinner tonight. What are they going to cook?	Find two people who are going to go to the library after this class. What are they going to do there?
Find two people who are going to play the same sport this week. What sport are they going to play?	Find someone who is going to move to another city within a year. What city is she or he going to move to?	Find someone who is going to go to the movies today. What movie is she or he going to see?
Find someone who is going to get his or her hair cut in the next two weeks. Where is he or she going to get it cut?	Find two people who are going to watch TV tonight. What are they going to watch?	Find two people who are going to celebrate their birthdays next month. What are their birthdates?

ACTIVITY 2: WRITING/SPEAKING

STEP 1 Write fortune cookie "fortunes" for your teacher and five of your classmates. Write each fortune on a small slip of paper, and give each one to the appropriate person.

STEP 2 The people who receive fortunes will read their fortunes aloud and the rest of the class will decide if they think the fortunes will come true.

ACTIVITY 3: WRITING

What are your predictions for the next ten years? What do you think will happen in the world? What do you think will happen in your country?

STEP 1 Write a brief report on your predictions. Your report should include a short introduction to your topic. It is not necessary to use *will* and *be going to* in every sentence you write!

STEP 2 When you finish writing, read your report carefully and check your use of *will* and *be going to*. Remember, it is often possible to use either one.

We have written the beginning of a report to give you some ideas, but you probably have better ideas of your own.

LIFE IN THE FUTURE

Nobody knows exactly what will happen in the future, but in my opinion, there will be many important changes in the world in the next ten years. Some of them will be good and some of them will be bad. In this short report, I am going to talk about some of my predictions for the future of the world, as well as the future of my country.

First, let me tell you about my predictions for the world. . . .

ACTIVITY 4: SPEAKING/ LISTENING

STEP 1 Listen to the tape of three different people talking about their goals and future plans. About how old do you think each speaker is? Take a guess. Take notes on what each speaker says in the chart below.

SPEAKER	AGE	FUTURE PLANS AND GOALS
Speaker 1		
Speaker 2		
Speaker 3		

STEP 2 Think about your own goals and future plans. Are they similar to those of any of the three speakers? Explain to a partner.

STEP 3 Listen to the tape again. Write down all the examples you hear of the future with *will* and *be going to*.

ACTIVITY 5: SPEAKING/ LISTENING

STEP 1 In this activity, you will interview several young North Americans about their goals and future plans. If possible, try to interview at least three young people who are at different stages of their lives: college students, high school students, and children. Find out what they are going to do when they leave school.

STEP 2 Report your findings to the class.

STEP 3 If possible, tape your interviews. Later listen to your tape and take note of the different ways these native speakers talk about the future. Make a list of the most interesting plans and share them with the rest of the class.

ACTIVITY 6: LISTENING/SPEAKING

In this activity, you will create a chain story about your teacher's next vacation.

STEP 1 Your teacher will start by telling you where he or she is going for his or her next vacation and one thing he or she is going to do:

Teacher: I'm going to Hawaii for my vacation, and I am going to climb a mountain.

STEP 2 The next person repeats the first part and adds another statement about the teacher's vacation until everyone in the room has added to the description.

▶ **EXAMPLE:** *Student 1:* (Teacher's name) is going to Hawaii; he or she is going to climb a mountain; he or she is going to swim in the ocean, too.

UNIT 4

ASKING QUESTIONS

Yes/No, Wh-, Tag Questions, Choice Questions

UNIT GOALS:
- To know how to form questions (*Yes/No, Wh-,* choice and tag) and what they mean
- To know the uses of different intonation patterns for various question types

▶ OPENING TASK
Any Questions?

STEP 1 Teachers usually ask students a lot of questions about all kinds of things, but students don't always get the same opportunities.

STEP 2 What questions would you like to ask **your** teacher? Work alone or with other students to complete the questions on this page.

▶ **R**eview of *Yes/No* Questions

EXAMPLES	EXPLANATIONS
(a) *Question*: Are you Brazilian? *Answer*: Yes, I am./No, I'm not. **(b)** *Question*: Do you understand? *Answer*: Yes, I do./No, I don't.	When you ask a *Yes/No* question, you expect the answer *yes* or *no*. *Yes/No* questions end with rising intonation.
subject *be* **(c)** *Statement*: He is tired. *be* *subject* *Question*: **Is** he tired? **(d)** **Are** you ready to go? **(e)** **Am** I too late for dinner? **(f)** **Was** the plane on time? **(g)** **Were** they mad at me?	**Yes/No questions with be:** Invert the subject and the verb (move the verb **in front of** the subject).
subject *verb* **(h)** *Statement*: They speak Turkish. *do* *subject* *base verb* *Question*: **Do** they **speak** Turkish? **(i)** NOT: Speak they Turkish? **(j)** **Does** the bus **stop** here? **(k)** **Do** you **take** credit cards? **(l)** **Did** the President **know** about this?	**Yes/No questions with other verbs:** Put the appropriate form of *do* **in front of** the subject. Put the base form of the verb **after** the subject.
subject *be* *verb + -ing* **(m)** *Statement*: They are leaving. *be* *subject* *verb + -ing* *Question*: **Are** they **leaving**? **(n)** **Is** your computer **working** today? **(o)** **Are** they **coming** with us? **(p)** **Was** it **raining** there? **(q)** **Were** her parents **visiting**?	**Yes/No questions with verbs in the progressive:** Invert the subject and *be* (move the *be* verb in front of the subject). For information on *Yes/No* questions with present perfect and past perfect, see Units 13, 14, and 19.

EXAMPLES	EXPLANATIONS
subject modal base verb **(r)** *Statement*: It will rain. *modal subject base verb* *Question*: **Will** it **rain**? **(s)** **Would** you **repeat** that? **(t)** **Can** you **help** me?	**Yes/No questions with modals:** Invert the modal and the subject (put the modal in **front of** the subject).
(u) *Statement*: She asked him out. *Question*: She asked him out? **(v)** You're from England? **(w)** Sasha can come? **(x)** He's 40 years old? Yes, he is.	**Statement form of *Yes/No* questions:** A statement said with rising intonation is also a type of *Yes/No* question. This type of question is common in informal conversation. When a statement form question is used, the speaker usually expects the listener to agree.

EXERCISE 1

Get together with a partner and make a list of all the *Yes/No* questions you both wanted to ask your teacher in the Opening Task on page 49. Write them here or in a notebook and add three more *Yes/No* questions to ask your teacher. You will have an opportunity to ask these questions later in the unit.

_____

_____

_____

_____

_____

_____

_____

_____

_____

_____

_____

_____

_____

_____

▶ **R**eview of **W***h*-Questions

EXAMPLES	EXPLANATIONS
(a) Q: What is your name? A: Elena. *Who What When Where* *Why Whose Which How*	A *Wh*-question usually begins with a *Wh*-word and expects the speaker to give information rather than *yes* or *no* in the answer.
(b) Where do you come from? ↘ **(c)** When did you arrive? ↘ **(d)** How many languages do you speak? ↘	*Wh*-questions usually end in falling intonation.
(e) Q: Why are you late? A: Because I missed the bus. *Wh-word be subject* **(f)** **Where is** the restroom? **(g)** **What was** her name? **(h)** **Who are** his friends?	**Wh-questions with *be*:** Choose a *Wh*-word. Invert the subject and the verb.
(i) **What's** the time? **(j)** **Where's** my car?	In informal speech, *is* is often contracted to *'s* in *Wh*-questions.
(k) Q: When did she get here? A: Just a few minutes ago. *Wh-word do subject base verb* **(l)** **Who(m) do** you **love**? **(m)** **What does** a judge **do**? **(n)** **Where did** Nicole **live**?	**Wh-questions with other verbs:** Choose a *Wh*-word. To form the question, follow the *Wh*-word with a form of *do*.
(o) Q: What time can you leave? A: As soon as this class is over. *Wh-word modal subject base verb* **(p)** **How long can I stay**? **(q)** **When will she come**?	**Wh-questions with modals:** Choose a *Wh*-word. To form a question, put the modal directly after the *Wh*-word and before the subject.

EXERCISE 2

Get together with a partner and write down all the *Wh*-questions that you wanted to ask your teacher in the Opening Task. Write them on a piece of paper and add three more. You will have an opportunity to ask them later in the unit.

EXERCISE 3

Bruno and Ken are friends. Bruno has just introduced Ken to his cousin, Marta. Ken is very interested in getting to know more about her, so now he is asking Bruno all about her.

Get together with a partner and look at the answers that Bruno gave. What questions do you think Ken probably asked? Write them in the appropriate place.

Ken: (1) _____ ?

Bruno: Yes, I think she does.

Ken: (2) _____ ?

Bruno: No, she doesn't.

Ken: (3) _____ ?

Bruno: Usually around midnight.

Ken: (4) _____ ?

Bruno: Not usually.

Ken: (5) _____ ?

Bruno: In Buenos Aires.

Ken: (6) _____ ?

Bruno: Three times a week, I think.

Ken: (7) _____ ?

Bruno: No, she isn't.

Ken: (8) _____ ?

Bruno: Yes, I'm pretty sure she was.

Ken: (9) _____ ?

Bruno: Last year, or maybe the year before. I can't remember exactly.

Ken: (10) _____ ?

Bruno: I have no idea. You'll have to ask her that question yourself.

Now change partners. Read the questions that you wrote while your new partner reads Bruno's answers. When you finish, change roles to read your partner's dialogue. Compare your questions with a partner's. Does Marta seem like a different person? In what ways?

Wh-Questions that Focus on the Subject

EXAMPLES	EXPLANATIONS
(a) Q: **Who(m)** did you call? A: I called Tony. *object* **(b)** Q: **Who** called you? A: Martin called me. *subject*	This question asks about the object. *Who* is more common in informal speech. *Whom* is very formal. This question asks about the subject.
Wh-word Verb **(c)** Q: **Who** lives here? A: Shan lives here. **(d)** Q: **Who** told you? A: Herb did.	For *Wh*-questions about the subject, put the appropriate *Wh*-word in front of the verb. Do not use *do* in the question.
(e) Q: **What** annoys her? A: Everything. **(f)** Q: **What** music annoys her? A: Heavy metal. **(g)** Q: **What** bands annoy her? A: Aerosmith and Megadeth.	Use *what* to ask a general question about something. Use *what* + a noun when you want a more specific answer. Make the verb singular or plural to agree with the noun.

EXERCISE 4

Get together with another student or someone in your class for this exercise. First read the report below. Next, think of the questions you need to ask your friend in order to complete the report. Write the questions in the "Question Box." Ask your partner all of the questions without showing them to him or her. Finally, use the answers that your friend gives you to complete the report.

Report:

My friend (1) _____ is from (2) _____ and
speaks (3) _____ languages: (4) _____ . S/he was
born in (5) _____ and s/he has (6) _____ brothers
and sisters. Her/his favorite subjects in school were (7) _____ .
S/he is taking this class because (8) _____ . In her free time,
s/he likes to (9) _____ . Her/his favorite (10) _____
is/are (11) _____ . When s/he first came here,
(12) _____ surprised her/him. After s/he finishes school,
s/he hopes to (13) _____ . (14) _____
make(s) her/him happy, but (15) _____ make(s) her/him angry.
Finally, there is one more thing I'd like to tell you about my friend:
(16) _____ .

QUESTION BOX	
1 _____ ?	2 _____ ?
3 _____ ?	4 _____ ?
5 _____ ?	6 _____ ?
7 _____ ?	8 _____ ?
9 _____ ?	10 _____ ?
11 _____ ?	12 _____ ?
13 _____ ?	14 _____ ?
15 _____ ?	16 _____ ?

EXERCISE 5

Chris and Robin have been living together for a long time. Chris wants Robin to help clean the house. Read their conversation below and make a question to go with each of Chris's answers. When you're finished, compare your questions with other students' questions.

1. **Robin:** _____?

   Chris: The closet door is closed because the paint's dry, and so I put everything back in there.

2. **Robin:** _____?

   Chris: The broom is in the closet, along with the mop, and some cleaning supplies.

3. **Robin:** _____?

   Chris: The vacuum cleaner is probably still in the basement where you left it.

4. **Robin:** _____?

   Chris: We need to clean the house because we're having some people over for dinner tonight.

5. **Robin:** _____?

   Chris: Pat, Sam, and their kids are coming, and of course our neighbors, the Smiths.

6. **Robin:** _____?

   Chris: They met them in the Smiths' garden.

7. **Robin:** _____?

   Chris: They met them there yesterday morning when we were gone.

8. **Robin:** _____?

   Chris: The Smiths were planting flowers.

9. **Robin:** _____?

   Chris: Pat and Sam are getting here by car.

10. **Robin:** _____?

    Chris: I told everyone to be here around 7:00. We'd better get busy; we don't have a lot of time to get this place cleaned up.

▶ *Wh*-Questions with Rising Intonation: Checking Information

EXAMPLES	EXPLANATIONS

(a) A: Where are you from? ↘
   B: Vanuatu.
(b) A: **Where** are you from? ↗
   B: Vanuatu. It's in the south Pacific.
(c) A: Michael Jackson was here last night.
   B: **Who** was here last night? ↗
   A: Michael Jackson.
	Most *Wh*-questions end with falling intonation.
	
	A *Wh*-question with rising intonation shows that you are not sure about what you heard or that you want to check that you heard something correctly. The *Wh*-word is also stressed (said strongly).

(d) A: Michael Jackson was here last night. B: **Who?** ↗	Sometimes, just the *Wh*-word (with rising intonation) is used.

EXERCISE 6

Complete the conversation with appropriate *Wh*-questions. For each question, draw an arrow ↗ or ↘ to show if the question ends with falling or rising intonation.

Albert: So, what did you think of the new Eisentraut movie?

Leslie: It was O.K., I guess, but I expected something more from a movie that cost $200 million to make.

Albert: (1) _____?

Leslie: $200 million. Amazing, isn't it? It's hard to imagine that amount of money.

Albert: (2) _____?

Leslie: It's an action movie set in the future, but I thought it was rather slow-moving. In fact, I almost fell asleep a couple of times.

Albert: (3) _____?

Leslie: It's about two hours, maybe a little longer. Luckily the seats were really comfortable.

Albert: (4) _____?

Leslie: At that new movie theater on Fourth Street, across from the parking garage. It only opened a couple of weeks ago, so it's got a state-of-the-art sound system, thick carpets, terrific popcorn. . . .

Albert: (5) _____?

Leslie: Twelve dollars.

Albert: (6) _____?

Leslie: Twelve dollars . . . I'm not kidding! I can't believe I spent twelve bucks on a movie that really wasn't very good.

► # Choice Questions

EXAMPLES	EXPLANATIONS
(a) A: Are you **a graduate student or a professor?** B: I'm a graduate student. **(b)** A: Do you live in **a dorm or an apartment?** B: I live off campus, in an apartment.	A choice question has two or more possibilities, or options. The speaker expects you to choose one of these options in your answer. You can add more information in your answer if you want.
(c) Does Tina walk ⁄ to school or take ＼ the bus? **(d)** A: Are you from Malaysia or from Indonesia? B: Neither. I'm from Singapore.	Choice questions have a different intonation pattern from *Yes-No* questions. *Yes-No* questions have rising intonation at the end; choice questions have rising intonation in the middle and falling intonation at the end.
(e) A: Would you like coffee or tea? B: I'll have some tea, please. **(f)** A: (Do you want) paper or plastic? B: Paper, please.	Choice questions are often used to get information quickly or to make offers (please see Unit 16 for more information on making offers with *Would . . . like*). In informal conversation, the first part of the question is sometimes dropped. Answers to choice questions are often very short. Adding *please* to your answer makes it more polite.

EXERCISE 7

Thongchai is a new student from Asia. You want to find out some information about him. Complete the following choice questions with options that are similar in meaning and form.

1. Are you from Thailand or _____?

2. Do you speak Chinese or _____?

3. Do you eat noodles or _____ for breakfast?

4. Do you live _____ or _____?

5. Are you going to study _____ or _____?

6. Do you walk to class or _____?

7. Do you like to play tennis or _____?

Practice asking and answering the questions you completed with a partner.

EXERCISE 8

Guess where each of the choice questions on the left was probably asked. Choose from the places or situations listed on the right.

Questions	Places/Situations
1. Paper or plastic?	A. a cash register in a department store
2. Would you like cole slaw or french fries with that?	B. a job interview
3. Do you want premium grade or regular?	C. a gas station
4. Will that be cash or charge?	D. a small shop selling hats and T-shirts
5. First class or economy?	E. an airline office
6. Did you say "large" or "extra-large"?	F. a fast-food restaurant
7. Do you prefer mornings or evenings?	G. a check-out counter in a supermarket

Practice asking and answering the questions with a partner. Imagine yourself in each place or situation, and use more than one way of answering.

▶ **Tag Questions**

EXAMPLES	EXPLANATIONS
statement tag **(a)** He is nice, **isn't he**? **(b)** She isn't here, **is she**? **(c)** We're late, **aren't we**? **(d)** They like it, **don't they**? **(e)** NOT: They like it, like they? **(f)** You didn't go, **did you**?	A tag question is a statement, followed by a short question (a tag). Tag questions are often used in conversation. The speaker expects a *Yes* or *No* answer. The verb in the tag agrees with the subject.
statement: tag: *affirmative + negative* **(g)** They play tennis, **don't they**? **(h)** The car was hot, **wasn't it**? **(i)** NOT: The car was hot, was not it? **(j)** Our teacher will help, **won't he**? **(k)** She is sleeping, **isn't she**? **(l)** We can wait, **can't we**? **(m)** I am right, **aren't I**? **(n)** NOT: I am right, amn't I?	An affirmative statement has a negative tag. The speaker thinks that the answer will probably be *yes*. The verbs in negative tags are contracted.
statement: tag: *negative + affirmative* **(o)** Your friends don't drive, **do they**? **(p)** It wasn't hot, **was it**? **(q)** You won't help, **will you**? **(r)** The baby isn't sleeping, **is she**? **(s)** We can't wait, **can we**?	A negative statement has an affirmative tag. The speaker thinks that the answer will probably be *no*. The verbs in affirmative tags are not contracted.

EXAMPLES	EXPLANATIONS
(t) Q: You're not cold, **are you**? A: No, I'm not. **(u)** NOT: Yes, I'm not. **(v)** Q: You're cold, **aren't you**? **(w)** A: Yes, I am. **(x)** NOT: No, I am.	When you answer a tag question, respond to the statement, not to the tag. If you agree with the statement: Answer *no* to a negative statement. Answer *yes* to an affirmative statement.
(y) Q: She left, **didn't she**? A: (Yes,) she did. OR: Right. OR: I think so. **(z)** Q: They won't call, **will they**? A: (No,) they won't. OR: I doubt it. OR: Probably not. OR: I don't think so. OR: No way.	It's not always necessary to use the words *yes* or *no* in your answers. *No way* is very informal.

EXERCISE 9

Complete the following statements with an appropriate tag.

1. You got there late, _____?

2. Your brother speaks French, _____?

3. It was cold, _____?

4. Teachers give too much homework, _____?

5. The bus isn't coming, _____?

6. Barry doesn't live here anymore, _____?

7. Nurses work very long hours for very little pay, _____?

8. We made a mistake, _____?

9. You didn't tell her, _____?

10. She will do it, _____?

11. I'm late, _____?

12. Your mother is coming too, _____?

13. The car won't start, _____?

EXERCISE 10

Deb and Sylvie are talking on the phone and making plans for their friend Bouzid's birthday. Work with a partner.

Fill in the blanks with an appropriate tag question and then put the conversation in order. Write the order of the conversation below. We have done some of them for you.

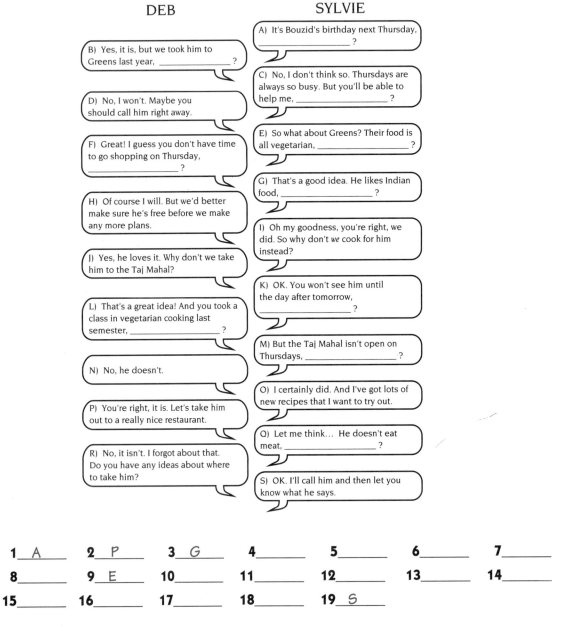

DEB   SYLVIE

A) It's Bouzid's birthday next Thursday, _____ ?

B) Yes, it is, but we took him to Greens last year, _____ ?

C) No, I don't think so. Thursdays are always so busy. But you'll be able to help me, _____ ?

D) No, I won't. Maybe you should call him right away.

E) So what about Greens? Their food is all vegetarian, _____ ?

F) Great! I guess you don't have time to go shopping on Thursday, _____ ?

G) That's a good idea. He likes Indian food, _____ ?

H) Of course I will. But we'd better make sure he's free before we make any more plans.

I) Oh my goodness, you're right, we did. So why don't we cook for him instead?

J) Yes, he loves it. Why don't we take him to the Taj Mahal?

K) OK. You won't see him until the day after tomorrow, _____ ?

L) That's a great idea! And you took a class in vegetarian cooking last semester, _____ ?

M) But the Taj Mahal isn't open on Thursdays, _____ ?

N) No, he doesn't.

O) I certainly did. And I've got lots of new recipes that I want to try out.

P) You're right, it is. Let's take him out to a really nice restaurant.

Q) Let me think… He doesn't eat meat, _____ ?

R) No, it isn't. I forgot about that. Do you have any ideas about where to take him?

S) OK. I'll call him and then let you know what he says.

1 __A__   2 __P__   3 __G__   4 _____   5 _____   6 _____   7 _____

8 _____   9 __E__   10 _____   11 _____   12 _____   13 _____   14 _____

15 _____   16 _____   17 _____   18 _____   19 __S__

You can find the answers to this exercise on page A-16.

▶ **T**ag Question Intonation

EXAMPLES	EXPLANATIONS
(a) Q: His name is Tom, isn't it? ↘ A: Yes, it is. **(b)** Q: It's not going to rain today, is it? ↘ A: No, it isn't. **(c)** Q: His name is Tom, isn't it? ↗ **(d)** Q: It's not going to rain today, is it? ↗	Falling intonation in tag questions shows that the speaker is fairly sure that the information in the statement is true. The speaker is also sure that the listener will agree. A person making an affirmative statement with falling intonation (a) expects the answer *yes*. A person making a negative statement with falling intonation (b) expects the answer *no*. Rising intonation in tag questions shows that the speaker is not sure if the information in the statement is true.

EXERCISE 11

Go back to the conversation in Exercise 10. With a partner, draw arrows ↗ or ↘ to show falling or rising intonation in the tags. One of you will take Sylvie's part and the other will take Deb's. Read the exercise aloud to practice intonation. Finally, get together with another pair and listen to each other's performances.

EXERCISE 12

Your teacher will ask some tag questions. Circle **Y** if you think the expected answer is **yes** and **N** if you think the expected answer is **no**.

1. Y N   **4.** Y N   **7.** Y N

2. Y N   **5.** Y N   **8.** Y N

3. Y N   **6.** Y N   **9.** Y N

EXERCISE 13

Read each tag question aloud, using the intonation as marked. For each question, tell whether the speaker expects a certain answer, and if so, what the speaker expects the answer to be, *yes* or *no*. Answer the question the way you think the speaker expects it to be answered.

	(a) Is the speaker fairly sure what the answer will be?	*(b)* If *yes* to (a), answer the question
1. It's going to rain today, isn't it? ↗		
2. You don't know where my umbrella is, do you? ↘		
3. You're driving today, aren't you? ↗		
4. It's not my turn to drive, is it? ↗		
5. You made lunch for me, didn't you? ↘		
6. I didn't forget to thank you, did I? ↗		
7. I'm pretty forgetful, aren't I? ↘		

EXERCISE 14

Your teacher has been nominated for a "Teacher-of-the-Year Award" and will appear at a press conference to answer questions from journalists and reporters. You and your classmates are all newspaper reporters; you need to write a profile of your teacher for your paper and want to get as much information from him or her as possible.

STEP 1 Get together with two or three other students. As a group, choose six questions that you would most like to ask your teacher at the press conference. You can use some of the questions you wrote in Exercise 1, Exercise 2, and the Opening Task if you want to, or you can make completely new questions. Important note:

- Two questions must be *Yes/No* questions.
- Two questions must be *Wh*-questions.
- Two questions must be tag questions.

STEP 2 When you have decided on your questions, your teacher will hold the press conference, but she or he **will only answer your questions if they are correctly formed and if the intonation is appropriate.** If another group asks a question that your group wanted to ask, you must ask a different question (your teacher will not answer the same question twice). Write your questions **and the answers** below. If possible, tape the "press conference" and listen to the tape to check your intonation and your teacher's answers.

Questions	Answers

Use Your English

ACTIVITY 1: SPEAKING/LISTENING

STEP 1 Your teacher is going to stick a piece of paper on your back and on the backs of your classmates. Get up and walk around the class, looking at what is written on your classmates' backs.

STEP 2 Your job is to guess what is written on your back. You can find this out by asking questions. You can also answer the questions that your classmates ask you about what is written on their backs. For the first five minutes, you can only ask *Yes/No* questions. Refuse to answer any question that is not a *Yes/No* question. When your teacher gives you a signal, you can ask any kind of question that you like. Here are some possible *Yes/No* questions to ask: Is this a person? Is this person male or female? Is this an object? Is it expensive? Is this an animal? Is this food? Here are some possible *Wh*-questions: How big is this? Where was she or he born? What color is this?

ACTIVITY 2: SPEAKING/WRITING

The international student office at your school is preparing a short guide for students who have just arrived in this country. The purpose of this guide is to give new students a clear idea of what to expect when they arrive here. You have been asked to write a chapter called "Most Commonly Asked Questions."

Get together with two or three other students and make a list of all the questions that people in this country usually ask you. Compare your lists with those of other students in the class. Use the information from your classmates to make a list of the questions that people here usually ask international students and that new students should be ready to answer.

ACTIVITY 3: SPEAKING/WRITING

Some of your friends here are thinking of taking a trip. Work in groups with at least one person whose country is not in North America, if possible. Have that person share questions that people in your country usually ask visitors from other countries. Make a list and compare the questions with those of students from different countries and cultures. What differences and similarities do you find?

ACTIVITY 4: WRITING/READING

STEP 1 In this activity you cannot speak, but you can write. Sit down next to a student that you do not know very well. Spend a couple of minutes thinking about some of the things you would like to know about this person. Take a piece of paper and write **one** question for your partner to answer. Pass the question to your partner. Read the question that your partner gives you. Without speaking, write your answer to the question and write another question for your partner to answer. **Do not speak at all**.

STEP 2 Exchange papers with your partner. Read your partner's answer to your question and answer his or her question to you. Continue writing questions and answers to each other until your teacher tells you to stop. Now you can speak!

Optional: With your partner's permission, share some of the information from your silent interview with the rest of the class.

STEP 3 Look back over the questions that you and your partner wrote. Were you able to use any of the kinds of questions discussed in this unit?

ACTIVITY 5: SPEAKING/LISTENING

Your English teacher has just quit her job and is now sunning on a beach in Tahiti. Your class is desperately searching for a new teacher. You have decided to take matters into your own hands and interview teachers yourselves. One of your classmates is an applicant for the position. Ask him or her some questions about his or her experience, interests, and future goals. Listen to your classmate's answers. They may help you ask other questions.

ACTIVITY 6: LISTENING/ WRITING

A friend of yours has applied for a job teaching English in Latvia. She cannot travel to Latvia for a job interview, so the school has to interview her by phone. You are at her house when the school calls. You can hear her half of the conversation (the answers that she gives), but you can't hear the questions that the interviewer asked.

STEP 1 Listen to her half of the conversation on the tape. In the first column, write the questions that you think the interviewer **probably** asked. Then listen to the complete interview to compare your questions with the ones the interviewer **actually** asked. Use the second column to write any questions that are different from the ones in the first column.

1) PROBABLE QUESTIONS	2) ACTUAL QUESTIONS

ACTIVITY 7: SPEAKING/LISTENING

At school, you have recently lost a very unusual and very valuable piece of jewelry, perhaps a ring or necklace. Now you are sitting in class, and you notice that the person sitting beside you is wearing a ring or necklace just like the one you lost. Of course, you would like to ask the person some questions about it to find out if it might be yours.

You might want to role-play this in teams. One team can serve as coaches for the person who has lost the piece of jewelry. The other team can serve as coaches for the person who is wearing the piece of jewelry.

ACTIVITY 8: SPEAKING/LISTENING/WRITING

With your classmates, brainstorm and write a list of questions that are useful for people learning English, in or outside the classroom setting. Which are the three most useful questions?

To get you started, here are some examples of questions that students have found useful:

- What does _____ mean?
- Can you repeat that, please?

ACTIVITY 9: SPEAKING/LISTENING

Bring in a photograph and give it to your teacher. Each student will look at one photograph for thirty seconds and then give it back to the teacher. Other students will then ask the student questions about the picture he or she studied and try to guess the situation. Try to use all types of questions: *Yes/No*, *Wh-*, statement form, choice, and tag. The person who brought in the picture can then tell the class whether their guesses were correct or not.

Tape yourself as you ask the questions. Afterwards, listen to the tape and check to see if you were able to use the kinds of questions discussed in this unit.

MODALS OF PROBABILITY AND POSSIBILITY

Could, May, Might, Must

UNIT GOALS:

- To use *could, may, might, must,* and *couldn't/can't* to show how certain you are about a present situation
- To correctly form statements and questions to describe probability and possibility in the present and past
- To correctly use the progressive with modals of probability and possibility
- To use *could, may, might, probably, will/be going to, may not,* and *might not* to talk about future probability and possibility

▶ **OPENING TASK**
Identify the Mystery Person

One evening toward the end of March, a New York taxi driver found that someone had left a briefcase on the back seat of his cab. When he opened it, he found that the briefcase was empty, except for the things you can see on the next page.

STEP 1   With a partner, examine everything on this page carefully. Can you find any clues about the identity of the owner of the briefcase? Use the chart below to write down your ideas and to show how certain you are about them.

GUESSES	HOW CERTAIN ARE YOU?		
	Less than 50% Certain (it's possible)	90% Certain (it's probable)	100% Certain (it's certain)
Name			
Sex			
Age			
Marital Status			
Occupation			
Likes and Interests			
Family and Friends			
Habits			
Recent Activities			
Future Plans			
Anything else?			

MARCH

SUNDAY	MONDAY	TUESDAY	WEDNESDAY	THURSDAY	FRIDAY	SATURDAY
1	2 Board meeting 10:30 send papers to Washington	3 meeting 8 lunch Sally leave for NYC 7:00	4 Ash Wednesday NYC EXECUTIVE	5 MEETING	6 return from NYC meeting 10:30 drinks Bob Theatre 8:30	7 wedding anniversary Dinner 8
8 golf 9:30	9 report on NYC meeting due	10 Sally's Birthday meeting with Vice president 2 p.m. movie 8	11 arrive 14.50	12 Paris meeting	13	14 Call Sally
15 Purim	16 Accountant Lunch Robert Haywood Call Paris Office	17 St. Patrick's Day OPERA 9:30	18 Visitors from Tokyo office dinner Japanese restaurant 7 p.m.	19	20 Export meeting	21 Spring begins tennis 2 p.m. Mike Kids home from school
22 golf 9:30	23 Japanese Class	24 Doctor: 8 sales meeting 10:30	25 9:00 Accountant tennis Mike	26 Lunch SALLY	27 Doctor: 9 10:00 sales meeting Japanese Class	28 check passport
29 TOKYO?	30	31				

STEP 2   Now get together with a group and share your ideas about the identity of this mystery person, showing how certain you feel about each one.

Modals of Probability and Possibility: Could, May, Might, Must   **71**

▶ **U**sing *Could, May, Might,* and *Must* to Show How Certain You Are about a Present Situation

EXAMPLES	EXPLANATIONS
Situation: He's got a baseball hat on. *Less Certain* ↑ (a) He **could** play baseball. (b) He **might** play baseball. ↓ (c) He **may** play baseball. *More Certain* Situation: She is wearing a white coat. *Less Certain* ↑ (d) She **could** be a doctor. (e) She **might** be a doctor. ↓ (f) She **may** be a doctor. *More Certain*	*Could, may, might,* and *must* show how certain or not you are about a present situation. **Possible (less than 50% certain)** Use *could, might* or *may* to express possibility (to show that you believe something is possible, but you are not very certain if it is true or not). You are making a guess. *May* shows that you are a little more certain that something is true.
Situation: He's wearing a baseball hat. He's carrying a baseball glove. (g) He **must** play baseball. Situation: She is carrying a stethoscope. (h) She **must** be a doctor.	**Probable (about 90% certain)** Use *must* to express probability (to show that you believe something is probably true). You are **almost** certain that this is true. You are drawing a conclusion, based on what you know.
Situation: It's the middle of a baseball game. He is throwing a ball to his teammate. (i) He **plays** baseball. Situation: She performed surgery on my mother in the hospital and saved her life. (j) She **is** a doctor.	**Certain (100% certain)** These are facts. You are completely certain about these situations. Do not use *could, may, might,* or *must.* For information on other ways of using *could, might, may,* and *must,* see Units 10, 11, and 17.

EXERCISE 1

Look at the situations below and complete the sentences to show how certain the speaker is about each one.

Situation	Possible
She always wears a purple hat.	**Less Certain** ↑ 1) She _____ like purple. 2) She _____ like purple. ↓ 3) She _____ like purple. *More Certain*

Situation	Probable
She always wears a purple hat and a purple coat.	4) She _____ like purple.

Situation	Certain
She always wears purple clothes, she drives a purple car and lives in a purple house, surrounded by purple flowers.	5) She _____ purple.

Situation	Possible
He's carrying a French newspaper.	**Less Certain** ↑ 6) He _____ be French. 7) He _____ be French. ↓ 8) He _____ be French. *More Certain*

Situation	Probable
He's carrying a French newspaper and he's speaking French to the people with him.	9) He _____ be French.

Situation	Certain
He's carrying a French newspaper and he's speaking French to the people with him. He was born in France and has a French passport.	10) He _____ French.

Compare your answers with a partner's and then check what you have written with the information in Focus 1.

▶ Modals of Probability and Possibility

EXAMPLES	EXPLANATIONS
subject + modal + verb **(a)** Jack **could** live here. **(b)** **NOT:** Jack could lives here. **(c)** Alex **might** know him. **(d)** **NOT:** Alex mights know him. **(e)** Shirley **may** be at home. **(f)** **NOT:** Shirley maybe at home.	**Affirmative Statements** Modals come before the base form of the verb. Modals have only one form. They do not take *s*. *Maybe* is not a modal.
subject + modal + not + verb **(g)** She **must not** like cats. **(h)** Bo **might not** know that. **(i)** That's impossible! Ron **couldn't** be in Las Vegas. I saw him just a few minutes ago. He **can't** be there. **(j)** I'm not very sure where Sid is. I think he **could** be in Reno.	**Negative Statements** *May not*, *might not*, and *must not* are not usually contracted when they express possibility or probability. *Couldn't/can't* shows that you strongly believe that something is impossible. They are usually contracted. *Couldn't* therefore expresses very strong certainty. However, *could* expresses very weak certainty; it shows that you are not very certain if something is possible.
modal + subject + verb **(k)** **Could** Sid be in Reno? **(l)** **Might** Cathy know about this?	**Questions** *May* and *must* are not used in questions about possibility and probability.
Question: *Answer:* **(m)** Does he take the train? — I'm not sure. He **might**. **(n)** Does Sue like Thai food? — She **may not**. She doesn't like spicy food very much. **(o)** Is Jay at home? — He **might be**. He's not in his office.	**Short Answers** Use the modal by itself in short answers. Use the modal + *be* in short answers to questions with *be*.

EXERCISE 2

Turn back to the Opening Task on page 71. Make statements about the owner of the briefcase. Use *must, may, could, might, couldn't,* or *can't* to show how certain you feel. Share your opinions with your classmates and be ready to justify them as necessary.

▶ **EXAMPLE:** NAME: I*n my opinion, the owner of the briefcase might be called C. Murray because this name is on the boarding pass. However, this boarding pass could belong to somebody else.*

1. SEX: In my opinion, the owner of the briefcase _____
because _____
_____ .

2. OCCUPATION: I believe she or he _____
because _____
_____ .

3. MARITAL STATUS: This person _____
I think this because _____
_____ .

4. LIKES AND INTERESTS: _____
_____ .

5. HABITS: _____
_____ .

6. AGE: _____
_____ .

EXERCISE 3

Add an appropriate short answer to the questions in these conversations.

1. A: Where's Mike? Is he angry?

   B: I don't know. He _____. He didn't say much before he left.

2. A: Does Perry drive to school?

   B: I'm not sure. He _____.

3. A: Does Elka like dogs?

   B: She _____ (not). I know that she doesn't like most animals.

4. A: Do you know if Frankie drinks coffee?

   B: Good question. She _____, but I don't really know.

5. A: Is Connie married?

   B: I think she _____, but nobody seems to know for sure.

6. A: Do you know if Hanh still lives with his parents?

   B: He _____ (not) anymore. I think he was planning on moving out last spring.

7. A: I'm looking for someone to translate this letter into Turkish. Does George speak Turkish?

   B: He _____. He lived there for five years, but I'm not sure how much he remembers.

▶ Modals of Probability and Possibility in the Past

EXAMPLES	EXPLANATIONS
subject + modal + have + past participle (a) Vi **may have left.** (b) I'm not sure how Liz went home last night; she **could have taken** a cab. (c) There's nobody here; everyone **must have gone** out.	**Affirmative Statements** Choose the appropriate modal + *have* + past participle to show how certain you are about something that happened in the past.
subject + modal + not + have + past participle (d) I **may not have seen** him. (e) Selena **might not have been** in town last week. (f) Darius **couldn't have robbed** the store. He was at home with me all evening.	**Negative Statements:** Choose the appropriate modal + *not* + *have* + past participle to show how certain you are that something did **not** happen in the past.
modal + subject + have + past participle? (g) **Could** she **have known?** (h) **Might** the police **have followed** the stolen car?	**Questions:** Choose the appropriate modal + subject + *have* + past participle to ask about possibility and probability in the past. Remember that *must* and *may* are not usually used in questions about possibility or probability.

(i) Q: Did Jerry talk to Kramer last night?
   A: I'm not sure. He **may have.**
 	
(j) Q: Did Bernadette remember to go to the store?
   A: She **must have.** The refrigerator is full of food.
	Short answers:
	Use the appropriate modal + *have* in short answers.

(k) Q: Was Vinny depressed? A: It's hard to say. He **might have been.** (l) **NOT:** He might have.	Remember to use the appropriate modal + *have been* in short answers to questions using *be*.

EXERCISE 4

Turn back to the Opening Task. Make statements showing how certain you are about the person's past activities. Use *must, may, could, might, couldn't,* or *can't* to show how certain you feel. Be ready to share and justify your opinions.

EXERCISE 5

In trying to solve crimes, detectives generally examine evidence carefully and then draw conclusions based on what they observe. Sometimes their conclusions are stronger (or more certain) than at other times, depending on the evidence they have examined. Creative detectives (like Sherlock Holmes) are famous for examining all possibilities in a case. What might Sherlock Holmes conclude about the following people?

▶ **EXAMPLE:** **1.** A woman with a yellow forefinger:

She must be a heavy smoker. OR *She might be a painter, and she might have lost her paintbrush.*

Can you think of any other possibilities? Be ready to share your ideas with your classmates.

2. A very short man with bowlegs: _____

_____

3. A man with a very red nose: _____

_____

4. A woman with rough, hard hands: _____

_____

5. A woman with a fur coat, diamonds, and chauffeur-driven limousine:

_____

_____

6. A man with soft, white hands: _____

_____

7. A man with a lot of tattoos: _____

_____

▶ # Modals of Probability and Possibility with the Progressive

EXAMPLES	EXPLANATIONS
subject + modal + be + verb + -ing **(a)** He **might be sleeping.** **(b)** Q: What's Lisa doing these days? A: I'm really not sure. She **may be working** in Latvia. **(c)** Something smells good! Albert **must be cooking** dinner. **(d)** You **must know** the Van Billiard family. They live in Amherst. **(e)** **NOT:** You must be knowing the Van Billiard family.	Use modals with the progressive to make a guess or draw a conclusion about something in progress at or around the time of speaking. Remember that some verbs cannot be used in the progressive. For more information, see Unit 2.
subject + modal + have been + verb + -ing **(f)** He **may have been sleeping.** **(g)** Mo **must have been working** on his car; his hands are really dirty.	Use this form to make a guess or draw a conclusion about something that was in progress before the time of speaking.

EXERCISE 6

Look back at the situations in Exercise 5. Can you make any statements about the people in these situations using *must, may, might,* or *could* with a progressive form? Use present forms (to talk about what you think they might be doing now) or past forms (to talk about what you think they might have been doing before now). For example: *The woman with a yellow forefinger might be a cook. She might have been cooking curry and she could have been using her finger to taste the food. She might be going home now to take a shower.* You may not be able to use these forms with all of the situations. Compare your ideas with a partner's.

EXERCISE 7

The police are investigating a murder. What might Sherlock Holmes conclude about the following pieces of evidence? Get together with a partner to come up with a theory. After that, share your conclusions with the rest of the class, using *must, may, could, might,* or *couldn't/can't* to show how certain you feel. Finally, take a vote to decide who has the most interesting theory. How probable do you think this theory is?

> The victim was found in her bedroom on the second floor of her house. The front door and her bedroom door were locked from inside. There were two wine glasses on the table in her room; one was empty, the other was full. There was an ashtray with several cigarette butts in it. The victim had a small white button in her hand and several long, blond hairs. Her watch was found on the floor; it had stopped at 11:30. The drawers of the victim's desk were open, and there were papers all over the floor. Nothing appeared to be missing.

EXERCISE 8

You are a reporter for your local newspaper. The editor has asked you to report on the murder described in Exercise 7. Explain what you think happened and why you believe this to be so. Make a headline for your report. Display your headline and your report so that your classmates can compare the different theories about the murder.

▶ # Future Probability and Possibility with Modals

MEANING

EXAMPLES	EXPLANATIONS
(a) There are a few clouds in the sky; it **could** **might** **may** rain later.	Use *could*, *might*, or *may* to express future possibility.
(b) Cheer up! She **might** call tomorrow.	
(c) We **may** see them next month.	*May* shows that you are a little more certain that something will happen.
(d) Q: Where's Anna? A: She'**ll probably** get here soon.	Use *will* or *be going to* with *probably* to show that you are almost certain that something will happen in the future. Do not use *must*.
(e) NOT: She must get here soon.	
(f) Q: What's Jim going to do after he graduates next year? A: He'**s probably going to** travel around the world on a motorcycle.	
(g) NOT: He must travel round the world on a motorcycle.	
(h) Look! The sun's coming out. It **may not** rain after all.	Use *may not* or *might not* to show that it is possible that something will **not** happen. Do not use *could not*.
(i) NOT: It could not rain after all.	
(j) Fran **might not** come to the airport with us tomorrow.	
(k) NOT: Fran could not come to the airport with us tomorrow.	

EXERCISE 9

Work with a partner and turn back to the Opening Task. From the evidence given, what can you say about the person's future plans? Use *will/be going to*, *probably*, *may, could, must,* or *may not/might not* as necessary. Be prepared to share and justify your answers.

EXERCISE 10

Work with a partner and choose the best way to complete each sentence. Discuss the reasons for your choice. Be prepared to share your answers with the rest of the class.

1. A: Where's Rose?

   B: I'm not sure. She _____ in the library.
   is   might be   must be

2. A: My daughter just got a scholarship to Stanford!

   B: You _____ be very proud of her.
   could   must   might

3. A: How does Sheila get to school?

   B: I don't really know. She _____ the bus.
   might take   takes   must take

4. A: It's really cold in here today

   B: Yes. Somebody _____ the window open.
   must leave   might leave   must have left

5. A: I wonder why Zelda always wears gloves.

   B: I don't know. She _____ some kind of allergy.
   may have had   has   may have

6. A: Have you heard the weather forecast?

   B: No, but look at all those dark clouds in the sky. I think it

   _____ rain.
   could   must   is probably going to

7. A: Did my mother call while I was out?

   B: I'm not sure. She _____ .
   might have   might   did

8. A: Ellen gave a violin recital in front of five hundred people yesterday. It was her first public performance.

   B: Really? She _____ very nervous.
   could have been   must be   must have been

9. A: Are you coming to Jeff's party?

   B: I'm not sure. I _____ go to the coast instead.
   must   will   might

10. A: Can I speak to Professor Carroll?

    B: She's not in her office, and she doesn't have any more classes today, so

    she _____ home.
    might go   must have gone   will probably go

11. A: Jenny's sneezing again.

    B: Yes, she _____ a terrible cold.
must have   must be having   must have had

12. A: Look, Maynard's sitting outside his own apartment. Isn't that weird?

    B: Not really. He _____ his keys and now he's waiting for his wife to come home.
may be losing   may have lost   may have been losing

13. A: Is Myrna working in the city today?

    B: She _____ . I'm not sure.
could   could have   could be

14. A: I can hear the water running in the bathroom.

    B: Yes, Bira _____ another shower.
must take   must have taken   must be taking

15. A: What's up? You look worried.

    B: I am. My dog's sick. I think he _____ eaten some poison.
maybe   may have been   may have

16. A: Have you heard? Mel's father died last night.

    B: Poor Mel. He _____ feeling terrible. They were very close.
must   must be   must have been

17. A: Dean just won a million dollars in the lottery.

    B: He _____ . He never buys lottery tickets.
must not have   could not   couldn't have

18. A: Does Isaiah still share a house with his sister?

    B: I don't know. He _____ .
might be   might   might have

EXERCISE 11

Look back at the Opening Task. Who do you think the "Mystery Person" is? What do you think happened to him or her? Complete the following newspaper article with your ideas about what might have happened. Remember to use *must, may, could, might,* or *couldn't/can't* to show how certain you feel.

Missing Mystery Person

It has been a week since New York taxi driver Ricardo Oliveiro found a briefcase on the back seat of his cab. It has been a week of guessing and speculation: Who is the owner of this briefcase and where is he or she now? Several different theories have been proposed, but so far the most interesting is the one which follows . . . .

Use Your English

ACTIVITY 1: SPEAKING/LISTENING

Can you guess what these drawings represent? Get together with a partner and see how many different possible interpretations you can come up with for each drawing. Classify your interpretations as "Possible," "Probable," and "Certain." Compare your answers with the rest of the class. (You can find the "official" answers on page A-16.)

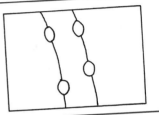

ACTIVITY 2: SPEAKING/LISTENING

The purpose of this activity is to confuse your classmates. Form teams and create five different drawings of familiar things seen from an unusual point of view. Exchange papers. Each team receives drawings from another team. As a team, see how many different interpretations you can make for each drawing. Write each beside the appropriate drawing, showing how probable you think your interpretation is.

When you have made your guesses, exchange papers with another team until everyone has had a chance to "interpret" all the drawings. Which team got the most "correct" interpretations? Which team had the most interesting interpretations?

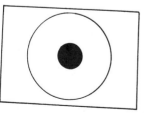

It could be a donut.
It might be a hat from above.
It could be an eyeball.

ACTIVITY 3: SPEAKING/LISTENING

Get together with a partner and examine the photographs below. What's going on? Who are the people? Create a story showing what you think might have happened and what might happen next. You can use the photographs in any order that you like. Compare your story with those of your classmates. In what ways do their interpretations differ from yours?

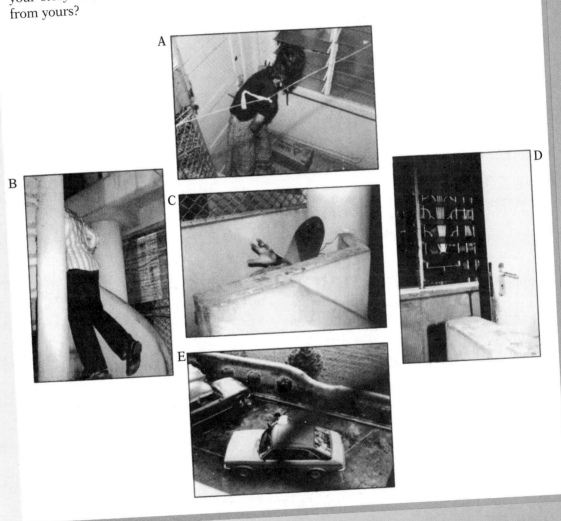

ACTIVITY 4: SPEAKING/LISTENING

STEP 1 Show the photographs from Activity 3 to a native speaker of English. Ask him or her to tell you what she or he thinks might have happened and what might happen next. Tape the answers he or she gives. Listen to your tape and be ready to tell your classmates what the person says. How many different stories are there? Which one is the most interesting?

STEP 2 Listen to your tape again and write down any sentences with examples of the language from this unit.

ACTIVITY 5: LISTENING

STEP 1 Listen to the tapes of two different people talking about the photographs on page 85. As you listen to their stories, write the letter of each photograph on the chart to show which one comes first, second, and so on.

	SPEAKER 1 Photograph	SPEAKER 2 Photograph
First		
Second		
Third		
Fourth		
Fifth		

Which story is the most interesting, in your opinion?

STEP 2 Listen to the tape again and write down any sentences with *may, might, could,* or *must* that show how certain the speaker feels.

ACTIVITY 6: SPEAKING/LISTENING

In the Opening Task, you looked at the contents of somebody's briefcase and made guesses about his or her identity. The purpose of this activity is to create your own "mystery person." Form groups and collect a number of items that somebody might carry in his or her pockets (tickets, bills, photographs, business cards, etc.). Choose between eight to ten items, put them in a bag, and bring them to class. Exchange bags with another group. With your group, examine the contents of your bag and try to decide on the possible identity of the owner, using the same categories as in the Opening Task. When everyone is ready, share your conclusions with the rest of the class, showing how certain you are. Remember, your class-mates might ask you to justify your conclusions, so be ready to justify each one.

ACTIVITY 7: WRITING

Write a profile of the "mystery person" your group presented to the class in Activity 6. Make sure you have an introduction and that you provide evidence to support your conclusions. When you finish writing, read your profile to see how much of the language discussed in this unit you were able to use.

Past progressive and simple past with time clauses

When, While, and As Soon As

UNIT GOALS:
- To choose between past progressive and simple past
- To form past progressive correctly
- To understand the meaning of *when*, *while*, and *as soon as*
- To correctly form clauses with *when*, *while*, and *as soon as*

▶ **O P E N I N G   T A S K**
Miami Murder Mystery

Last night Lewis Meyer died at his home in Miami. Phil Fork, a police detective, was the first person to arrive at the house after Mr. Meyer died. This is what he found:

Mr. Meyer's wife, Margo, told Fork: "It was an accident. My husband took a shower at about 10:00 P.M. After his shower, he slipped on a piece of soap and fell down."

Do you believe her?

What probably happened?

Look at the picture and work with a partner. Decide whether the following statements are **probably** true (T) or **probably** false (F). Be ready to share your answers with your classmates and to explain your choices.

1.	Mr. Meyer died after Phil Fork arrived.	T	F
2.	Mr. Meyer died when Phil Fork arrived.	T	F
3.	Mr. Meyer died before Phil Fork arrived.	T	F
4.	Mr. Meyer brushed his teeth before he died.	T	F
5.	Mr. Meyer was brushing his teeth when he died.	T	F
6.	Mr. Meyer was taking a shower when he died.	T	F
7.	Mr. Meyer took a shower before he died.	T	F
8.	Mr. Meyer died when he slipped on a piece of soap.	T	F
9.	Somebody hit Mr. Meyer over the head while he was brushing his teeth.	T	F
10.	The murder weapon is still in the bathroom.	T	F

You are the detective. In your opinion, how did Mr. Meyer die?

With your partner, use the picture and your answers above to try to solve the mystery. Make as many guesses as you like. For example: *We think somebody killed Mr. Meyer while he was brushing his teeth. This is how it happened.* . . . Be ready to share your ideas with the rest of the class. Write your ideas here:

What really happened:

▶ **Past Progressive and Simple Past**

EXAMPLES	EXPLANATIONS
(a) Phil Fork **arrived** at 10:30. **(b)** Mrs. Meyer **drank** several cups of black coffee.	Use the simple past for an action that started and finished in the past. For a list of irregular past forms, see Appendix 5 on page A-13.
(c) Phil Fork **was eating** dinner at 10:00. **(d)** Mr. Meyer **was brushing** his teeth at 10:00.	*Was eating* and *was brushing* are past progressive. Use the past progressive for an action that was in progress at a specific time in the past.
(e) Mr. Meyer **was brushing** his teeth when the murderer **entered** the room. **(f)** Phil Fork **was eating** dinner when he **heard** about the murder.	Use the past progressive with the simple past to show that one action began first and was still in progress when the second action happened. It is possible that the first action continued after the second action finished.
(g) Mrs. Meyer **was talking** on the phone while her husband **was taking** a shower. **(h)** Phil Fork **was reading** a newspaper while he **was eating** dinner.	Use the past progressive with the past progressive to show two actions in progress at the same time.

EXERCISE 1

Look back at what you wrote in the Opening Task on page 89. Did you use the past progressive and the simple past? If you did, underline all examples of the past progressive, circle all examples of the simple past, and check with your teacher to see if you used them correctly. If you didn't use these forms at all, write three sentences about Mr. Meyer's murder using the past progressive and the simple past. Check with your teacher to see if you used these forms correctly.

▶ **Past Progressive**

STATEMENT	NEGATIVE	QUESTION
I She He It ⎫ **was sleeping.**	I She He It ⎫ **was not sleeping. (wasn't)**	**Was** ⎰ I she he it ⎱ **sleeping?**
We You They ⎫ **were sleeping.**	We You They ⎫ **was not sleeping. (weren't)**	**Were** ⎰ we you they ⎱ **sleeping?**

EXERCISE 2

Get together with a partner and complete this newspaper report of Mr. Meyer's murder. Use information from the Opening Task on page 88 and your own ideas about what happened to help you.

DAILY NEWS

BATHROOM MURDER

"I am innocent!" says Mrs. Meyer.

Last night police arrested Margo Meyer for the murder of her husband, Lewis. On her way to the police station, Mrs. Meyer told reporters: "I am innocent. I loved my husband very much. I didn't kill him."

According to Mrs. Meyer, on the night of his death, her husband _____

_____ when

_____ .

However, Detective Phil Fork and his colleagues have a different theory about how Mr. Meyer died. According to them, _____

_____

_____ while _____

_____ .

▶ *When, While,* and *As Soon As*

EXAMPLES	EXPLANATIONS
(a) **While** Mr. Meyer was getting ready for bed, Mrs. Meyer drank several cups of black coffee. OR **(b)** Mrs. Meyer drank several cups of black coffee **while** Mr. Meyer was getting ready for bed.	*When, while* and *as soon as* give information about time. You can use them **either** at the beginning of a sentence **or** in the middle. *While* introduces an action in progress. It means "during that time." It is usually used with the past progressive. However, many people now use *when* in place of *while*, especially in conversation.
(c) Mrs. Meyer called the police **when** she found the dead body. OR **(d)** **When** Mrs. Meyer found her husband's body, she called the police.	*When* introduces a completed action. It is usually used with the simple past. In (c) and (d), *when* introduces the action that happened first: **First** Mrs. Meyer found the body and **then** she called the police.
(e) Mrs. Meyer came to the door **as soon as** Phil Fork arrived. OR **(f)** **As soon as** Phil Fork arrived, Mrs. Meyer came to the door.	*As soon as* introduces a completed action and means "immediately after."

EXERCISE 3

Make meaningful statements about Mr. Meyer's murder by matching information from A with information from B. The first one has been done for you.

A	B
1. Mrs. Meyer called the police	she said that she was innocent.
2. While she was waiting for the police to arrive	Mrs. Meyer took him to the scene of the crime.
3. As soon as Phil Fork heard about the murder	as soon as her husband died.
4. When Fork asked to see the body	while the police were taking her to jail.
5. While Fork was searching the bathroom for clues	while he was brushing his teeth.
6. He saw that Mr. Meyer died	she placed a bar of soap on the bathroom floor.
7. When Fork accused Mrs. Meyer of murder	he rushed to the Meyers' house.
8. A crowd of news reporters tried to interview Mrs. Meyer	he became suspicious of Mrs. Meyer's story.

EXERCISE 4

Look again at the sentences you created in Exercise 3. For each one, underline the part of the sentence that gives information about time. This is the part of the sentence that answers the question "When?" For example: *Mrs. Meyer called the police <u>as soon as</u> her husband died*.

Time Clauses with
When, While, As Soon As,
Before, and After

EXAMPLES	EXPLANATIONS
Dependent Time Clause — *Main Independent Clause*	A time clause is a **dependent** clause; this means that it is not complete by itself. It needs the rest of the sentence (**the main** or **independent** clause) to complete its meaning.
(a) When Amy returned home, — everyone ran out to greet her.	In order to understand *When Amy returned home,* we need more information.
(b) While my father was cooking dinner, our guests arrived.	A time clause can come at the beginning of a sentence (b) **or** at the end (c). If the time clause comes at the beginning of the sentence, use a comma between the time clause and the main clause.
(c) Our guests arrived while my father was cooking dinner.	**When** ～～～～, ～～～～
	If the main clause comes at the beginning of the sentence and the time clause comes last, do not use a comma between the two clauses (c).
	～～～～**when** ～～～～

EXERCISE 5

Turn back to the sentences you created in Exercise 3. Write them below and add commas, as necessary.

1. _____.

2. _____.

3. _____.

4. _____.

5. _____.

6. _____.

7. _____.

8. _____.

EXERCISE 6

Check (✓) the sentence—(a) or (b)—closest in meaning to each statement.

1. While Mr. Meyer was brushing his teeth, someone entered the room.

   (a) Mr. Meyer finished brushing his teeth before someone entered.

   (b) Mr. Meyer was alone when he started brushing his teeth.

2. When he got Mrs. Meyer's call, Phil Fork left his office and drove to her house.

   (a) Mrs. Meyer called before Phil Fork left his office.

   (b) Mrs. Meyer called after Phil Fork left his office.

3. As soon as he got into his car, he took out a cigarette and lit it.

   (a) He was smoking when he got into the car.

   (b) He started to smoke after he got into his car.

4. While Fork was driving to the Meyers' house, he was listening to his favorite opera on the radio.

   (a) He drove his car and listened to the radio at the same time.

   (b) He turned on the radio when he reached the Meyers' house.

5. When he got there, a number of police officers were searching the house for clues.

   (a) They started when he got there.

   (b) They started before he got there.

6. As soon as Fork started to question Mrs. Meyer, she burst into tears.

   (a) She was crying when he started to question her.

   (b) She started to cry when he began to question her.

7. Phil Fork carefully reviewed all his notes when he went home.

   (a) He went home first.

   (b) He reviewed his notes first.

EXERCISE 7

Work with a partner and write down five things you know about John Lennon.

Here is some more information about John Lennon's life. The wavy line (∿∿∿) indicates an action in progress. X indicates a completed action.

1. attend high school ∿∿∿ ―――― X his mother dies	2. attend high school ∿∿∿ ―――― X meet Paul McCartney
3. study at art school ∿∿∿ ―――― X form the Beatles	4. perform in clubs in Liverpool ∿∿∿ ―――― X sign his first recording contract
5. live in London ∿∿∿ ―――― X fall in love with Yoko Ono	6. work for peace and write new songs ―――― ∿∿∿ X die
7. leave his apartment ―――― ∿∿∿ X one of his fans shoots him	

Use this information to finish the short biography below. Fill in the blanks, using the simple past or the past progressive. The first one has been done for you as an example.

John Lennon was one of the most famous singer/songwriters of his time. He was born in Liverpool, England, in 1940, but his childhood was not very happy.

(1) _His mother died_ while _he was attending high school_. Life was difficult for John after his mother's death, but after a time things got better. (2) _____ while _____ . Soon Paul introduced him to George Harrison, and they began to play in a band together. After John left high school, he became an art student. (3) While _____ , _____ . After forming the Beatles, John married his first wife, Cynthia, and they had a son, Julian. (4) _____ when _____ . John and the Beatles moved to London and became very famous throughout the world. (5) _____ while _____ . A couple of years later, the Beatles split up. John and Yoko got married and moved to the United States, where their son Sean was born. John (6) _____ when _____ . On December 8, 1980, (7) _____ while _____ . John Lennon died in 1980, but he still has lots of fans all over the world.

EXERCISE 8

Complete the sentences in the story below using the words in parentheses. Use the simple past or the past progressive.

1. Yesterday morning at 10:00, Marie _____ (go) to see the dentist.

2. While she _____ (wait) for her appointment, her old friend Lin _____ (come) into the dentist's waiting room.

3. Before Marie _____ (get) her new job at the software company, she and Lin _____ (work) together at the bank.

4. When Marie and Lin _____ (see) each other in the waiting room, they _____ (be) surprised and delighted.

5. They _____ (realize) that they had not seen each other for several months.

6. While they _____ (wait) for their appointments, they _____ (talk and laugh) about old times.

7. When it _____ (be) finally time for Marie to see the dentist, they _____ (not + want) to stop talking.

8. Just before Marie _____ (leave) the waiting room, they _____ (make) a date to see each other again.

9. While Marie _____ (leave) the waiting room, Lin _____ (say), "I hope you don't have any cavities!"

Use Your English

Nan Silviera has just written her first book:

As you can see below, the author's life story on the back of the book is not complete. Work with a partner to finish writing it.

STEP 1 Student A: Turn to page 102. Student B: Turn to page 103.

STEP 2 You both have information about Nan's life, but some of the information is missing. Do not show your pages to each other, but ask each other questions to get information about the parts marked "?".

STEP 3 Write down the information your partner gives you so that when you finish, you will have the complete story.

STEP 4 Use the information from your chart to write about Nan's life. You can use the biography on the back of her book to begin your story.

STEP 5 When you finish writing, check your work to see if you have used time clauses and the past progressive and simple past tenses appropriately.

About the author:
Nan Silviera graduated from Arizona State University in 1980. In 1981 she sailed across the Pacific single-handedly. After that, she ...

JOURNEYS
By
Nan Silviera

ACTIVITY 2: SPEAKING/LISTENING/WRITING

In this activity, you will be finding information about your classmates' lives by asking what they were doing at the times shown below. In the last box on the chart, add a time of your own choice (for example, on your last birthday, last New Year's Eve, etc.). Do not write information about yourself.

STEP 1 Think about the different students in your class. Can you guess what they were doing at these times? In the box marked *Guesses*, write what **you** think different people were doing at each time.

STEP 2 Go around the room and talk to as many people as possible to find out what they were really doing.

STEP 3 Write this information in the box marked *Facts*.

NOTE: Copy the chart into your notebook if you need more space to write. If your class is very big, you can make guesses about some of your classmates rather than all of them. If you don't want to give information about a certain time, you can say, "I'm sorry but I'd rather not talk about that time." If you can't remember, feel free to invent something.

Times	Guesses	Facts
at 8:30 P.M. last Sunday		
in May 1993		
five years ago		
ten years ago today		
????? (you choose a time)		

STEP 4 When you finish, review the information you collected. Choose the most interesting or surprising facts and make a short report (oral or written). Report on the facts, not on your original guesses. For example:

I recently asked my classmates about certain times in their lives. I was surprised by some of the things they told me. For example, ten years ago, while Sun Wu (she was only eight years old at that time) was going to elementary school, Tranh was working in his father's store. . . .

ACTIVITY 3: SPEAKING/WRITING

STEP 1 Take a large sheet of paper and make a time line for your own life like the one in Activity 1. Bring your time line to class and describe the story of your life to your classmates.

STEP 2 Exchange your time line with a partner. Use his or her time line to write the story of his or her life. How many differences and similarities can you find between your partner's life history and yours?

ACTIVITY 4: SPEAKING/ LISTENING/WRITING

The death of President John F. Kennedy in 1963 was an enormous shock to people in the United States and to people all over the world. Many people who were alive at that time can remember exactly what they were doing when they heard the news of Kennedy's assassination.

STEP 1 With a partner, interview one or two people who were alive at that time and find out what they were doing when they heard the news of Kennedy's death. If possible, tape-record your interviews. Before the interview, get together with your partner to make a list of possible questions. You can use the questions below or make other questions of your own, if you prefer.

QUESTIONS:

- What were you doing when you heard the news of President Kennedy's death?
- Where were you living at that time?
- Who were you with?
- What were you doing just before you heard the news of his death?
- What did you do after you heard about it?
- How did you feel?
- Do you remember what you were wearing?
- How old were you? What did you look like at that time?

STEP 2 Share your findings with the rest of the class.

STEP 3 Listen to your tape and write down any sentences with the simple past or the past progressive. Underline any time clauses in these sentences.

ACTIVITY 5: LISTENING

For this activity, you will hear three people talking about what they were doing when President Kennedy was killed.

STEP 1   Listen to the tape and take notes in the chart below.

Speaker	Place	Activity
Speaker 1		
Speaker 2		
Speaker 3		

STEP 2   Listen to the tape again and write down any sentences with past progressive or simple past.

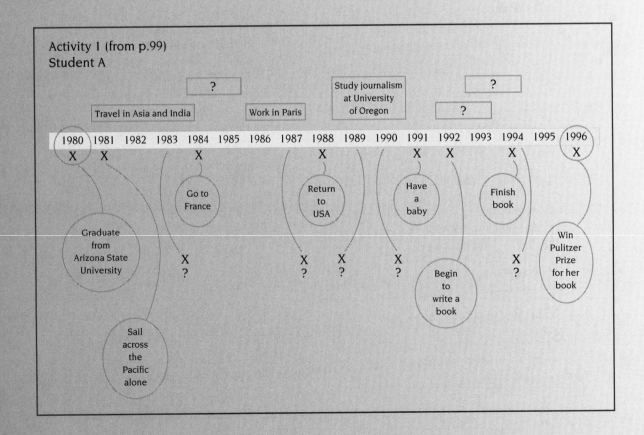

Activity 1 (from p.99)
Student A

Activity 1 (from p.99), continued
Student B

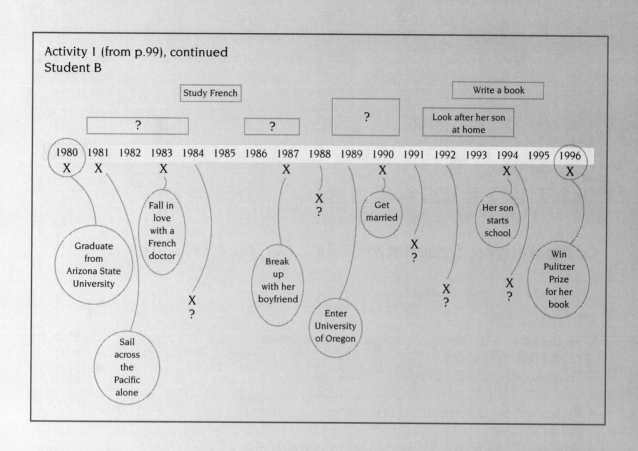

SIMILARITIES AND DIFFERENCES

Comparatives, Superlatives, As . . . As, Not As . . . As

UNIT GOALS:

- To know how to use comparatives and superlatives to express differences
- To know the meaning of *as . . . as* and *not as . . . as*
- To know how to form sentences with *as . . . as* and *not as . . . as*
- To use *as . . . as* and *not as . . . as* to make tactful comparisons

▶ OPENING TASK
Friends

Can you guess the names of the people in this picture? Work by yourself or with a partner and use the information in the chart and the list of clues on the next page to identify each person. Write their names in the correct position on the picture.

The Left   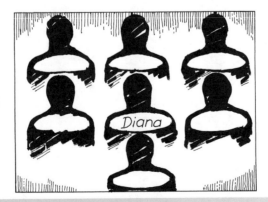   **The Right**

Name	Likes	Age	Hair	Occupation	Eyes	Height
LINDA	football	75	red	doctor	green	5'9 1/2"
BOB	coffee	21	brown	student	blue	5'9 1/2"
SUSAN	music	25	blond	student	green	5'1"
FRANK	cats	43	gray	artist	brown	6'4"
CARLA	food	28	black	singer	blue	5'5"
GEORGE	movies	44	bald	writer	brown	5'10"
DIANA	opera	58	brown	engineer	gray	5'10"

Clues

1. The oldest person is behind the youngest woman.
2. The tallest woman is behind someone who is thirty years younger than she is.
3. The shortest person is in front of someone with green eyes.
4. The tallest man is next to the tallest woman.
5. The 28-year-old singer is not next to anybody.
6. The person who likes coffee is not quite as tall as the person next to him on the right.
7. The man who is on the right of the youngest person is behind the tallest person.
8. The youngest person is as tall as the person next to him on the left.

When you finish, check your answers with the rest of the class to see if you all agree. You can find the solution to the Opening Task on page A-16.

▶ **Expressing Difference: Comparatives and Superlatives**

EXAMPLES	EXPLANATIONS
(a) Susan is **the shortest**, and Frank is **the tallest**. Susan ⋯ Frank	*The tallest* and *the shortest* are superlatives. Superlatives show extremes of difference among people or things. They show which has the greatest amount of a certain quality in a group of people or things.
(b) George is **taller than** Linda. **(c)** Carla is **shorter than** George. Carla Linda George	*Taller than* and *shorter than* are comparatives. Comparatives show differences among people or things, but they do not show extremes of difference.

	Comparative	Superlative	Comparatives and superlatives can be used with all parts of speech:
young	young**er than**	**the** young**est**	• adjectives with one syllable
easy	eas**ier than**	**the** eas**iest**	• adjectives with one syllable + *-y*
difficult	**more** difficult **than**	**the most** difficult	• adjectives with two or more syllables
carefully	**more** carefully **than**	**the most** care-	• adverbs
weigh	weigh **more than**	weigh **the most**	• verbs
	weigh **less than**	weigh **the least**	
money	**more** money **than**	**the most** money	• nouns
	less money **than**	**the least** money	

George is a good singer, but I am not. **(d)** George sings **better than** I do. **(e)** Carla is **the best** singer in the family.	Not all comparative and superlative forms are regular. Examples (d) and (e) use irregular comparative and superlative forms of *good*.

EXERCISE 1

First fill in the blanks with a word or word ending and then use the information from the Opening Task to decide if the statements are true (T) or false (F).

1. The oldest woman is taller _____ the oldest man.   T   F
2. George is tall _____ than the person beside him.   T   F
3. Diana is young _____ _____ the man beside her on the right.   T   F
4. George is tall _____ _____ Frank.   T   F
5. The singer is several years older _____ the person behind her.   T   F
6. The doctor is _____ old _____.   T   F
7. Bob is old _____ _____ the person in front of him.   T   F
8. The young _____ woman is in front of _____ old _____ woman. T   F
9. Frank is _____ tall _____ man, but he isn't _____ old _____ . T   F
10. _____ old _____ man is short _____ _____ the young _____ woman.   T   F

FOCUS **2**

Similarity and Difference:
▶ ## As . . . As and
Not As . . . As

EXAMPLES	EXPLANATIONS
Linda is about 5′9″. Bob is about 5′9″. **(a)** Linda is **as tall as** Bob. OR Bob is **as tall as** Linda. Linda Bob	To show similarity among people or things, you can use *as . . . as*. *Continued on next page*

EXAMPLES	EXPLANATIONS
(b) George is **exactly as tall as** Diana. OR Diana is **exactly as tall as** George. *5'10"* *5'10"* Diana George	To show that people or things are the same, you can add *exactly*.
George is 5'10". Bob is 5'9 1/2". **(c)** Bob is { almost not quite nearly practically just about } **as tall as** George. *5'9½"* *5'10"* Bob George	To show that people or things are very similar, add: *almost, not quite, nearly, practically,* or *just about.*
George is 5'10". Bob is 5'9 1/2". **(d)** Bob is **not as tall as** George.	To show differences among people or things, you can use *not as . . . as.*
Susan is 5'1". Diana is 5'10". **(e)** **nowhere near** Susan is **not nearly as tall as** Diana. **not anywhere near** *5'10"* *5'* Susan Diana	To show a great amount of difference, add: *nowhere near, not nearly,* or *not anywhere near.* *Nowhere near* and *not anywhere near* are only used in very informal conversation with friends.

EXERCISE 2

Get together with another student. Think of all the ways that you are similar and all the ways that you are different. You have five minutes to make as many sentences as you can, using *as . . . as* and *not as . . . as* to show these differences and similarities. Share your sentences with the rest of the class.

EXERCISE 3

Use the information in the Opening Task to write complete sentences about the following people. You can use a comparative, a superlative, *as . . . as* or *not as . . . as* in each sentence. Show the amount of difference or similarity as necessary.

1. Linda/Bob/height

   Linda is as tall as Bob. _____

2. Susan/Frank/height

_____

3. Linda/Diana/height

_____

4. Linda/Carla/height

_____

5. George/Susan/height and age

_____

6. Bob/George/height

_____

7. Frank/George/age

_____

8. Diana/Linda/age

_____

9. Frank/height

_____

10. Linda/age

_____

11. George/Diana/height

_____

▶ **U**sing *As . . . As* and
Not As . . . As

EXAMPLES	EXPLANATIONS
	As . . . as and *not as . . . as* can be used with all parts of speech:
(a) Susan is **not as tall as** Carla.	• adjectives
(b) Frank does not work **as quickly as** George.	• adverbs
(c) Linda does not have **as much money as** Diana.	• nouns
(d) Diana does not have **as many friends as** Carla.	
(e) George **works as** much **as** Linda.	• verbs
	In sentences using *as . . . as* or *not as . . . as*, the second *as* can be followed by:
(f) Susan works as hard as **Carla works.**	• clauses
(g) Carla is not as tall as **Linda is.**	
(h) Susan works as hard as **Carla does.**	
(i) Susan works as hard as **Carla.**	• reduced clauses
(j) Carla is not as tall as **her younger sister.**	• noun phrases
(k) Susan works as hard as **I/you/he/she/ we/they.**	• subject pronouns
(l) Susan works as hard as he **works.** OR	In sentences where the verb is repeated after the second *as*, you can use a form of *do* instead.
(m) Susan works as hard as he **does.**	
(n) Susan works **as hard as he.** OR	The subject pronoun (*he, she, I, we, you, they*) is very formal.
(o) Susan works **as hard as him.**	The object pronoun (*him, her, me, us, you, them*) is very common in conversation and informal writing.

EXAMPLES	EXPLANATIONS
(p) Susan's hair is not as short as **mine**. **(q)** Susan's hair is as long as **mine**. Susan's Hair / My Hair **(r)** Susan's hair is as long as me. Susan's Hair / Me	Remember to use a possessive pronoun where necessary. In examples (q) and (r), both sentences are correct, but there is a big difference in meaning!

EXERCISE 4

Correct the mistakes in the following sentences.

1. All her life, Hester has been lucky than her sister, Miriam.

2. Hester is not intelligent as Miriam but she was always more successful than Miriam in school.

3. For example, Hester's grades were always better than Miriam.

4. Both sisters are pretty, but many people believe that Miriam is prettier that her sister.

5. However, Miriam does not have as many boyfriends than her sister does.

6. They both have excellent jobs, but Miriam thinks her job isn't as interesting as her sister.

7. They both travel as part of their work, but Hester goes to more exciting places than Miriam is.

8. In spite of these differences, Miriam thinks that she is happier that her sister is.

9. However, Hester thinks that good luck is important than good looks and intelligence.

What do **you** think is the most important: good luck, good looks, or intelligence? Why do you think so? Share your ideas with your classmates.

EXERCISE 5

Work in a group to create a problem like the one in the Opening Task. First use the picture and blank chart to record your information and then write the clues. Each clue must contain at least one of the following: a comparative; a superlative; *as . . . as; not as . . . as.* Finally, exchange your problem with another group and see if you can solve each other's problems.

NAME	AGE	HEIGHT	OCCUPATION	LIKES

CLUES

_____

_____

_____

_____

_____

Making Tactful Comparisons with *As . . . As* and *Not As . . . As*

Sometimes it is important to be tactful (more polite and less direct) when you are making comparisons. The adjective you choose can show how tactful your comparison is.

EXAMPLES	EXPLANATIONS
Some adjectives commonly used in making comparisons:	When you use *as . . . as*, it is more usual to use an adjective that expresses "more." When you use an adjective that expresses "less," you draw special attention to it because it is an unusual use.
Express "MORE": / Express "LESS": *tall* / *short* *old* / *young* *large* / *small* *fast* / *slow*	
(a) Linda is **as tall as** Bob.	In (a), the use of *tall* is usual. It does not make us think about **how** tall or **how** short Bob and Linda are, but only that they are the same height.
(b) Linda is **as short as** Bob.	In (b), the use of *short* is unusual. It makes us think that both Bob and Linda are very short.
(c) Patricia is **as old as** Virginia.	In (c), the use of *old* is usual. It shows only that they are the same age.
(d) Patricia is **as young as** Virginia.	In (d), the use of *young* is unusual. It therefore puts special emphasis on *young*.
(e) Bob is **not as tall as** Frank. **(f)** Frank is **not as short as** Bob. Bob Frank	Both (e) and (f) show that Frank is taller than Bob. However, the use of *short* in (f) is unusual, so it draws special attention to the fact that Bob is short. It is more tactful and more polite to choose (e).
(g) Otis is **not quite as smart as** Rocky. **(h)** His latest book is **not quite as good as** his earlier ones.	When you want to be really polite and tactful, you can use *not quite as . . . as*.

EXERCISE 6

You are working in a company in Spain that does a lot of business with clients from North America. You speak both Spanish and English. Your boss speaks some English, but he often needs help, so he has asked you to assist him at a meeting with some important clients. Your company would very much like to do business with these clients, but there are several problems to discuss because the two companies are very different.

To prepare for the meeting, your boss wrote down some of the differences he wants to discuss. However, because he doesn't speak a lot of English, you feel that some of his statements sound rather direct and will probably offend the clients. You decide to change these statements so that they will be less direct and more tactful. Use the adjectives in parentheses with *not as . . . as*. Add *not quite* if you want to be even more tactful. The first one has been done for you.

1. Your company is smaller than ours. (large)
   Your company is not as large as ours.

2. Your factories are more old-fashioned than ours. (modern)
   _____

3. Your workers are lazier than ours. (energetic)
   _____

4. Your products are less popular than ours. (well known)
   _____

5. Our advertising is more successful than yours. (effective)
   _____

6. Your designs are more conservative than ours. (up-to-date)
   _____

7. Your production is slower than ours. (fast)
   _____

8. The quality of your product line is lower than ours. (high)
   _____

9. Your factories are dirtier than ours. (clean)
   _____

10. Your factories are more dangerous than ours. (safe)
    _____

EXERCISE 7

Omar is president of the International Students' Association at an American college located in a small town in the Midwest. The Chamber of Commerce has asked him to give a speech to local businesses on international students' reactions to life in America. He has made a survey of the international students on campus, and he is using the results of the survey for his speech. Some of the comments are not very complimentary, but he feels the local community should know what international students really think. He therefore decides to edit some of the more direct comments so that they will be informative but not offensive. He is having problems with the following statements.

Can you help him make these statements more tactful and polite?

1. In America, people are less sincere.
   In America, people are not quite as sincere.

2. People in my country are much friendlier and more hospitable.

3. Americans are often very rude; people in my country are never rude.

4. The cities here are dirtier and more dangerous than at home.

5. Americans are lazy compared to people in my country.

6. American food is tasteless compared to the food in my country.

7. The nightlife in this town is really boring compared to the nightlife at home.

8. People here watch too much television. We watch much less TV at home.

Do you agree or disagree with these comments?
Do you have any comments of your own that Omar could include in his speech? Add them here:

Use Your English

ACTIVITY 1: WRITING

Write a brief guide for American families who want to become host families for students from other countries. Think about a country you know something about. What should American host families know about the differences between the culture and customs of that country and those of the United States? Be tactful where necessary!

ACTIVITY 2: SPEAKING/LISTENING

There are many common idioms in English that use the construction *as . . . as.*

Here are some common ones:

- as stubborn as a mule
- as happy as a clam
- as strong as an ox

Interview several native speakers of English and ask them to tell you as many of these idioms as they can remember. Then ask them to give you an example of when they might use each idiom.

Idiom	Example of When to Use This Idiom
as _____ as _____	

Choose one of these idioms to explain to your classmates.

ACTIVITY 3: SPEAKING/LISTENING

The purpose of this activity is to think of as many differences as possible between two objects. Your teacher will tell you what you are to compare. Form teams. You have five minutes with your team to make a list of as many differences as possible. After five minutes, the teams take turns sharing their differences. The team with the most differences scores a point. Your teacher will then give you the next two objects to compare. The team with the most points is the winner.

STEP 1 To score a point, your comparison must be meaningful **and** accurate.

STEP 2 You cannot repeat a comparison that another team has already given. However, you **can** express the same idea, using different words. For example:

Team A says: A *Harley Davidson is more expensive than a Honda motorcycle.*

Team B can say: A *Honda isn't as expensive as a Harley Davidson.*

Team C can say: A *Honda is cheaper than a Harley Davidson,* and so on.

If possible, try to tape your team as you play this game. Afterwards listen to the tape and see how many comparative, superlative, and (*not*) *as . . . as* forms you used.

ACTIVITY 4: LISTENING/ SPEAKING

STEP 1 Before you listen to the tape for this activity, get together with a partner. Make a list of all the differences you can think of between a pizza and a hot dog. Write them on the left side of the chart.

What's the Difference Between a Pizza and a Hot Dog?

_____ and I	Terry and Robin
A pizza is more expensive than a hot dog.	

STEP 2 Listen to the tape. You will hear two people, Terry and Robin, comparing a pizza and a hot dog. Add the differences they describe to the right side of the chart. How many differences did you and your partner find? How many did Terry and Robin find?

STEP 3 Now listen to the tape again, and write down any sentences with comparative, superlative, or (not) as . . . as forms in them.

ACTIVITY 5: SPEAKING/LISTENING

Choose one set of objects that you compared in Activity 3 (or example, a bicycle and a car). Ask three different native speakers to compare these two objects and tape their replies. Listen to the tape. Did the native speakers make more comparisons than you did? Or did you make more comparisons than them? Compare your findings with those of the rest of the class.

Listen to your tape again and write down any sentences with examples of comparative, superlative, and (not) as . . . as forms.

ACTIVITY 6: SPEAKING/LISTENING

In North America, it is very common to honor people with special awards for achievements in different fields. For example, the film industry presents Oscars every year for "the best picture," "the best director," and so on. This year, your school has decided to give several special awards to students and teachers for different achievements.

You and your classmates are members of the committee that will decide who should get these awards.

STEP 1 Get together with two or three other students and make a list of awards you would like to give. Decide on who should receive these awards. They don't have to be serious awards. For example, you can give awards for "the best dressed student"; "the most talkative student"; "the most creative dancer"; "the student who is the most likely to become president of his/her country," and so on. You can also give awards to other people on campus or to places that you like in the community ("the teacher who gives the most homework"; "the best hamburger"; "the quietest place to study"; "the best place to meet other students"; "the most romantic place to go on a first date," and so on).

STEP 2 When you are ready, hold your own awards "ceremony" to announce the winners and present your awards.

Tape your group when you present your "awards." Listen to the tape and check to see if you were able to use superlatives correctly.

ACTIVITY 7: WRITING

Your school wants to prepare a short guide for new international students. You have been asked to write a chapter on the best places in town for international students. You can decide on what you want to include in this chapter. Some of the "awards" from Activity 6 may help you here.

Write your chapter for the guide. If you wish, you can include illustrations (photographs, maps, drawings). Share your chapter with the rest of the class.

MEASURE WORDS AND QUANTIFIERS

UNIT GOALS:

- To understand special measure words used with foods
- To correctly use measure words with count and noncount nouns
- To know how to use common quantifiers

▶ **OPENING TASK**
Getting Ready for a Potluck Dinner

Jim has been invited to a potluck dinner—a meal where each guest brings a dish. The hostess asked him to bring cookies and a salad for six people. Jim wants to make everything himself. He already has these ingredients in his kitchen.

INGREDIENTS

mustard	chocolate chips
sugar	tomatoes
salt	flour
lettuce	olive oil
hard-boiled eggs	butter
cheese	eggs
vinegar	garlic

STEP 1 Help Jim decide which ingredients he can use in each dish. Write each ingredient in a box below.

Salad	Salad Dressing	Chocolate Chip Cookies

STEP 2 How much of each ingredient should Jim use? Write an amount beside each ingredient. Remember, there will be six people at the party.

STEP 3 Are there any **other** ingredients you would include? Add them to the boxes above, with suggested amounts.

▶ **M**easure Words with Food

CONTAINERS

Some measure words are **containers** that we can find in a store.

a bottle of (ketchup, soy sauce)

a jar of (peanut butter, mustard)

a box of (crackers, cereal)

a bag of (potato chips, flour)

a carton of (milk, eggs)

a can of (tuna fish, soup)

Some measure words are **portions.** They describe food items as they are commonly served.

a slice of (bread, cheese)

a scoop of ice cream

a piece of (candy, cake)

a pat of butter

a piece of bacon

In North America, these **measurements** are common in recipes:

a cup of (rice, water, flour)

a tablespoon of (salt, sugar, water)

a teaspoon of (salt, sugar, water)

a pinch of (pepper, salt)

Some measure words talk about the **shape** or **appearance** of the food item.

an ear of corn

a head of lettuce

a head or bulb of garlic

a clove of garlic

a bunch of grapes

a loaf of bread

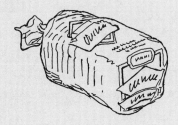

a bar of chocolate

EXERCISE 1

Turn back to the Opening Task on page 121. Look at the ingredients and the amounts. Did you use the right measure words? Make any necessary corrections.

EXERCISE 2

Turn back to the Opening Task and look carefully at the ingredients. Some of these are count nouns (tomatoes) and some are noncount nouns (flour). Write C beside each count noun and NC beside each noncount noun.*

FOCUS **2**

▶ Measure Words with Count and Noncount Nouns

Measure words express specific quantities. They also allow us to make noncount nouns countable.

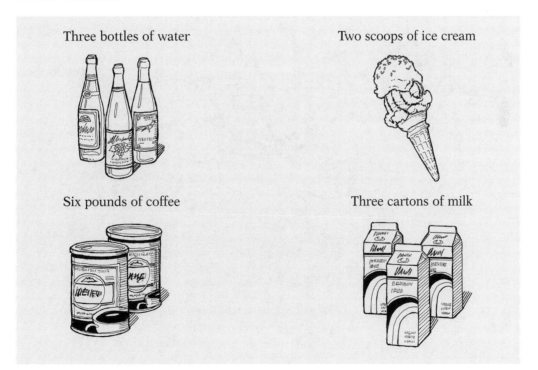

Three bottles of water

Two scoops of ice cream

Six pounds of coffee

Three cartons of milk

*For more information on count and noncount nouns, see *Grammar Dimensions* Book 1, Unit 4.

Most measure expressions follow this pattern.*

A/An/One Two Three	+	Measure Word (Singular/Plural)	+	of	+	Noun (Noncount/ Plural)
a		cup		of		milk
a		pound		of		apples
two		cups		of		milk
two		pounds		of		apples

*Exception: specific numbers (including *dozen*):
       a dozen eggs NOT: a dozen of eggs
       ten strawberries NOT: ten of strawberries

EXERCISE 3

These are the recipes that Jim finally used. Complete the missing parts. (The picture may help you.)

Jim's Super Salad

1 large (a) _____ of red lettuce

1 medium-sized (b) _____ of romaine lettuce

1 large cucumber, cut into (c) _____

6 tomatoes, cut into quarters

1/2 (d) _____ of Swiss cheese, cut into small strips

1 (e) _____ cooked chicken, shredded into small pieces

2 hard-boiled eggs, shelled and cut into quarters

1. Line a large salad bowl with red lettuce leaves.
2. Tear the romaine lettuce leaves into medium-sized pieces.
3. Place in the bowl in layers: slices of cucumber and tomato, cheese, lettuce, and chicken.
4. Add olives and eggs. Cover and refrigerate for one hour. Toss with Jim's Super Salad Dressing just before serving.

Jim's Super Salad Dressing

1 (a) _____ Dijon mustard   1/2 (d) _____ salt

4 (b) _____ red wine vinegar   1/2 (e) _____ pepper

1 (c) _____ sugar   1/2 (f) _____ olive oil

1. Put the mustard into a bowl. Whisk in vinegar, sugar, salt, and pepper.
2. Slowly add the oil while continuing to whisk the mixture.

Jim's Granny's Old Time Chocolate Chip Cookies

1/2 (a) _____ butter
1 (b) _____ brown sugar
3/4 (c) _____ granulated sugar
2 eggs
2 (d) _____ flour

1 (e) _____ baking soda
1 (f) _____ vanilla extract
1 (g) _____ salt
1 1/2 (h) _____ chocolate chips

1. Preheat the oven to 350°F. Grease a cookie sheet.
2. Cream the butter and both the sugars together until light and fluffy. Add the eggs and vanilla and mix well.
3. Sift the flour, baking soda, and salt. Mix thoroughly.
4. Add the chocolate chips.
5. Form into cookies. Place on a cookie tray and put on the middle rack of the oven for 8–10 minutes.
6. Cool for 5 minutes.
7. Enjoy! (This recipe makes about 40 cookies.)

Turn back to the Opening Task on page 121 and look at the ingredients (and the amounts) you suggested for these dishes. How many differences can you find between your suggestions and Jim's recipes? Whose recipe do you think will taste better?

EXERCISE 4

Last week Matthew ate a delicious spaghetti sauce at his friend Nancy's house. He enjoyed it so much that Nancy lent him the recipe so that he could make a copy of it. However, Nancy has obviously used this recipe many times and it is quite difficult to read. Can you help Matthew figure out the recipe? Fill in the missing words below.

Spaghetti Sauce

(from Nancy's kitchen)

First, cut 3 _____ of bacon into small pieces and cook over a very low heat. Stir in 1/2 _____ of ground meat along with 4 _____ garlic and 2 _____ onion, chopped up very finely. Add 1 _____ salt, a pinch of cayenne pepper, and 2 _____ of fresh herbs. Mix in two 8-ounce _____ tomato sauce. Let it cook on low heat for about 30 minutes. Serve over fresh pasta.

If you were making this recipe yourself, would you change or add anything? Share any changes or additions with your classmates. Try to be as precise as possible.

▶ **Common Quantifiers**

AMOUNT	EXAMPLES	EXPLANATIONS
all	**(a)** **All** of the dishes at the potluck were delicious. **(b)** He spends **all** of his money on wine.	Some quantifiers (words that talk about quantity/number or amount) can be used with **both count and noncount nouns.** Use *all* to mean *everything* or *everyone*.
most	**(c)** **Most** of the people in North America take vacations in the summer. **(d)** **Most** of my money has been spent.	*Most* means *almost everyone* or *almost everything*.
many/much	**(e)** We heard that **many** people were coming. **(f)** We don't have **much** time. **(g)** A: Were **many** people hurt? **(h)** B: No, not **many**.	*Many* is used only with count nouns to talk about a large number. Use *much* with noncount nouns to talk about a large amount. *Many* and *much* are usually used in questions or negative statements.
a lot of/lots of/a great deal of	**(i)** We make **a lot of** trips back and forth over the mountains. **(j)** I heard that there was **lots of** new snow. **(k)** **A great deal of** current information is available on the Internet.	Use *a lot of* or *lots of* with very large numbers or amounts, and with either count or noncount nouns. *Lots of* is used in informal situations. Use *a great deal of* in formal situations, and only with noncount nouns. It means the same as *a lot of* or *lots*.
some	**(l)** We needed **some** information about the weather. **(m)** We were glad that we had put **some** new snow tires on our car.	*Some* is a smaller amount or quantity than *a lot of/lots of*. *Some* is used with both count and noncount nouns.

AMOUNT	EXAMPLES	EXPLANATIONS
several	(n) We couldn't travel on **several** days last winter because the mountain passes were closed.	*Several* is used only with count nouns. *Several* means more than a small number.
a few/a little *few/little*	(o) In a **few** days, we'll be ready to go. (p) There was **a little** snow on the mountains. (q) Let's buy **a little** food and **a few** cans of soda. (r) We have **few** friends and **little** money. (s) **Few** people know that she has **little** time left.	*A few* means more than two, but not many more. *A few* and *a little* have similar meanings. *A little* is used only with noncount nouns and *a few* is used only with count nouns. *Few* and *little* refer to the same amounts or numbers as *a few* and *a little*; however, they have a negative meaning. They mean *almost none*. *Few* is used only with count nouns, *little* only with noncount nouns.
a couple (of)	(t) I'd like to get **a couple of** blankets to keep in the car. (u) Let's ask **a couple (of)** people to come with us.	*A couple of* means two, but it is sometimes used informally to mean two or more. *A couple of* is used only with count nouns. In informal English, *of* is sometimes omitted.
none/no	(v) **None of** the people went to the meeting. (w) We heard that there was **no** new snow.	*None* means *not any*, and is used with count nouns. *No* has the same meaning, and is used with noncount nouns.

EXERCISE 5

Find a partner and take turns asking each other questions about your native countries or countries you know about. Use the topics in (A) to ask general questions. In your answers to the questions, give specific examples to explain what you mean. You must use a quantifier (from Focus 3) in your answer. Column (B) gives you ideas for quantifiers you can use in your answers, but you may use others.

▶ **EXAMPLE:** Q: Is clothing expensive in (Vietnam)?

A: No, not really. A *lot of* people go to the big cities to buy clothes. There are *lots of* factories in the cities, so you can usually find clothes that are pretty cheap.

(A) TOPIC	(B) QUANTIFIER
1. clothing	some lots of/a lot of
2. tourist attractions	a few a couple of
3. holidays	most some
4. climate	no/none a great deal of
5. fast-food restaurants	some several
6. technology	a few many
7. English speakers	most a lot of
8. entertainment	all much

EXERCISE 6

Some of the sentences in the following letter have errors with nouns and with quantifiers. Find the errors and correct them. When you have finished, check your answers with another student.

Dear Nell,

I think I'm going to like my new job. So far it's interesting, and I hope that it stays that way! There are several of people who work in the same office with me. At the moment I share a desk with Jessica, who just started a couple week ago, but our office manager just ordered new furnitures so that soon we will each have a desk of our own. There are lot of people in the building who share desks *and* computers, so I feel pretty lucky to have my own to work on.

Every morning Martha, the staff assistant, brings us each a cup of coffee. She already knows that I like sugars in my coffee but no milks. Martha also brings the mails to us, *and* she likes to give us many advice about how to be efficient. Two times a day I get at least fifty letter which I have to respond to, so I do listen to Martha's advices. A few her ideas have really been useful!

Some days I can do most of my business on the computer. Other days I need a little more informations from my customers, so I need to talk to them on the telephone. Every day there are some problem that I cannot handle. If there are only couple of problems, my coworker helps, but on the days when there are lot of problems, we call in Anna, the office supervisor. Already there have been several time when even Anna couldn't handle the problems, and so she has had to call in *her* supervisor.

So you can see that I'm busy, and at this point, I'm *not* bored.

Talk to you soon—

Love,

Elliott

Use Your English

ACTIVITY 1: WRITING/SPEAKING

This "recipe" was written by an English teacher:

"Recipe" for the Perfect Student

Ingredients:
1 cup of motivation
1 cup of determination
1/2 cup of patience
1/2 cup of tolerance
1 cup of laughter
1 cup of imagination
1 1/2 cups of willingness to make a guess
1 cup of independence
1 1/2 cups of cooperation with others
1 pinch of fun

Combine ingredients and stir gently to bring out the best flavor.

What do you think the teacher meant by this?

Get together with a partner and create a "recipe" of your own. Here are some ideas, but you probably have plenty of your own:

- Recipe for a long-lasting marriage
- Recipe for the perfect partner
- Recipe for the perfect teacher
- Recipe for the perfect house
- Recipe for the perfect mother/father

Share your recipes with the rest of the class.

ACTIVITY 2: SPEAKING

STEP 1 Work in small groups or with a partner to think of someone famous that everyone in your class knows. Imagine that this person is traveling. What would be in this famous person's suitcase? Make a list of these things, and be sure to include the amounts (*a lot, some, several, a few*).

STEP 2 Then read your list to the other groups in your class, and have them guess who the famous person is. If they can't guess, add more quantifiers in order to make the identity of the famous person clear.

ACTIVITY 3: SPEAKING

Your class is scheduled for a weekend trip in a nearby park. Transportation is provided, and a few small cabins are available. But you will need to decide what food to bring, and also what other things you will need. Here are some ideas: sleeping bags, cooking pots, eating utensils (plates, cups, silverware), firewood (in the winter), sports equipment, depending on the season (fishing poles? swimsuits? skis?).

Work in groups and come up with a list. Be specific about the quantities. Compare lists to make sure you haven't forgotten anything!

ACTIVITY 4: SPEAKING/LISTENING/WRITING

STEP 1 Organize an international potluck. Everyone in the class should prepare a dish, preferably from his or her country. Bring the dish to class to share and enjoy with your classmates, or, if possible, try to arrange your potluck at somebody's house so you can watch each other cook. After the meal, have each person describe their recipes. Tape-record this description.

STEP 2 Listen to the tape and write down these recipes. Collect all the recipes for an international cookbook. Make copies and distribute them to the class.

ACTIVITY 5: LISTENING

Listen to the tape of a person describing a recipe for a traditional North American dish.

STEP 1
1. What dish is the speaker describing?
2. When is this dish usually eaten?
3. What are the important ingredients in the dish?

STEP 2 Listen to the tape again, and this time write down the ingredients and amounts. Work with a partner to make sure that you understand what each ingredient is, and then take turns reading each ingredient and the amount aloud. If you decide to make this dish, it is important that your recipe is accurate!

For each ingredient with a measure word, check to see what kind of measure word is used:

- If it is a **container**, mark it with a C.
- If it is a **portion**, mark it with a P.
- If it is a **shape/typical state**, mark it with a S.
- If it is a **measurement**, mark it with a M.
  - Do you recognize the measurements?
  - Do you know what a teaspoon/tablespoon/cup is?

ACTIVITY 6: SPEAKING/LISTENING

The purpose of this activity is to do some research about various dishes and their recipes. The dishes below are very popular in North America, but different people sometimes have quite different recipes for the same dish. Your goal is to discover some of these variations.

Brownies   Potato Salad   Cheesecake   Cranberry Sauce

Divide into groups and choose **one** of these dishes. (If you prefer, you can select a dish that isn't on this list, preferably one that you don't know how to make.) Interview several different native speakers by asking them to tell you how to make the dish you have chosen. If possible, tape-record your interview. Get together with your group and compare the directions you have gathered. How many differences can you find? Be ready to share your findings with the rest of the class.

UNIT 9

DEGREE COMPLEMENTS

Too, Enough, **and** *Very*

UNIT GOALS:

- To understand the meaning of *enough*, *not enough*, and *too*
- To form correct sentences with *enough*, *not enough*, and *too*
- To know how to use *too much*, *too many*, *too little*, and *too few*
- To understand the difference between *too* and *very*

▶ **O PENING TASK**
Looking for Somewhere to Live

Maria is looking for a place to rent. She is looking for a two-bedroom, unfurnished house or apartment with lots of light and plenty of closet space. She cannot pay more than $900 a month.

STEP 1 When she first looked at the classified ads in the newspaper, she was very confused by some of the strange abbreviations. Can you help her? Get together with a partner and try to guess what these abbreviations mean:

apt   *kit*   **BR**   **DR**   *sm*   *lg furn*   *unfurn*   *mo*

STEP 2 She read all the ads and decided to go and look at the following places. After she saw each place, she made notes about what she liked and didn't like. Match her notes to the appropriate classified ads.

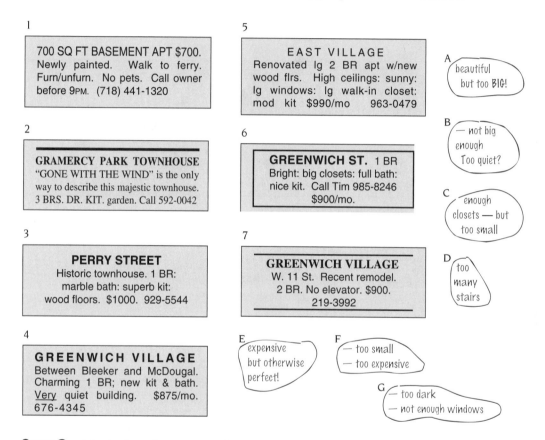

1

700 SQ FT BASEMENT APT $700. Newly painted. Walk to ferry. Furn/unfurn. No pets. Call owner before 9PM. (718) 441-1320

2

GRAMERCY PARK TOWNHOUSE "GONE WITH THE WIND" is the only way to describe this majestic townhouse. 3 BRS. DR. KIT. garden. Call 592-0042

3

PERRY STREET Historic townhouse. 1 BR: marble bath: superb kit: wood floors. $1000. 929-5544

4

GREENWICH VILLAGE Between Bleeker and McDougal. Charming 1 BR; new kit & bath. <u>Very</u> quiet building. $875/mo. 676-4345

5

EAST VILLAGE Renovated lg 2 BR apt w/new wood flrs. High ceilings: sunny: lg windows: lg walk-in closet: mod kit $990/mo   963-0479

6

GREENWICH ST. 1 BR Bright: big closets: full bath: nice kit. Call Tim 985-8246 $900/mo.

7

GREENWICH VILLAGE W. 11 St. Recent remodel. 2 BR. No elevator. $900. 219-3992

A beautiful but too BIG!

B — not big enough Too quiet?

C enough closets — but too small

D too many stairs

E expensive but otherwise perfect!

F — too small — too expensive

G — too dark — not enough windows

STEP 3 Maria lost her notes about the two following ads. What do you think she probably wrote? Write about each one.

MODERN 1 BR APT LOTS OF STORAGE SPACE SPECTACULAR VIEWS $1000

GREAT KIT!! 4 BR basement apt. 20 minute walk to subway $795

STEP 4 Look back at all the ads and all Maria's notes. Which place do you think she probably chose? Why?

► *Enough, Not Enough, Too*

EXAMPLES	EXPLANATIONS
(a) There are **enough** closets. **(b)** This apartment is big **enough** for both of us.	*Enough* shows something is sufficient. You have as much as you need and you do not need any more. *Enough* usually shows that you are satisfied with the situation.
(c) There are **not enough** windows in this apartment. (I want more windows!) OR: There are**n't enough** windows in this apartment. **(d)** The bedroom is **not** big **enough.** (I want a bigger bedroom!) OR: The bedroom is**n't** big **enough.**	*Not enough* shows that something is insufficient. In your opinion, there should be more. *Not enough* usually shows that you are not satisfied with the situation.
(e) The rent is **too** high. (It is more than I want to pay.) **(f)** The kitchen is **too** small. (I want a bigger one.) **(g)** That coffee is **too** hot. (I can't drink it.) **(h)** He speaks **too** fast. (I can't understand him.) **(i)** She's **too** young to drink. (She has to be 21 to drink alcohol in this state.)	*Too* shows that something is **more** than you want or need OR that it is **less** than you want or need. It depends on the meaning of the word that follows. *Too* usually shows that you are not satisfied with the situation.

EXERCISE 1

Look back at the notes you wrote in Step 3 of the Opening Task on page 137. Did you use *too, not enough,* or *enough*? If not, rewrite the notes and see if you can use *too, enough,* or *not enough* in them.

In your opinion, what would Maria say about these apartments? Where possible, use *too, enough,* and *not enough*.

1. Tiny but charming studio apartment. Large skylights. Limited storage space.

_____

_____

2. Gorgeous penthouse apartment. Fabulous views of Central Park. 3 bedrooms, 2 bathrooms. Dining room and roof garden. $1800.

_____

3. Bright two-bedroom apartment. Big closets. Next to fire station. $825.

_____

_____

EXERCISE 2

In this exercise, people are talking about problems that they are having, and their friends are responding by saying what they think caused these problems. For example:

Read the list of problems and the list of causes below. What do you think caused the problems? Work with a partner and match the problems and their causes.

PROBLEMS	CAUSES
1. My feet really hurt.	You don't go to the dentist often enough.
2. I'm broke!	Maybe you shouted too much at the ball game.
3. I failed my math test.	You didn't add enough salt.
4. I've gained a lot of weight recently.	Perhaps your shoes aren't big enough.
5. I never feel hungry at mealtimes.	You spend too much money.
6. I can't sleep at night.	Your stereo is too loud.
7. I have a sore throat.	You don't get enough exercise.
8. This soup is tasteless.	You eat too many snacks.
9. My neighbors are always angry with me.	You drink too much coffee.
10. My teeth hurt.	You didn't study enough.

▶ *Enough, Not Enough, Too*

EXAMPLES	EXPLANATIONS
	Place *enough* or *not enough:*
(a) This house is **big enough.** That apartment is **not big enough.**	• after adjectives
(b) Po speaks **clearly enough.** Tan does **not** speak **clearly enough.**	• after adverbs
(c) She **ate enough.** He **did not eat enough.**	• after verbs
(d) We have **enough money.** They **do not** have **enough money.**	• before nouns
	Notice how *enough* can be used with:
(e) She is **(not) old enough to vote.**	• an adjective + an infinitive
(f) They studied **hard enough to pass** the test, but they did**n't** study **hard enough to get** a good score.	• an adverb + an infinitive
(g) We **(don't) earn enough to pay** the rent.	• a verb + an infinitive
(h) I (don't) have **enough chocolate to make** a cake.	• a noun + infinitive
(i) She is **too young.** **(j)** They work **too slowly.** **(k)** This tea is **too hot to drink.** **(I)** We worked **too late to go** to the party. **(m)** That book is **too difficult for me to understand.** **(n)** He walked **too fast for the children to keep up.**	Place *too* before adjectives and adverbs. *Too* + adjective or adverb is often followed by an infinitive. *Too* + adjective or adverb is often followed by *for* + noun/pronoun + infinitive.

EXERCISE 3

Complete the following appropriately, using *too*, *enough*, or *not enough*. There are many different ways to make meaningful responses in this exercise. Compare your answers with a partner's and see how many different responses you can make.

1. A: Why are you wearing so many sweaters?

   B: Because this room *is too cold/isn't warm enough* .

2. A: Does your brother have a car?

   B: No, he's only fourteen! He's _____ .

3. A: Why did they move?

   B: They're expecting a baby, and their old house _____ .

4. A: Would you like some more pie?

   B: No, thanks. It's delicious, but I _____ .

5. A: Can we count on your support in next month's election?

   B: I'm sorry, but I _____ . I won't be eighteen until next year.

6. A: What's wrong?

   B: My jeans _____ . I can't get them on.

7. A: Waiter!

   B: Yes, sir?

   A: We can't eat this. It _____ .

8. A: Let me help you carry that.

   B: Thanks. This suitcase _____ .

► *Too Much* and *Too Many;* *Too Little* and *Too Few*

EXAMPLES	EXPLANATIONS
(a) Walt has **too much money.**	Use *too + much* with noncount nouns.
(b) There are **too many students** in this class.	Use *too + many* with count nouns. *Too much* and *too many* show that there is more than you want or need. They show that you are not satisfied with the situation.
(c) There's **too little time** to finish this.	Use *too + little* with noncount nouns.
(d) The class was canceled because **too few students** enrolled.	Use *too + few* **with count nouns.** *Too little* and *too few* show that there is less than you want or need. They show that you are not satisfied with the situation.

EXERCISE 4

Read the following description of a wedding reception where everything went wrong. Underline all the words or phrases that show there was not enough of something. Where possible, replace these with *too little* or *too few* and change the verbs as necessary.

My sister's wedding was a disaster. First of all, she decided to get married very suddenly, so there <u>wasn't enough time to</u> plan it properly. Nevertheless, about
was too little time to
fifty of her friends came to the reception in her studio. Unfortunately, there wasn't enough room for everyone, so it was rather uncomfortable. She only had a few chairs, and our ninety-six-year-old grandmother had to sit on the floor. My father had ordered lots of champagne, but there weren't enough glasses, so some people didn't get very much to drink. In addition, we had several problems with the caterers. There wasn't enough cake for everyone, but there was too much soup! We also had problems with the entertainment. My sister loves Latin music, so she hired a salsa band; however, it was hard to move in such a small space, and my sister got upset when not enough people wanted to dance.

I got into trouble too. I was the official photographer, but I didn't bring enough film with me, so now my sister is mad because she only has about ten wedding photographs—and all of them are pictures of people trying to find a place to sit down!

EXERCISE 5

You and your friends decided to give a big party. You made lots of plans, but unfortunately, everything went wrong and the party was a total disaster. Get together with one or two other students and make a list of all the things that can go wrong at parties. Use this list to make a description of **your** disastrous party, using *too, too much, too many, too little, too few,* or *not enough.* Share your description with the rest of the class and decide who had the "worst" possible party.

FOCUS **4**

▶ *Too* **versus** *Very*

EXAMPLES	EXPLANATIONS
(a) This writing is small.	*Very* adds emphasis, but *too* shows that something is more than is necessary or desirable.
(b) This writing is very small.	In (b) the writing is small, but I can read it.
(c) This writing is too small.	In (c) the writing is smaller and I cannot read it.
	In these situations, *too* shows that you are unable to do something, but *very* does not.

EXERCISE 6

Complete the following with *too, too + to,* or *very,* as appropriate.

1. A: Are you really going to buy that motorcycle?

B: Yes. It's <u>very</u> expensive, but I think I've got enough money in the bank.

2. A: Why aren't you drinking your tea?

B: I can't. It's _____ hot _____ drink.

3. A: Can I borrow your truck when I move to my new apartment?

B: Sure.

Use Your English

ACTIVITY 1: SPEAKING

ACTIVITY 1: SPEAKING

Work with a partner or in teams to play this version of tic-tac-toe.

STEP 1 Decide who will be "X" and who will be "O" and toss a coin to see who will start the game.

STEP 2 For each round of the game, select a different topic from the list below.

STEP 3 Choose the square you want to start with. With your team, agree on a meaningful sentence expressing the idea written in the square and relating to the topic of the round. For example: TOPIC: This classroom. *"This classroom is very small," "There aren't enough chairs in this classroom," "There are too few windows in this classroom,"* and so on.

STEP 4 The first team to get a line is the winner.

TOPICS

1. This campus
2. Television
3. North America
4. This town or city

very	too + to	too
too few	not enough	too much
enough	too many	too little

146   UNIT 9

ACTIVITY 2: SPEAKING/WRITING

STEP 1 Look at the chart below. If you were responsible for making the laws in your community, at what ages would you permit the following activities? Write the ages in the column marked *Ideal Age*.

STEP 2 Go around the room and collect information from your classmates about the ages at which these activities are permitted in the parts of the world (countries, states, provinces) that they know about. You can include information about this country (or state or province) as well. Write this in the last column.

ACTIVITY	IDEAL AGE	REAL AGE / WHERE
drive a car		
drink alcohol		
vote		
join the military		
get married		
own a gun		
leave school		

STEP 3 When you have collected the information, prepare a report (oral or written) on the differences and similarities you found among different parts of the world. Include your own opinions about the ideal ages for these activities and give reasons to support them. Remember to announce the purpose of your report in your introduction and to end with a concluding statement. You can use these headings to organize your information:

Introduction: Purpose of this report
Most interesting similarities among parts of the world:
Most interesting differences among parts of the world:
Your opinions on ideal ages, with reasons to support them:
Brief concluding statement:

STEP 4 If you make a written report, remember to read it through carefully after you finish writing. Check to see if you were able to use any of the language in this unit. If you make an oral report, record your presentation and listen to it later. Write down any sentences that you used containing *too, very, not enough,* or *enough.*

ACTIVITY 3: SPEAKING

The purpose of this activity is to share opinions on different social issues. Work with a partner and look at the issues listed below. For each one, think about what is sufficient (enough), what is insufficient (not enough), and what is excessive (too much) in this country and in other countries you and your partner know about. For example, you might think that public transportation in this country is too expensive and that there is not enough of it, but that public transportation in Egypt is very inexpensive but too slow. Record your opinions in your notebook. Be ready to share your ideas with the rest of the class.

Public Transportation
Health Care
Law and Order
Education
Care of the Elderly

Housing
Employment
Access for Disabled People to Public
    Buildings and Transportation

ACTIVITY 4: WRITING

Choose **one** of the social issues you discussed in Activity 3. Review the information you collected on different countries. In your opinion, which country has the best solution? Which country, in your opinion, is the least successful in dealing with this issue? Write a short report, describing the best and worst solutions. Give reasons to support your opinions. Remember to introduce your topic; we have suggested one possibility below, but you can probably think of a better way. When you finish writing, read your report carefully and check to see if you were able to include any of the language discussed in this unit.

In the modern world, many countries are trying to find solutions to the same social issues, and it is interesting to see that different countries and cultures deal with these issues in different ways. In my opinion, some countries have better solutions than others. To illustrate this point, I will talk about _____ (social issue) and show how _____ (country) and _____ (country) both deal with it.

ACTIVITY 5: SPEAKING/LISTENING

STEP 1 Use the information from Activity 3. As a class, choose four topics that interest you. Then, by yourself or with another student, interview a native speaker of English about these topics. Record your interview. Listen to your tape and make a brief summary of the person's opinions. Share your findings with the rest of the class. What similarities and differences did your class find in these interviews?

STEP 2 Listen to your tape again and write down any sentences containing examples of language discussed in this unit.

ACTIVITY 6: LISTENING

STEP 1 Does the world already have too many people? Listen to the tape of two people (a man and a woman) discussing the topic of overpopulation. Write a sentence telling which speaker you agree with and why.

I agree with _____ because _____.

STEP 2 Listen to the tape again. Write down as many phrases containing *too, enough,* and *very* as you can.

UNIT 10

GIVING ADVICE AND EXPRESSING OPINIONS

Should, Ought To, Need To, Must, Had Better, Could, **and** *Might*

UNIT GOALS:

- To use *must, had better, need to, should, ought to, could, might,* and imperatives to give advice appropriately
- To use *should, ought to,* and *should not* to express opinions

▶ OPENING TASK
How to . . .

In North America, many "self-help" books are published every year. These books give people advice on how to improve their lives.

STEP 1 With a partner, look at the books below. What kinds of advice do you expect to find in each one? Be ready to share your ideas with the rest of the class.

STEP 2 Now read the sample passages from these books and match each one to the book you think it probably comes from.

A

As an important first step, you really ought to eliminate red meat. This may be hard at first, but you will be amazed to find that there are many healthy—and delicious—alternatives.

B

This is never as easy as it sounds, so you should be prepared to put time and effort into it. For example, doing volunteer work is one way to meet people who share your interests, and you may get to know them better as you work on projects together.

C

It's easier than you think. To really make a difference, you should start slowly and establish a routine. Think about one thing that you can easily do (carpool? recycle paper, cans, and glass?) As soon as this becomes a habit, you should start to think about what to do next.

D

You should never settle into a regular, predictable routine. Surprise each other with fun activities, like picnics after work or moonlight barbecues on the beach.

E

You ought to make every effort to motivate yourself to stay on your diet! Buy a dress that is just a little bit too small for you and hang it in your closet. You should look at it every day and dream of the time when it will really fit you.

F

You shouldn't draw attention to yourself. Choose conservative but attractive styles. Navy blue is a good color choice. Remember that you ought to look competent and professional at all times.

STEP 3 With your partner, choose **one** of these self-help books. What advice would **you** give on the topic? Write at least three pieces of advice below:

BOOK:

Three pieces of advice we would give:

  1.

  2.

  3.

▶ **G**iving Advice with *Should, Ought To, Shouldn't*

EXAMPLES	EXPLANATIONS
(a) A: I'm so tired. B: You **should/ought to** get more sleep. **(b)** A: I can't understand my teacher. B: You **ought to/should** talk to her about it.	*Should/should not* and *ought to* are often used to give advice (to tell someone what you think is a good or bad idea for him or her to do). Use *should* or *ought to* to show that you think something is a good idea. *Ought to* is usually pronounced as *oughta* in spoken English.
(c) A: I have a terrible cough. B: You **should not (shouldn't)** smoke so much.	Use *should not (shouldn't)* to show that you think something is a bad idea. *Ought to* is not usually used in negatives or in questions in American English.
(d) Nami works too hard. She **should/ought to** take a vacation. **(e)** **NOT:** She shoulds/oughts to take a vacation.	*Should* and *ought to* are modal auxiliaries. They do not take third person *s*. For more information about the form of modals, see Unit 5.

EXERCISE 1

Look at the advice that you and your partner wrote in the Opening Task on page 151. Did you use *should, ought to, should not*? Check to see if you used them correctly. If you didn't use them at all, rewrite your advice to include them.

Share your advice with the rest of the class. Do not tell your classmates which book you were thinking about when you wrote the advice and see if they can guess correctly.

Using *Need To* and Imperatives to Give Advice

EXAMPLES	EXPLANATIONS
(a) A: My tooth hurts. B: You **need to** see a dentist.	*Need to* + base verb can also be used to give advice. It is stronger than *should* or *ought to*.
(b) A: My tooth hurts. B: You **should/ought to** see a dentist.	*Need to* is not a modal verb.
(c) A: My tooth hurts. B: **Go** to a dentist. **(d)** A: I can't sleep. B: **Don't drink** so much coffee! **(e)** A: I can't sleep. B: You **shouldn't** drink so much coffee.	You can also use an imperative to give advice. An imperative is much stronger and much more direct than *need to*. If you do not know the person you are addressing very well, it is usually better to use *should/shouldn't* or *ought to*.

EXERCISE 2

> ### HEINLE & HEINLE
> *the specialized language publisher*
> A Thomson Learning Company
>
> We are proud to announce an exciting new book, *by* language learners
> *for* language learners
>
> ### HOW TO BE A BETTER LANGUAGE LEARNER
>
> Language learners from all over the world give you advice
>
> about ways to learn a second, third, or fourth language.
>
> This book will change the way you learn languages...

You have been asked to contribute to this exciting new "self-help" book. First, think about your own experience as a language learner. Then, write down at least three important things that you think someone who wants to learn **your** language should or should not do. Get together with a partner and compare your lists. How many similarities and differences can you find in your advice? Share your advice with the rest of the class.

▶ *Should* and *Ought To* versus *Must*

EXAMPLES	EXPLANATIONS
(a) Alma: I can't sleep at night. Bea: You **should** drink a glass of milk before you go to bed.	*Should* and *ought to* shows that something is a good idea. In (a), Bea is giving advice, but Alma is not obliged to follow that advice; she is free to do what she pleases.
(b) Dora: Do I need to get a special visa to visit Taiwan? Wen: Yes, you **must** go to the Taiwanese consulate here and get one before you leave. You **must not** try to enter the country without one.	*Must* is stronger. In (b), it is obligatory for Dora to follow Wen's advice. She is not free to do what she pleases. For more information about this use of *must*, see Unit 11.

EXERCISE 3

Oscar has just bought a used car. Complete the following, using *should, shouldn't, must,* or *must not* as appropriate. Different people may have different opinions about some of these, so be ready to justify your choices.

1. He _____ get insurance as soon as possible.

2. He _____ take it to a reliable mechanic and have it checked.

3. He _____ get it registered.

4. He _____ drive it without insurance.

5. He _____ drink and drive.

6. He _____ wear a seat belt.

7. He _____ lock the doors when he parks the car.

8. He _____ keep a spare key in a safe place.

► *Should* and *Ought To*
versus *Had Better*

EXAMPLES	EXPLANATIONS
(a) You **should** go to all your classes every day. **(b)** You **had better** go to all your classes every day.	You can also use *had better* to give advice. *Had better* is much stronger than *should* and *ought to*, but not as strong as *must*. In (a), it is a good idea for you to do this. In (b), if you don't go, something bad will happen.
(c) You **should** see a doctor about that. (It's a good idea.) **(d)** You**'d better** see a doctor about that. (It's urgent.) **(e)** You **must** see a doctor about that. (It's obligatory.)	*Had better* often shows that you think something is urgent. *Had better* is often contracted to *'d better*.
(f) *Teacher to student:* If you want to pass this class, you **had better** finish all your assignments. **(g)** *Student to teacher:* If you come to my country, you **should** visit Kyoto. **(h)** **NOT:** You had better visit Kyoto.	*Had better* is often used in situations where the speaker has more power or authority (for example, boss to employee or teacher to student). In these situations, *had better* sounds like an order or a command. If you want to be sure that you sound polite, use *should* or *ought to*.
(i) You **had better** finish this tomorrow. **(j)** I **had better** leave now. **(k)** He **had better** pay me for this.	*Had better* refers to the present and the future. It does not refer to the past (even though it is formed with *had*).
(l) She**'d better not** tell anyone about this. **(m)** You**'d better not** be late.	Notice how the negative is formed.

EXERCISE 4

Complete the following with *should, ought to, must,* or *had better,* as necessary.

1. **Inez:** How can I register to take the TOEFL?

   Patsy: First you _____ complete this application form.

2. **Naoko:** I want to get a good score on the TOEFL, but I'm not sure how to do that.

   Kate: I think you _____ take every opportunity to practice your English.

3. **Yu-shan:** I'm sorry I haven't been coming to class recently. My father is in town.

   Advisor: You _____ start attending class regularly if you want to stay in this program.

4. **Herbert:** I think I'm getting the flu.

   Eleanor: You _____ go to bed and drink plenty of orange juice.

5. **Claudia:** I've lost my credit card.

   Rafael: You _____ report it immediately.

6. **Doctor:** You _____ take these pills four times a day. If you forget one, you will feel a lot worse.

7. **Audrey:** I just can't sleep at night.

   Shannon: You _____ try drinking herbal tea just before you go to bed.

8. **Carmen:** I'd love to visit Poland.

   Cherry: Well, first of all you _____ get a special visa.

9. **Debbie:** I've got a sore throat.

   James: You _____ try not to talk too much.

10. **Lois:** You _____ clean up your room. If you don't, there'll be trouble.

EXERCISE 5

Circle your choice in each of the following sentences.

1. You (should not/must not) smoke when you are in a movie theater in the United States.

2. While you are in Los Angeles, you (had better/should) try to visit Disneyland.

3. In the state of Michigan, people under the age of twenty-one (should not/must not) try to purchase alcohol.

4. People (should/had better) wear helmets when they ride bicycles.

5. Look, the bus is coming! We (should/had better) run if we want to catch it.

6. Everybody who comes into the United States (must/should) show a valid passport or picture ID.

7. I've just spilled coffee on the new rug. I (should/had better) clean it up right away before it stains.

8. Professor Katz gets really angry when students chew gum in class. You (had better/should) get rid of your gum before we get there.

9. Tourists visiting my hometown in the spring (had better/should) bring cameras, as it's very beautiful at that time of year.

10. My brother wants to have more friends. He (must/should) join the tenants' association; maybe he can make some friends there.

FOCUS **5**

▶ ***Should*** **versus** ***Could*** **and** ***Might***

EXAMPLES	EXPLANATIONS
(a) A: I heard there's a new movie playing in town. B: Yeah, you **should** see that movie. It's great. **(b)** A: I don't know what to do on Friday night. B: You **could** see a movie.	You can also use *could* to give advice. *Could* is not as strong as *should* because it only expresses choices or possibilities. *Could* does not show that the speaker thinks that something is a good idea to do or that it is the right thing to do.
(c) If you want to improve your Spanish, you **could** take classes, you **might** listen to Spanish-speaking stations on the radio, you **could** find a conversation partner, or you **might** take a vacation in Mexico.	We often use *could* or *might* to express many different possibilities, without saying which one we think is best.

EXERCISE 6

Your friends always come to you when they have problems because you usually have lots of great ideas about what to do.

STEP 1   For each problem, write down as many possible solutions as you can think of, using *could* and *might*.

STEP 2   Get together with two or three other students and compare your ideas. Decide who has the best solution to each problem and write it down, using *should*.

▶ **EXAMPLE:**   Your neighbors play loud rock music all night.

Possibilities: *You could talk with them. You could play very loud opera in the morning when they are still asleep. You might move. You might buy ear plugs. You could call the police.*

In our opinion, the best solution: *You should buy ear plugs.*

1. Your friend's husband snores. Possibilities: _____

   _____

   In our opinion, the best solution: _____

   _____

2. Your friend's father is planning to come and visit for a few days. Unfortunately, he is a heavy smoker and your friend's roommates are nonsmokers who do not permit smoking in the house. Possibilities: _____

   _____

   In our opinion, the best solution: _____

   _____

3. A classmate has just spilled coffee on her favorite white shirt. She doesn't know what to do. Possibilities: _____
   In our opinion, the best solution: _____

   _____

4. Your friend can't sleep at night. She feels exhausted every morning and doesn't have enough energy to do anything all day. Possibilities: _____

   _____

   In our opinion, the best solution: _____

   _____

5. One of your classmates wants to learn more about American culture and customs and would really like to make friends with some Americans. He doesn't know how to start. You have lots of ideas. Possibilities: _____

   _____

   In our opinion, the best solution: _____

   _____

6. Your partner never has enough money. At the end of the month, he is always broke. He comes to you for some ideas about what to do. Possibilities: _____

   _____

In our opinion, the best solution: _____

_____

7. Two of your friends are taking a university class. The professor speaks very fast and they find it hard to follow the lectures. They are afraid that they are going to flunk the class. Possibilities: _____

_____

In our opinion, the best solution: _____

8. Your friend's fiancee has two dogs. She has had these dogs since she was a child and is very attached to them. Unfortunately, your friend is allergic to dogs. He loves his fiancee very much, but the dogs are making him sick. He doesn't want to upset her. Possibilities: _____

_____

In our opinion, the best solution: _____

_____

EXERCISE 7

The following story is a well-known logic problem. Get together with some of your class-mates and decide on the best solution.

A woman went shopping. First she bought a large piece of cheese. Then she stopped at a pet store to buy a white mouse for her nephew's birthday. Just as she was leaving the store, she saw an adorable black and white cat. She couldn't leave the store without it, so she bought the cat as well.

Unfortunately, her car is parked a long way from the pet store, and it's only possible for her to carry one thing at a time. What could she do in order to get everything to her car? How many solutions can you find?

She could _____

_____

_____

There are no parking areas near the pet store, so she cannot move her car, and there is nobody around to help her. Unfortunately, cats eat mice and mice eat cheese. This means that if she leaves the cat with the mouse, the cat will eat the mouse, and if she leaves the mouse with the cheese, the mouse will eat the cheese. What should she do? What is the best solution to her problem?

She should _____

_____

_____

You can find the solution to this problem on page A-17.

There are many different versions of this problem. Do you know one? Share it with the rest of the class.

▶ *Should* and *Ought To* versus *Might, Could, Need To, Had Better,* and *Must*

EXAMPLES	EXPLANATIONS

WEAK
 	
↑
    might
    could
    should/ought to
    need to
    had better
↓   must
 	
STRONG
	All these verbs can be used to give advice. However, they express different degrees of strength.

EXERCISE 8

Read the following situation and follow the instructions given:

Jennifer is an American student. As she is planning to major in international business, she decided that it would be important for her to know how to speak Japanese. She managed to get some money from her father and left for Japan for six months.

She has now been in Tokyo for three months, taking classes in Japanese language and conversation. When she first arrived, she missed home a lot, so she quickly made friends with other Americans she met. Instead of living with a Japanese host family, she decided to move in with two other American women and now she spends all her time with her new friends. She takes Japanese classes every day, but she seldom spends any time with the students who do not speak any English. As a result, she rarely speaks Japanese and has not made much progress in the language. She hasn't learned much about Japanese culture either.

Jennifer is having a great time in Tokyo with her American friends, but now she's in a terrible panic. Her father has just called to tell her that he will be coming to Tokyo on business, and he wants her to help him while he is there. He wants her to help interpret for him, as well as advise him on Japanese culture and customs. She is feeling very anxious about meeting her father. . . .

First, make a list of all the possible solutions to Jennifer's problem that you can think of in two minutes. Then get together with two or three other students and share your solutions. Look at all the possibilities and then select the best three. Be ready to share these with the rest of the class and to justify them as necessary.

▶ Expressing Opinions with *Should, Ought To,* and *Should Not*

EXAMPLES	EXPLANATIONS
(a) Iryna believes that more people **should** drive electric cars. **(b)** In Mune's opinion, couples **ought to** live together for a while before they marry. **(c)** Most of my friends think that we **shouldn't** eat meat.	You can also use *should, ought to,* and *should not* to express your opinions about what you think is right or wrong.

EXERCISE 9

In your opinion, which of the following occupations should receive the highest salaries? Number the occupations in order of the highest to the lowest salaries (Number 1 is the highest salary).

TV news announcer	plumber	politician
firefighter	emergency room doctor	elementary school teacher
professional football player	model	plastic surgeon
member of the clergy	CEO of a large company	police officer
attorney	bus driver	nurse

   When you finish, compare your answers with a partner's. Be ready to share and justify your opinions with the rest of the class.

Use Your English

ACTIVITY 1: SPEAKING/ LISTENING

STEP 1 Sometimes, for fun, people give each other advice on the best way to accomplish a negative goal; for example, the best way to lose your job or how to annoy your neighbors. Get together with another student and choose one of the following humorous topics. How many different ideas can you come up with?

- How to get a traffic ticket
- How to get rid of your boyfriend or girlfriend
- How to avoid learning English
- How to get an F in this class
- How to annoy your roommate

STEP 2 With your partner, make a poster presentation on the topic you chose. Take a large poster-sized sheet of paper or card and use it to make a poster that expresses your ideas. You can use graphics, pictures, and diagrams to make your poster informative and eye-catching. Display your poster and use it to explain your ideas to the rest of the class.

STEP 3 Record yourself as you make your poster presentation. Listen to your tape and write down all the sentences where you used *should, shouldn't, ought to, need to, must, had better, might,* or *could.* Did you use them appropriately?

ACTIVITY 2: SPEAKING

Many American newspapers have advice columns. People write to these columns for help with their problems. Three famous ones are "Dear Abby," "Ann Landers," and "Miss Manners." Clip any advice columns you can find in various newspapers and bring them to class. Cut off the answers to the letters and circulate the letters without their replies. In groups, try to come up with helpful advice. Share your responses with the rest of the class. Compare your advice with the advice the professionals gave.

ACTIVITY 3: WRITING

In groups, write a letter to "Dear Abby," asking for advice on a particular problem. Exchange your problem letter with another group and write solutions to their problem. Share both problem and solution with the rest of the class.

ACTIVITY 4: WRITING

Write a short report, giving advice to someone who is planning to visit your hometown, your country, or the community where you grew up. Advise him or her on places to visit, clothes to wear, things to bring, things to do, and how to act.

Remember to start your report with an introductory statement. For example: *My hometown/country, (name), is very interesting, and if you follow my advice, I am sure that you will have an enjoyable and rewarding visit. . . .*

When you finish writing, check and see if you have used *should, shouldn't, must, ought to, might, need to, could,* and *had better*. It is not necessary to use one in every sentence, as this would sound very unnatural!

ACTIVITY 5: SPEAKING

Is honesty always the best policy? Should we **always** tell the truth? Think about the following situations. Share your opinions on each one with your classmates. How many people share your point of view? How many have different ideas?

1. You saw your best friend's girlfriend out on a date with someone else. Should you tell your friend what you saw? Why? Why not?

2. A classmate cheated on the last test. Should you tell your teacher? Why? Why not?

3. Your friend has a new haircut. She is really happy with her new "look," but you don't like it at all. In fact, you think it makes her look quite ugly. She asks for your opinion. Should you tell her what you really think? Why? Why not?

4. You catch your eight-year-old son telling a lie. Should you tell him that it is wrong to lie? Why? Why not?

ACTIVITY 6: SPEAKING/WRITING

STEP 1 Read the following and circle *should* or *should not* to express the point of view that is closest to your own opinion on the topic.

1. School uniforms should/should not be obligatory.

2. Animals should/should not be used in laboratory experiments.

3. Doctors should/should not reveal the identity of AIDS patients to the patient's employer or school.

4. Mothers should/should not work outside the home when their children are young.

5. A woman should/should not take her husband's family name when she marries.

6. Smoking should/should not be permitted in public places.

STEP 2 Choose the topic that interests you the most and then go around the room until you find one or two other students who share your opinion on that topic. Form a group with these students and brainstorm all the reasons and examples you can think of to support your point of view and then write them down. Choose the strongest ones, with the best examples, and use them to make a short report (oral or written) presenting your opinion. Share your report with the rest of the class and be ready to justify your position as necessary.

STEP 3 If you make a written report, read your report carefully and underline every example you can find of the modal auxiliaries from this unit.

If you choose an oral report, record your report. Listen to your tape and write down every sentence where you use one of the modal auxiliaries from this unit.

ACTIVITY 7: LISTENING

In this activity, you will hear a taped interview on the topic of smoking. Listen to the person's opinion. Does she think smoking should be banned in public places? What other ideas does she express? Check (✔) the statements you think the speaker agrees with.

_____ Smoking should be banned in public places.

_____ People should not be able to buy cigarettes in drug stores and supermarkets.

_____ Parents should not smoke at home in front of children.

_____ Teachers need to teach students about the dangers of smoking.

Listen to the tape again. Write down any sentences that contain examples of the verb forms in this unit.

ACTIVITY 8: SPEAKING/LISTENING

Many people have strong opinions about smoking. Ask five different native speakers of English questions like these: "What's your opinion about smoking in public places?" "Do you think it's a good or bad idea to ban smoking in public places?"

Tape their answers. Listen to your tape and be ready to share the information that you collect with the other people in your class. What do most of the people you interviewed think about this topic?

Listen to your tapes. What are some of the ways people express their opinions? Write down any sentences that contain examples of the verbs from this unit.

MODALS OF NECESSITY AND PROHIBITION

Have To/Have Got To, Do Not Have To,
Must/Must Not, Cannot

UNIT GOALS:

- To use *must*, *have to*, and *have got to* to show something is necessary
- To use *must not* and *cannot* to show something is prohibited
- To choose between *have to* and *have got to*
- To use *do not have to* to show something is not necessary
- To use *have to* for *must* in the past

▶**O**PENING TASK
Visiting the United States

STEP 1 A friend of yours from Jamaica is planning a short vacation in California. As he is a Jamaican citizen, he will have to deal with Immigration and Customs when he enters the United States.

He doesn't have much room to pack a lot of things because he's planning to travel with just a backpack. Here are some of the things he is thinking of taking with him:

a passport	a map of the U.S.	an umbrella
a surfboard	fireworks	a business suit
fresh fruit	a laptop computer	hiking boots
an international driver's license	a credit card	
traveler's checks	a tourist visa	
books about Jamaica	California guide books	
a return airline ticket	photographs of his home town	
	many reggae (Jamaican music) tapes and CDs	

STEP 2 Use the boxes below to help him organize the things he wants to take to the United States. Work with a partner and put them in the boxes where you think they belong.

#1 It's necessary and obligatory: You can't enter the United States without this: You must take this with you.	#2 It's prohibited by law: You must not take this into the United States.
#3 It's a good idea to bring this: You should take this with you.	#4 It's O.K. to bring this, but it isn't really necessary: You don't have to take this.

STEP 3 Can you and your partner add any other things to this list? Try to think of at least five more items and put them in the appropriate boxes.

STEP 4 With your partner, write sentences about one or two items in each box, explaining why you think they belong there.

▶ Modals of Necessity, Prohibition, and Permission

EXAMPLES	EXPLANATIONS
(a) You **must** have a passport. OR **(b)** You **have to** have a passport. OR **(c)** You **have got to** have a passport.	Use *must, have to,* or *have got to* to show something is necessary and obligatory (something that is strongly required, often by law).
(d) You **must not (mustn't)** bring fresh fruit into the United States. OR **(e)** You **cannot (can't)** bring fresh fruit into the United States.	Use *must not (mustn't)* or *cannot (can't)* to show something is prohibited and absolutely not permitted (often by law). In the past, use *couldn't* . In the future, use *won't be able to*.
(f) You **can** bring a surfboard.	Use *can* to show that something is permitted. In the past, use *could*. In the future, use *will be able to*.
(g) You **should** bring a credit card.	Use *should* to show something is a good idea. For more information about this use of *should* see Unit 10.
(h) You **don't have to** bring a surfboard.	Use *do not (don't) have to* to show something is permitted, but not necessary. You can do this if you want to, but you are not required to.

EXERCISE 1

Look back at the sentences you wrote in Step 4 of the Opening Task. Did you use *must, have to, have got to, should, can, can't, mustn't,* and *don't have to* ? If you did, check to see that you used them correctly. If you didn't use them, rewrite the sentences.

▶ **EXAMPLE:** *He must have a valid passport—it is required by law.*

In the rest of this unit, you will have the opportunity to practice all of these in more detail.

▶ Modals and Phrasal Modals:
Must, Have To, and
Have Got To

EXAMPLES	EXPLANATIONS
(a) International students **must** get visas before they enter the United States.	*Must* is a modal and does not change to agree with the subject.
(b) My Jamaican friend **must** get a tourist visa before he goes to the United States on vacation.	
(c) International students **have to** get visas before they enter the United States.	*Have to* is a phrasal modal. It changes to agree with the subject.
(d) My Jamaican friend **has to** get a tourist visa before he goes on vacation in the United States.	*Have to* and *has to* are usually pronounced "hafta" and "hasta" in fast speech and informal conversation.
(e) International students **have got to** get visas before they enter the United States.	*Have got to* is a phrasal modal. It changes to agree with the subject.
(f) My Jamaican friend **has got to** get a tourist visa before he goes to the United States on vacation.	*Have got to* and *has got to* are usually pronounced "'ve gotta" and "'s gotta" in fast speech and informal conversation.
(g) **Do** we **have to** go? **Does** she **have to** go too?	Notice how questions with *must, have to,* and *have got to* are formed. Use *do/does* with *have to*.
(h) **Have** we **got to** go? **Has** she **got to** go too?	Use *has/have* with *have got to*. Do not use *do/does*.
(i) **Must** we go? **Must** she go too?	Do not use *do/does* with *must*. However, *must* is rarely used in questions in American English.

EXERCISE 2

Many road signs are used internationally, but some used in the United States are confusing for tourists from other countries. What do you think the following road signs mean? Complete the sentences, using *have to* and *have got to* in your answers.

1.  In the United States, drivers _____
when they see this sign.

2.  Also, when they see this one, they_____
_____

3.  This sign tells you that you _____
_____

4.  A driver who sees this sign _____
_____

5.  Be careful when you see this one. It means that you
_____

6.  Q: What happens when there are two or three cars waiting at this sign?

A: The car that arrives last _____

_____

How many of these road signs are also found in your country? Are there are any road signs from your country that are not found in North America? Draw the signs and write sentences showing what you have to do when you see them.

EXERCISE 3

Work with a partner and decide which of the following are necessary and obligatory to do if you want to get a driver's license in the United States.

- speak English very well
- know how to drive
- practice before the test
- take an eye test
- take a written test
- have a medical examination
- have a passport or birth certificate as ID

- pass a driving test
- have a high school diploma
- own a car
- study the information booklet from the DMV (Department of Motor Vehicles, the department that issues driver's licenses)
- have an international driver's license

EXERCISE 4

Your friend wants to know what he has to do to get a driver's license. Make statements to explain what it is necessary for him to do if he wants to get a driver's license in the United States; then explain what it is necessary for him to do if he wants to get a driver's license in your country.

▶ *H*ave To versus Have Got To

USE

EXAMPLES	EXPLANATIONS
(a) Joe **has to** go on a diet.	Both *have to* and *have got to* show that something is necessary and obligatory. However, many people use *have got to* when they want to emphasize that something is **very** important and **very** necessary.
(b) Joe **has got to** follow a very strict diet because he has a serious heart condition. (If he doesn't follow the diet, he will die.)	
(c) You **have to** pay your phone bill once a month.	
(d) You **have got to** pay your phone bill immediately. (If you don't, the phone company will disconnect the phone.)	
(e) Hey Steve, you**'ve got to (gotta)** see this movie. It's really great.	In very informal conversation among friends, some people use *have got to* to show they think something is a really good thing to do. In (e), Steve's friend is not saying that Steve is obliged to see the movie; she is just strongly advising Steve to see it.

EXERCISE 5

Make a statement for each situation below. Work with a partner and decide which you would use for each one, *have to* or *have got to*.

1. Your sister's four-year-old son takes a nap every day and goes to bed at 8:00 every night. But today he didn't take a nap, and it's now 10:00 P.M.

She says to her son, "You _____ go to sleep now."

2. The last time your friend went to the dentist was four months ago. He doesn't think he has any problems with his teeth, but he feels he should probably go to the dentist for a checkup.

He says, "I _____ make an appointment to see the dentist sometime soon."

3. You haven't been reading the assignments for your history class, and you did very badly on the first two quizzes. You are afraid that you'll fail the course.

You tell your classmate, "I _____ study every day if I don't want to fail my history class."

4. Your roommate is making dinner. She has just put a loaf of bread in the oven. Suddenly she realizes that she doesn't have an important item that she needs for dessert.

She says, "I _____ go to the store. If I'm not back in ten minutes, can you take the bread out of the oven? It _____ come out at 7:00 or it'll be ruined."

5. You are at a friend's house. You are feeling a little tired and want to go to sleep early.

You say, "I _____ leave now. I'll see you after class tomorrow."

FOCUS **4**

Using *Cannot (Can't)* and *Must Not (Mustn't)* to Show Something Is Prohibited or Not Permitted

EXAMPLES	EXPLANATIONS
(a) You **cannot (can't)** bring fresh fruit into the United States. OR **(b)** You **must not (mustn't)** bring fresh fruit into the United States. **(c)** You **cannot (can't)** smoke in here. OR **(d)** You **must not (mustn't)** smoke in here.	Use *cannot* and *must not* to show that something is completely prohibited or not permitted (often by law). *Cannot* is more common than *must not* in American English. *Cannot* and *must not* are usually contracted to *can't* and *mustn't* in fast speech.
(e) Herbert, you **must not (mustn't)** eat any more of those cookies!	*Must not/mustn't* is also often used as a strong command in situations where you want someone to obey. In (e), eating cookies is not prohibited by law, but the speaker **really** wants Herbert to stop eating them.

EXERCISE 6

STEP 1 Look at the cartoon. Write statements in your notebook, using *cannot* and *must not* to describe each prohibited activity.

STEP 2 With your partner, make signs for your classroom, showing classroom "rules." Write a caption for each sign, using *must, must not,* and *cannot*. For example: *You can't smoke in this room.* Display your signs. Take a vote to see which ones your classmates want to put on your classroom walls.

EXERCISE 7

These photographs were taken in New York City. Photograph A is a sign on a newsstand and Photograph B is a sign in the window of a convenience store. With a partner, try to figure out what the two signs mean. What is the difference between the two photographs? Work with your partner and try to complete the summary below.

PHOTOGRAPH A   **PHOTOGRAPH B**

Reprinted with permission from Mark Chester, *No in America*, Taylor Publishing Co, Dallas (1986).

In Photograph A, you _____

but in Photograph B, you _____

FOCUS **5**

▶ ***M****ust* and *Have To* versus
Must Not, Cannot, and
Do Not Have To

EXAMPLES	EXPLANATIONS
(a) To enter the United States you **must** have a valid passport. OR **(b)** To enter the United States you **have to** have a valid passport.	**Showing something is necessary and obligatory:** Use either *must* or *have to*. In this situation, they have the same meaning.
(c) You **cannot** bring fireworks into the United States. OR **(d)** You **must not** bring fireworks into the United States. **(e)** **NOT:** You don't have to bring fireworks into the United States.	**Showing something is prohibited:** Use *cannot* or *must not*. Do not use *do not have to*. In negative sentences, they do **not** have the same meaning. In this situation, *must not* means it is prohibited.
(f) You **don't have to** bring a surfboard to California because you can rent one there. **(g)** **NOT:** You must not bring a surfboard to California because you can rent one there. **(h)** There are aren't any classes on Saturdays, so we **don't have to** come to school.	**Showing something is not necessary:** Use *do not have to*. Do not use *cannot* or *must not*. In this situation, *do not have to* means you can do something if you want to, but you are not obliged to do it if you don't want to.

EXERCISE 8

Look back to what you wrote in Exercise 7. Check to see if you used *have to, must,* or *do not have to* correctly. Rewrite your sentences if necessary.

EXERCISE 9

Your teacher wants to visit the country you come from and needs your help. How many different "helpful" statements can you make using *must, have to, have got to, cannot, must not, should, can,* and *do not have to*? For example: You don't have to have a tourist visa to visit Spain, but you must have a valid passport. All visitors have to carry their passports at all times; this is the law.

EXERCISE 10

The magazine article below is about traffic laws in different European countries.

STEP 1 Before you read the article, look at the following statements. Do you think they are <u>probably</u> true or <u>probably</u> false? Circle T (for true), or F (for false). After you finish reading, look at the statements again and change your answers if necessary.

1. In Germany, you mustn't use bad language or make rude and insulting gestures if you get angry with other drivers. T F
2. You must be careful when you honk your horn in Greece. T F
3. You have to honk your horn when you pass another car in Gibraltar. T F
4. You cannot flash your lights at other drivers in Luxembourg. T F
5. In Scandinavian countries, you cannot drive with your headlights on during the day. T F
6. You have to drive more slowly at night in Austria. T F
7. In Romania, you don't have to keep your car clean. T F

How not to collide with local road laws

If you are planning on driving in Europe, you should know that driving laws and customs vary greatly from country to country.

Be careful not to allow frustration with other drivers to develop into swearing or offensive gestures in Germany: They are illegal. Displays of anger are not welcome in Greece, either. It is unlawful to honk your horn too loudly (although this may surprise many visitors to Athens!). In Gibraltar, using your horn at all is completely prohibited.

In Luxembourg, the law says that drivers have to flash their lights each time they pass another car. In Scandinavian countries, you have to drive with your headlights dimmed during the day, but in Poland, this is obligatory only in winter.

Make sure you fill your tank before you get on the Autobahn in Germany: It is illegal to run out of gas. Speed limits vary too, not just from country to country, but within countries as well. Beware of speed limits that change from one moment to the next. For example, in Austria, speed limits are lower at night and in France, the speed limit on the freeways drops from 130 kmh to 110 kmh when it rains. (And if the French police catch you speeding, you have to pay a massive on-the-spot fine!)

But perhaps the strangest law of all is from Romania, where you must not drive your car if it is dirty.

Adapted from *The European* (Magazine Section), 6/9/95.

STEP 2   Make statements using *must, have to, cannot, mustn't,* or *do not have to* about the following topics from the article.

1. Driving in Poland during the winter: _____

   _____

2. Driving on the Autobahn in Germany: _____

   _____

3. Driving on the freeways in France: _____

   _____

STEP 3   Are there any traffic laws that are sometimes confusing to visitors to the country you come from? Describe them to the rest of your class, using *must, have to, cannot, must not,* and *do not have to* where you can.

> # Talking about the Present, Past, and Future with *Have To* and *Must*

PRESENT	PAST	FUTURE
must	—	must
have to	had to	have to/will have to
do not have to	did not have to	do not have to/will not have to

EXAMPLES	EXPLANATIONS
(a) Olympic athletes **have to** train every day. **(b)** Olympic athletes **must** train every day. **(c)** High school athletes **don't have to** train every day.	Use *must (not), have to,* and *do not have to* to show that something is (or is not) necessary in the present.
(d) He **had to** train hard last night. **(e)** He **didn't have to** cross-train last year.	Notice that there is no past tense form of *must* when it shows necessity. Use *had to* to show that something was necessary in the past.
(f) He **must** start a special diet tomorrow. OR **(g)** He **has to** start a special diet tomorrow. OR **(h)** He **will have to** start a special diet to-morrow.	You can use *must, have to,* or *will have to* to talk about events that will be necessary in the near future.
(i) He **doesn't have to** start a special diet tomorrow. **(j)** He **will not (won't) have to** start a spe-cial diet tomorrow.	You can also use negative forms *do not have to* or *will not have to* to talk about the near future.

EXERCISE 11

Maggie and her friend Jan are talking about jobs. Maggie is describing a job she had last summer. Complete their conversation with *have to*, and *do not have to* in the present, past, or future.

Maggie: The worst job I ever had was last summer, when I worked as a waitress in that tourist restaurant down by the aquarium.

Jan: Oh really? What was so terrible about it?

Maggie: For a start, I (1) _____ get up at 5:00 A.M. and, as I didn't have a car then, I (2) _____ walk.

Jan: Why didn't you take the bus?

Maggie: It doesn't start running until 7:00, and I (3) _____ be at the restaurant by 6:30 to set the tables for breakfast.

Jan: That's tough. Did they make you wear a silly uniform or anything?

Maggie: No, thank goodness. We (4) _____ wear any special uniforms, except for hats. We all (5) _____ wear really stupid sailor caps. Mine was too small and it kept falling off.

Jan: So you're probably not planning on working there again next summer.

Maggie: Absolutely not. I'm earning twice as much at my present job, so with a bit of luck, I'll be able to save some money and I (6) _____ work at all next summer.

Jan: That sounds good. What's your present job like?

Maggie: It's much better. I start work at 11:00 A.M.

Jan: So you (7) _____ get up early. What about weekends?

Maggie: I (8) _____ work on weekends, but if I want to make some extra money, I can go in on Saturdays. It's ideal.

Jan: Maybe I should try to get a job there. Our landlord raised the rent last month and I just can't afford to stay there on my present salary.

EXERCISE 12

Read the four conversations below carefully and complete the missing parts with *must, (do not) have to,* or *have got to.*

Conversation A

Ann has just finished talking on the phone with Tom. When she hangs up the phone, her friend Bill wants to know about their conversation.

Bill: You sound worried. Is Tom having problems?

Ann: Tom's landlord sold the apartment house, so Tom

(1) _____ find another place to live.

Bill: Oh, that's too bad. When (2) _____ (he) move out of his apartment?

Ann: I think he (3) _____ move out by the end of the month.

Conversation B

Emily, a five-year-old, is playing outside. Her mother, who is watching from the house, suddenly runs out to her. A big car zooms by.

Emily's mother: Emily! You (4) _____ be more careful! Don't cross the street without looking for cars!

Emily: But I didn't see the car!

Emily's mother: You (5) _____ look in both directions before you cross the street.

Conversation C

Outside the classroom, you hear a conversation between your teacher and Wang, one of your classmates.

Your teacher: Wang, I'm afraid this is the last time I'm going to tell you this. You (6) hand in your homework on time.

Wang: I know, I know. But . . .

Your teacher: No more excuses! You really (7) _____ try to keep up with the class if you want to pass.

Conversation D

It's the end of the school year. Ron and Marion have just had their last class.

Ron: Vacation time at last! We (8) _____ come to school for two whole months!

Marion: Not me. My grades were bad, so I (9) _____ go to summer school all summer, without one single day off.

Ron: I know how that feels. I flunked physics two years ago, and I

(10)_____ read physics books while my friends were going to the beach every day.

Use Your English

ACTIVITY 1: SPEAKING

In Exercise 6, you saw some examples of signs. The local tourist board has asked you and your classmates to create some signs for tourists visiting the area. Get together with two or three other students and draw at least three signs. For example: *You mustn't feed the ducks. You must have exact change for the bus. You mustn't drink this water.* Draw each sign on a different piece of paper. Do not write anything next to the sign—your classmates must guess what it is. Look at their signs and write down what you think they mean.

ACTIVITY 2: SPEAKING

In this activity, you will be comparing your childhood memories with your classmates'. Think back to when you were a child. Write down five things you had to do then that you do not have to do now. Then write down five things you did not have to do then that you have to do now. Next, compare your list with those of two or three other classmates and be ready to report on your findings to the rest of the class.

YOU		YOUR CLASSMATES	
CHILDHOOD	Now	CHILDHOOD	Now
1	1	1	1
2	2	2	2
3	3	3	3
4	4	4	4
5	5	5	5

ACTIVITY 3: SPEAKING

Do you know how to get a driver's license in any other countries in the world? What do you have to do to get a license there? In what ways is it different here? Talk to your classmates and find out what they know. Be ready to report on your findings.

ACTIVITY 4: SPEAKING/LISTENING

STEP 1 Do you know what a person has to do in order to get any of the following?

- a green card (for permanent residence in the United States)
- a Social Security number
- a marriage license
- a license for a gun
- United States citizenship

With a partner, make a list of what you think a person must or has to do in order to get any of these.

STEP 2 Listen to the tape. You will hear somebody discussing **one** of the above topics. Which topic is the speaker talking about? What does she or he think someone has to do? Make notes on the chart below.

TOPIC	WHAT YOU HAVE TO DO

STEP 3 Now look at the list you and your partner made on the same topic. How many differences and how many similarities can you find?

STEP 4 Listen to the tape again. Write down any sentences containing examples of modals and phrasal modals expressing necessity and prohibition.

ACTIVITY 5: SPEAKING/LISTENING/ READING

STEP 1 Choose a topic from Activity 4 that you don't know anything about.

STEP 2 Interview three different native speakers of English and ask them to tell you what they know about the topic. For example, you can ask: What does somebody have to do if they want to get a license for a gun here? Tape-record your interviews. Afterwards, listen to your tape. Did all the people you interviewed tell you the same information? Or did they all tell you different things? Make a list of all the things they told you that a person has to do and share your findings with the rest of your class.

STEP 3 Listen to your tape again, but this time, listen for the language that was used. Write down any sentences containing *must, have to, must not, cannot, do not have to, have got to,* or *should.*

STEP 4 Go to a library and find all the information you can about your topic. Be sure to ask a librarian if you need help locating information. Alternatively, if you have access to a computer and the World Wide Web, you may be able to find all the information there. Take notes on what you read. Are there any differences between the information you found in the library (or on the World Wide Web) and the information that people told you? Make a list of any differences and be ready to share them with the rest of your class.

STEP 5 Write down any examples of the language practiced in this unit that you found in your reading.

ACTIVITY 6: WRITING

A friend of yours is interested in studying at a North American university. Write him or her a letter explaining what he or she will have to do in order to enter a university.

Expressing likes and dislikes

UNIT GOALS:

- To express similarity with *too/either* and *so/neither*
- To express similarity with *so* clauses
- To use short phrases to show agreement and weak agreement
- To express likes and dislikes with gerunds and infinitives

▶ O P E N I N G   T A S K
What Kind of Food Do You Like?

STEP 1 Work with a partner. One of you is A, the other is B. Talk about food that you like and don't like, and complete the chart together.

STEP 2 In the top left-hand box, write three kinds of food that A and B both like. In the top right-hand box, write three kinds of foods that A does not like, but B does. In the bottom left-hand box, write three kinds of food B doesn't like, but A does. In the last box, write three kinds of food that both A and B do not like.

A

	LIKES	DOESN'T LIKE
LIKES	(A likes and B likes too.)	(A doesn't like, but B does)
DOESN'T LIKE	(B doesn't like, but A does).	(B doesn't like, and A doesn't either.)

B

STEP 3 Share some of these findings with the class. Make statements with *like* and *dislike* (or *don't like*), such as:

I like _____ and _____ does too.

I don't like _____ but _____ does.

I don't like _____ and _____ doesn't either.

▶ Expressing Similarity with *Too* and *Either*

EXAMPLES	EXPLANATIONS
(a) I like fruit **and** Roberta **does too.**	To avoid repetition in affirmative sentences (sentences without *not*), use *and* (X) *do/does too.*
(b) **NOT:** I like fruit, and Roberta likes fruit.	
(c) Roberta doesn't eat meat and I **don't either.**	To avoid repetition in negative sentences (sentences with *not*), use *and* (X) *do/doesn't either.*
(d) **NOT:** I don't eat meat, and Roberta doesn't eat meat.	

EXERCISE 1

Check the statements you made in the Opening Task on page 185. Did you use *too* and *either* correctly? Did you use *neither* or *so*? If not, rewrite these statements using *too, either, neither,* and *so.*

▶ Expressing Similarity with *So* and *Neither*

EXAMPLES	EXPLANATIONS
(a) I like fruit **and so does** Roberta.	Another way to avoid repetition is with *and so do/does* (X) in affirmative sentences, and with *and neither do/does* (X) in negative sentences.
(b) Roberta doesn't eat meat **and neither do I.**	Invert subject and verb after *so* and *neither.*

EXERCISE 2

Now work with a different partner and share the information on your charts in the Opening Task. Use this information to complete the following report. Make sure that your statements are not only grammatical but also true.

My classmates and I have strong opinions about the kinds of food we like and dislike. For example, _____ and so

_____ . _____

and neither _____ . _____

too. _____ either.

We also found other similarities in our taste in food. _____

either. _____ neither

_____ . _____

so _____ . _____

too.

FOCUS **3**

▶ **Expressing Similarity with *So***

EXAMPLES	EXPLANATIONS
(a) I speak French and so **does** my mother. **(b)** My mother exercises every day and so **do** I.	Use *do* when you do not want to repeat the verb. Make sure that there is subject/verb agreement: I *do* she/he *does* they/you *do*
(c) I **can** speak French and so **can** she. **(d)** I **have** studied it and so **has** she. **(e)** I **am** happy and so **is** she.	Use an auxiliary verb (*can, have, should*) if the first verb uses one. Use *be* if the first verb is *be*.

EXERCISE 3

Match the first half of the sentences in column A with the second half in column B. Draw an arrow to show the connection. The first one has been done for you.

1. She is late
2. We saw it last night
3. They've never eaten there
4. She'll call you tomorrow
5. Barbara was looking sad
6. The children have seen that movie
7. You didn't do the right thing
8. I can't play tennis
9. Her bike wasn't cheap
10. Scott doesn't have any money
11. The secretary speaks Spanish

a. and so have I.
b. and Peter didn't either.
c. and my brother can't either.
d. and so is her boyfriend.
e. and we do too.
f. and her friend was too.
g. and so will I.
h. and neither do we.
i. and we haven't either.
j. and they did too.
k. and neither was her car.

FOCUS **4**

▶ **Showing Agreement with Short Phrases**

EXAMPLES	EXPLANATIONS
(a) Tina: I love going to movies. Rob: **So do I.** **(b)** Tina: I never go to violent movies. Rob: **Neither do I.** **(c)** Tina: I can't stand watching violence. Rob: **I can't either.** **(d)** Tina: I prefer comedies. Rob: Really? **I do too.**	Short phrases such as *so do I, neither do I, I can't either* and *I do too,* are used to show agreement with somebody else's opinions and ideas. They are very common in informal conversation.

EXERCISE 4

Read the comic strip. Can you find the missing parts of the conversation in the list below? Write the letters in the appropriate cartoon bubble.

► **Short Phrases or Hedges**

EXAMPLES	EXPLANATIONS
(a) Sue: I love ballet. What about you? 　　Tien: **Kind of.**	If you do not agree strongly with the speaker's opinions, you can use hedges (*sort of, kind of*) in informal conversation. In fast speech, *sort of* sounds like "sorta"and *kind of* sounds like "kinda."
(b) Sue: Do you like opera? 　　Tien: **Sort of.**	
(c) Sue: I hate football. 　　Tien: **So do I.**	Hedges follow a question, while short phrases (*So do* I, I *don't either*) follow a statement.

EXERCISE 5

Claire and Chris have just met at a party and are finding out how much they have in common.

Look at the chart showing their likes and dislikes.

✔✔ = a lot　　　　　　　　　　✔ = a little

Use the information from the chart to complete the conversation using hedges where appropriate. The first one has been done for you.

	LIKES		DISLIKES
Chris	swimming ✔✔ cats ✔✔ cooking ✔✔	hiking ✔✔ music ✔ Chinese food ✔✔	TV ✔✔ getting up in the morning ✔✔ country music ✔✔
Claire	cats ✔ eating in restaurants ✔✔ Chinese food ✔✔	cooking ✔ music ✔✔ swimming ✔✔ hiking ✔	country music ✔✔ getting out of bed ✔✔ staying home ✔✔ watching TV ✔✔

Chris: Well, let me see . . . what are some of my favorite things? The ocean . . .
　　　I love swimming in the ocean.

Claire: (1) ___so do I___. Maybe we should go for a swim sometime.

Chris: Yes, that'd be great! Do you like hiking too?

Claire: (2) _____. In general, I prefer to be active. I mean, I don't
　　　like sitting at home and watching TV.

Chris: (3) _____. But I don't like getting up in the morning.

Claire: Well, (4) _____. Most people don't like getting out of bed in the morning! What about music? Do you like music?

Chris: (5) _____. I don't know too much about it, actually.

Claire: Really? I love all kinds of music, except for country. I hate country!

Chris: (6) _____. We certainly agree on that one! What else? I love cooking, do you?

Claire: (7) _____. I really prefer eating out in restaurants, especially in Chinatown. I really love Chinese food.

Chris: (8) _____. I've heard that the new Chinese restaurant on Grant Avenue is supposed to be really good.

Claire: (9) _____. Why don't we give it a try?

Chris: That sounds good. By the way, I have six cats. Do you like cats?

Claire: Well, (10) _____.

Chris: That's O.K.—as long as you don't *hate* them. . . .

EXERCISE 6

One way to meet people is through personal ads in newspapers or magazines. These personal ads appeared in a local newspaper. Read them quickly and then read the statements that follow. Circle T (true) if you think the statement is true and F (false) if you think it is false.

(A) COULD THIS BE YOU?
You are attractive, slim, and athletic. You like dancing, eating candlelit dinners, and walking on the beach by moonlight. Like me, you also enjoy camping and hiking. You love dogs and you don't smoke. If you are the woman of my dreams, send a photo to Box 3092.

(B) BEAUTY & BRAINS
Warm, humorous, well-educated SF loves walking on the beach, dancing, cycling, and hiking. Seeks intelligent life partner with computer interests. P.S.—I'm allergic to cats, dogs, and smoking. Box 875.

(C) I'VE GOT YOU ON MY WAVELENGTH
Athletic, professional, DF, animal lover seeks active man who knows how to treat a lady. Box 4021.

(D) A FEW OF MY FAVORITE THINGS:
Cooking for my friends, cycling, walking on the beach with my dog, wise and witty women. I can't stand: snobs, cheap wine, jogging, people who smoke, women who wear makeup. DM looking for a special woman. Box 49.

1. A likes walking on the beach and so do D and B.   T F
2. B does not like smokers and neither do A and C.   T F
3. Cooking for friends is one of B's favorite pastimes.   T F
4. D does not like women who wear makeup.   T F
5. D likes dancing, and A does too.   T F
6. A wants to find someone who likes hiking, and so does D.   T F
7. Jogging and cycling are two of B's favorite sports.   T F

Do you think any of these people would make a good couple? If so, why? If not, why not?

▶ # Likes and Dislikes with Gerunds and Infinitives

EXAMPLES	EXPLANATIONS
(a) **Cooking** is my favorite hobby. (b) I love **cooking.** Do you? (c) My favorite hobby is **cooking.**	*Gerunds* (nouns formed from verb + *-ing*) can be used as: • the subject of a sentence • the object of a sentence • the complement of a sentence (something needed to complete the sentence)
(d) I like **to cook.** (e) I don't like **to swim.** (f) I hate **to go** to the dentist. (g) AWKWARD: **To cook** is my favorite hobby.	*Infinitives* (*to* + verb) are also used in talking about likes and dislikes. In this context, infinitives are usually used as objects of sentences or as complements, but they sound awkward as subjects.
(h) I don't like **swimming.** (i) I hate **going** to the dentist	When talking about likes and dislikes, you can usually use infinitives or gerunds. The verbs *hate, like,* and *love* can be followed by either a gerund or an infinitive.

EXERCISE 7
Look back at Exercise 6.

1. Underline all the gerunds.

2. Check (✔) all the gerunds that are subjects and circle the gerunds that are objects or complements.

3. Replace the gerunds with infinitives where possible.

4. Rewrite sentence 2, using a gerund or an infinitive.

Use Your English

ACTIVITY 1: SPEAKING

The purpose of this activity is to share information with one other person and then to report to the rest of the class on what you find. In sharing information with your partner, try to find out **how many things you have in common.** Some ideas for starting your conversation are given below. When you have nothing more to say on this topic, decide on another one and find out what you have in common on that topic. Use the chart for your notes.

TOPIC	NOTES
family	some ideas: brothers and sisters?/ grandparents alive?/father older than mother?

ACTIVITY 2: SPEAKING

Form teams. Your job as a team is to find as many similarities as possible among the pairs of things listed below. The team that finds the most similarities is the winner.

1. an apple and an orange
2. learning a foreign language and learning to ride a bike
3. tennis and golf
4. hiking and jogging

ACTIVITY 3: SPEAKING

Form pairs or groups of three.

STEP 1 Think of fifteen to twenty statements using *so/too/either/neither*. Make sure they are meaningful. Write each statement on two cards, like this:

A	B
My parents live in Paris	and so does my sister
I don't like broccoli	and they don't either

Therefore, if you have twenty statements, you will have forty cards.

STEP 2 Get together with another pair or threesome. Place all the A cards in one pile and all the B cards in another pile. Shuffle each deck of cards carefully.

STEP 3 Put the A pile face-down on the table. Then distribute the B cards among the players. Do not look at the cards; place them face-down on the table in front of you.

STEP 4 The first player turns the first card from the A pile on the table and puts the first card from his or her B pile beside it. The player must not look at his or her card before putting it down on the table. The object of the game is to create meaningful sentences. If the two cards on the table do not make a meaningful match, the next player puts his or her B card down. The game continues in this way until a meaningful match is created. The first player to spot a match shouts "Match" to stop the game. If the match is acceptable, he or she collects all the B cards on the table. The next A card is then turned over and the game continues.

STEP 5 The player with the most cards at the end is the winner. This game should be played as quickly as possible.

ACTIVITY 4: SPEAKING/LISTENING

STEP 1 Make a chart similar to the one in the Opening Task on page 185 and find out more about your classmates' likes and dislikes. You can ask about movies/movie stars/types of music/singers/musicians/sports/writers/books. Tape-record your conversations or interviews.

STEP 2 Make a report on your findings. Listen to the tape to make sure your report is accurate. For example:

Recently I made a survey of my classmates' likes and dislikes. I asked them their opinions on several different topics and would now like to tell you about some of my findings . . .

STEP 3 Listen to the tape again. Did your classmates use short phrases such as I *do too, so do* I, I *don't either, neither do* I, *sort of,* and *kind of*? If not, what did they use instead to agree and disagree with each other?

ACTIVITY 5: LISTENING

Listen to the tape of people talking about what they like and dislike. Number the statements below in the order that you hear them. Mark the first statement as number 1 and so forth.

_____ I do too.

_____ So do I.

_____ I don't either.

_____ Neither do I.

_____ Sort of.

_____ Kind of.

ACTIVITY 6: WRITING

Write a personal ad for yourself like the ones in Exercise 6. Display the ads that the class writes and try to guess who wrote each ad.

PRESENT PERFECT WITH SINCE AND FOR

UNIT GOALS:

- To use present perfect to show a connection between past and present situations
- To form correct sentences with present perfect
- To know how to use for and since correctly
- To know which verbs not to use with present perfect

▶ OPENING TASK
Medical History

STEP 1   Quickly read the following medical form.

MEDICAL HISTORY
NAME: Michael James Harris
SEX: Male
DATE OF BIRTH: 5/13/56
MARITAL STATUS: Single
HEIGHT: 5 ft 11 in
WEIGHT: 185 lbs
SERIOUS ILLNESS(ES): None
TIME IN HOSPITAL: May 1973. Broke both legs in traffic accident
SMOKING: Stopped 10 years ago
EYESIGHT: Wears glasses for reading; started in 1987
DRINKING: 1 glass of wine with dinner
ALLERGIES: None
PRESENT PROBLEM: Headaches
WHEN PROBLEM STARTED: 2 months ago

STEP 2   Work with a partner and find details from Michael Harris's medical history to complete the following list. Find two things that happened in the past, two things that are true in the present, and two things that started in the past and have continued to the present. (The first one has been done for you.)

PAST

1.   He broke his legs. _____

2.   _____

PRESENT

1.   _____

2.   _____

FROM PAST TO PRESENT

1.   _____

2.   _____

▶ Present Perfect: Connecting Past and Present

EXAMPLES	EXPLANATIONS
PAST February: **(a)** I **moved** to New York. (simple past)	Use the simple past for completed actions in the past.
PRESENT September: **(b)** I **live** in New York now. (simple present)	Use the simple present for facts about present situations.
PAST AND PRESENT **(c)** I **have lived** in New York since February. **(d)** I **have lived** in New York for seven months. (present perfect)	Use the present perfect (*have* + past participle) to connect the past and present. One use of the present perfect is to tell us about something that began in the past and continues to the present. (For other uses of the present perfect, see Unit 14.)

EXERCISE 1

Use the information about Michael Harris from the Opening Task on page 197 to complete the doctor's report below. Circle the simple present, simple past, or present perfect.

Report on Michael Harris

Michael Harris spoke with me yesterday about serious headaches. He (1) (a) has (b) had (c) has had these headaches for two months. His previous medical history is good. He (2) (a) doesn't have (b) didn't have (c) hasn't had any serious illnesses. In 1973, he (3) (a) is (b) was (c) has been in the hospital for three weeks, when he (4) (a) breaks (b) broke (c) has broken both legs in a car accident. He (5) (a) doesn't smoke; (b) didn't smoke (c) hasn't smoked; now; he (6) (a) stops (b) stopped (c) has stopped ten years ago, and he (7) (a) doesn't smoke (b) didn't smoke (c) hasn't smoked since that time. He (8) (a) wears (b) wore (c) has worn glasses when he reads and he (9) (a) wears (b) wore (c) has worn them since 1987. He (10) (a) drinks (b) drank (c) has drunk a little wine with dinner every night.

I examined Mr. Harris and did several tests. I asked him to return next week.

▶ Forming the Present Perfect

To form the present perfect use *have/has* + past participle.*

STATEMENT	NEGATIVE	QUESTION
I You } **have gone.** We } **('ve)** They	I You } **have not gone.** We } **(haven't)** They	**Have** { I you } **gone?** we they
She } **has gone.** He } **('s)** It	She } **has not gone.** He } **(hasn't)** It	**Has** { she he } **gone?** it

*See Appendix 5 on page A-13 for the past participles of some common irregular verbs.

EXERCISE 2

Write the questions that the doctor probably asked Mr. Harris in order to get these responses.

▶ **EXAMPLE:** **1.** _Do you drink?_____

                 Yes, a little. I drink a glass of wine with dinner every night.

2. _____ ?

    Yes, I do. I wear them when I read.

3. _____ ?

    I started wearing them in 1987.

4. _____ ?

    Yes, I've worn them since 1987.

5. _____ ?

    No, I don't smoke now.

6. _____ ?

    I stopped ten years ago.

7. _____ ?

    No, I haven't smoked since that time.

8. _____ ?

    Yes, I have had these headaches for two months.

EXERCISE 3

Work with a partner. Ask and answer questions about each other's medical history. Feel free to make up information on the following topics, or use Michael Harris's medical form (on page 197) to answer questions.

serious illnesses	time in hospital
smoking	drinking
eyesight	allergies
present problem	when problem started

EXERCISE 4

Go back to Exercises 1 and 2. Look for the words *for* and *since*. In the boxes below, write down the word or words that directly follow *for* and *since*. The first example is *two months* with *for*, from Exercise 1.

Since	For
	two months

What does this tell you about the use of *since* and *for*? What kinds of words or phrases follow *since* and *for*?

▶ *For* and *Since*

EXAMPLES	EXPLANATIONS
(a) **for** two weeks **(b)** **for** ten years **(c)** **for** five minutes	*For* is used to show length of time (how long the period of time was).
(d) **since** 1985 **(e)** **since** my birthday **(f)** **since** I turned 40 **(g)** **since** Monday **(h)** **since** April	*Since* is used to show when a period of time began.

EXERCISE 5

What difference in meaning (if any) is there in each pair of statements? Discuss with a partner.

1. **(a)** He lived here for ten years.

   (b) He has lived here for ten years.

2. (It is May. He moved here three months ago.)

   (a) He has lived here for three months.

   (b) He has lived here since February.

3. **(a)** They have worked for the same company for a long time.

   (b) They worked for the same company for a long time.

4. (They met in 1988.)

   (a) They have known each other for over 10 years.

   (b) They have known each other since 1988.

5. (It is July.)

   (a) Anthony hasn't watched TV for six months.

   (b) Anthony stopped watching TV in January.

▶ *For and Since*

EXAMPLES	EXPLANATIONS
(a) She's worked here **(for)** several years.	The word *for* can be omitted in statements. *For* can also be omitted in questions.
(b) **(For)** how long have you lived here?	
(c) **Since** when have you lived here?	*Since* cannot be omitted. *"How long . . ."* is more common than *"Since when . . ."* in questions.
(d) **NOT:** When have you lived here?	
(e) I've lived here **since** January.	
(f) **NOT:** I've lived here January.	

EXERCISE 6

Look at the hotel register below. How many people are staying in the hotel right now? Who has stayed there the longest?

Hotel Beresford Arms

701 Polk Street ▪ San Francisco, CA 94109
(415) 493-0443   Date: 3/11

Guest	Check-in	Check-Out
Mr. Cruise	3/3	
B. Simpson	3/1	
Mr. and Mrs. Kowlowski	3/8	
Mr. and Mrs. Gordon	3/2	3/8
Ms. Chapman	3/2	
Mr. Nixon	3/2	3/5
Maria da Costa	3/6	
Yee Mun Ling	3/4	

Use the information from the register to make statements with the words given below.

1. Mr. and Mrs. Gordon/for

2. Maria da Costa/since

3. Yee Mun Ling/since

4. B. Simpson/for

5. Mr. and Mrs. Kowlowski/for

6. Ms. Chapman/since

7. Mr. Cruise/for

8. Mr. Nixon/for

▶ **V**erbs Not Used with Present Perfect and *For*

EXAMPLES	EXPLANATIONS
(a) Shin **arrived** in the U.S. three years ago. **(b)** **NOT:** Shin has arrived in the U.S. for three years. **(c)** Shin **has lived** in the U.S. for three years.	Some verbs talk about an action that happens all at once, an action that doesn't continue for a period of time. In (c) we understand that it is the living in the U.S. that continues, not the arriving.
begin arrive meet *end leave stop*	For the same reason, these verbs are not usually used with present perfect and *for*.

EXERCISE 7

Rewrite these sentences using the present perfect and *since* or *for*.

▶ **EXAMPLE:**   Karen wears glasses. She started to wear glasses when she was a child.

Karen has worn glasses since she was a child.

1. He works for the TV station. He started working there eight years ago.
2. They are married. They got married in 1962.
3. She knows how to fix a car. She learned how to do it a long time ago.
4. Tom rides his bike to work. He started to do it when his car broke down.
5. I wanted to go to China several years ago. I still want to go now.
6. My brother started painting when he was in college, and he still paints now.
7. I was afraid of bats when I was a child, and I am afraid of them now.
8. My mother is in France. She went there last week.
9. My sister runs two miles every morning before breakfast. She started to do this when she was fifteen years old.
10. They go to Cape Cod every summer. They started to do this twelve years ago.

EXERCISE 8

Fill in the blanks with *since* or *for* OR the appropriate form of the verb in parentheses.

Leroy and Paula are having a party. Two of their guests, Lee and Bob, have just met.

Lee: (1) <u>Have you known</u> (know) Leroy and Paula (2) _____ a long time?

Bob: I (3) _____ (know) Paula (4) _____ my senior year in college. I first (5) _____ (meet) Leroy at their wedding two years ago. What about you?

Lee: I'm a colleague of Leroy's. We (6) _____ (work) together (7) _____ several years.

Bob: Oh, Leroy (8) _____ (show) me some of your work last week. It's great.

Lee: Thanks. What do you do?

Bob: I (9) _____ (teach) French (10) _____ ten years, but I (11) _____ (quit) a couple of years ago. Now I'm an actor.

Lee: An actor! I thought you looked familiar.

Bob: Well, not really. I (12) _____ (not work) as an actor (13) _____ last October. In fact, last night I (14) _____ (start) to work as a waiter at the Zenon.

Lee: Really? I (15) _____ (eat) there last night. *That's* why you look familiar!

EXERCISE 9

Look for mistakes in the following passage. Correct any mistakes that you find. One has been corrected for you.

1. My sister is very good at languages. She studies

2. Italian at the language institute. She started studying

3. Italian in 1993, so she ~~studies~~ *has studied* Italian several years. When

4. she was a child, she wanted to learn Russian and she still

5. wants to learn it. She has wanted to learn Russian

6. since a long time, but Russian courses are not offered

7. at the language schools near her home. Two years ago

8. she has found out that the local community college offers

9. courses in Chinese, so she started learning Chinese.

10. Unfortunately, she doesn't have a car, so she takes the bus

11. to school since two years.

Use Your English

ACTIVITY 1: SPEAKING

Work in pairs or groups of three. Complete the following with information about your partner(s). Make a list of appropriate questions and then ask your partner(s) the questions. Here are some sample questions:

How long have you studied English?

How long have you lived in this town?

1. _____ for _____ hours.

2. _____ since _____.

3. _____ for _____.

4. _____ for _____ years.

5. _____ since _____.

ACTIVITY 2: SPEAKING/LISTENING

Work with a partner.

STEP 1 Read the statements below and try to match each statement to someone in your class. Write the name in the column marked *Guesses*.

STEP 2 Next, ask your classmates questions using *How long have you . . . ?* in order to find out who has done each thing the longest and shortest amounts of time. Fill in the answers in the column marked *Facts*.

GUESSES	WHO	FACTS
_____	has studied English the longest time?	_____
_____	has been married the longest time?	_____
_____	has owned his or her watch the longest time?	
_____	has known how to drive the longest time?	_____
_____	has known how to drive the shortest time?	_____
_____	has had the shoes she or he is wearing today the longest time?	_____
_____	has worn glasses the longest time?	_____
_____	has worn glasses the shortest time?	_____
_____	has had the same hair style the longest time?	_____

ACTIVITY 3: SPEAKING/LISTENING/WRITING

In this activity, you will find out how different countries are governed.

STEP 1 Get together with a group of classmates from different countries, if possible. First use the three charts to note and list information about your own country or another country you are familiar with. We have done some for you, as an example.

STEP 2 When you have all filled in the charts, begin sharing your information. Then use the charts to take more notes on what your classmates tell you. In the first two charts, check (✔) the appropriate box or write in the box marked *other*. In the third chart, write notes.

STEP 3 Be ready to share this information with the rest of the class.

Country	Type of Leadership				
	PRESIDENT	MONARCH*	PRIME MINISTER	MILITARY	OTHER
Great Britain		✔	✔		

*King, queen, emperor, etc.

Country	How Current Leader Came Into Power			
	ELECTION	SUCCESSION*	COUP**	OTHER
Great Britain	✔ (Prime Minister)	✔ (Queen)		

*Succession: the act of a position or title passing from one person to another, usually a relative

**Coup: a sudden or violent seizure of power by a group that has not been elected

Country	What Current Leader Has Done		
	LENGTH OF TIME THE CURRENT LEADER HAS BEEN IN POWER	BEST THING SHE OR HE HAS DONE WHILE IN POWER	WORST THING SHE OR HE HAS DONE WHILE IN POWER***

***Choose to talk about the leader of your country or another one for which you've listed information.

ACTIVITY 4

STEP 1 Listen to the job interview. Match the first part of each sentence in column A with the second part in column B.

1. I've been	a. a lot more than just manage the office.
2. I've done	b. the EDS.
3. I've overhauled	c. new, more efficient software.
4. I've reorganized	d. at the Smithton and Banks firm for seven years now.
5. I've implemented	e. the whole systems management.

STEP 2 Do you think the man will get the job? Why or why not? Discuss with a partner.

STEP 3 Listen to the tape again. This time, listen closely for the questions and statements with the present perfect. For each sentence with the present perfect, complete the following chart.

1. **Wendy's questions:**	
time expression (*how long*)	subject + verb phrase (*have/has* + verb)

2. **Patrick's statements:**	
subject + verb phrase (*have/has* + verb)	time expression (*for/since*)

ACTIVITY 5: SPEAKING/LISTENING

STEP 1 Find a classmate, a friend, or an acquaintance who is studying the same field as you, or who has or wants a job like yours. Conduct a practice job interview. You can work together to come up with questions, which should include **when** things happened and for **how long:** work experience, job history, and education. Feel free to make up information!

STEP 2 Decide who will be the "employer" (the interviewer) and who will be the "employee" (the interviewee). Take turns if there is time. Tape-record the interviews.

STEP 3 Listen to the recording. Write down all the sentences with the present perfect. In each case, was it used correctly? Were *since* and *for* used correctly? Were there cases where the present perfect should have been used but wasn't?

ACTIVITY 6: WRITING

STEP 1 Choose Activity 3 or Activity 5, whichever was most interesting to you. Write a brief report of two or three paragraphs, summarizing the information that you gathered in that Activity.

STEP 2 Exchange reports with a classmate and check to make sure that the present perfect was used correctly. Were there cases where the present perfect should have been used but wasn't?

PRESENT PERFECT AND SIMPLE PAST

Ever and Never, Already and Yet

UNIT GOALS:

- To use present perfect and simple past in the right situations
- To understand the meaning of *ever* and *never* in questions
- To use present perfect questions in the right situations
- To understand the meaning of *already* and *yet*

▶ **O PENING TASK**

Max's Passport

STEP 1 Work with a partner and look at the stamps on Max's passport to answer these questions:

a) How many different countries has Max visited?

b) When did he visit each one?

STEP 2 Now use Max's passport to complete the following:

Max has visited _____ countries in Asia, Europe,

(1)

and North America. He has been to _____ different

(2)

countries in Asia. In 1986, he went to _____ ,

(3)

_____ , and _____ . He has visited

(4) (5)

_____ and _____ twice. The first time he

(6) (7)

visited Japan was in _____ and the second time was in

(8)

_____ . He went to _____ in 1988 and

(9) (10)

1995. In 1990, he visited _____ . Max hasn't been to

(11)

Europe too ofen; he has been to _____ and

(12)

_____ only once.

(13)

▶ **P**resent Perfect versus Simple Past

EXAMPLES	EXPLANATIONS
(a) Last year, she **graduated** from high school.	Use the simple past to talk about something that happened at a **specific time** in the past.
(b) He **lived** in this house from 1980 to 1988.	Use the simple past to show when something happened.
(c) He **has been** to Mexico. **(d)** They **have run** a marathon.	Use the present perfect when you talk about something that happened in the past without mentioning the specific time it happened. The experience is more important than when it happened.
(e) I **have been** to Thailand. **I went** there about ten years ago and **traveled** all over. **I had** a great time. The Thai people **were** open and friendly to tourists.	Use the present perfect to introduce the general idea. Use the simple past to give specific details.

EXERCISE 1

There is a "classic" film festival in town featuring a number of famous American movies at several different movie theaters. Robert loves classic movies, and so he is planning to invite some friends to a movie on Saturday night. Naturally, he wants to suggest a movie that nobody has seen. Use the information below to help him choose.

FILM FESTIVAL

BALBOA	CORONET	METRO
38th & Balboa 555~8184	Geary & Arguelio 555~4400	Union-Webtser 555~1835
■ HIGH NOON	■ ON THE WATERFRONT	■ CASABLANCA
4:55 8:30 10:55	1:20 3:30 5:37 7:30	1:00 3:15 5:30 10:00
■ ROMAN HOLIDAY		REGENCY
6:50 10:25	GALAXY	Van Ness & Sutter
■ PSYCHO	Van Ness & Sutter 555~8700	555~6773
12:30 4:45 8:40 11:15	■ THE GODFATHER	■ THE GRADUATE
	6:10 8:30 10:55	4:40 7:40 10:30

Ann has seen the movie at the Coronet.

Patty and Mark went to the Metro last night.

Karen went to the Balboa on Tuesday to see the movie that started at 8:30.

Tom went to the Galaxy last weekend.

Carolyn and Terry have seen the movie at the Regency.

A couple of days ago Robert went to the Balboa and saw the movie that started at 8:40.

1. Which movie should they see?

2. Have **you** seen any of these movies?

3. Find out how many of your classmates have seen these movies.

EXERCISE 2

Use the information from Exercise 1 to make questions that fit with the following answers. The first one has been done for you.

1. _Did Carolyn and Terry go to the movies yesterday?_

   Yes, they did. They went to see *The Graduate* yesterday.

2. _____

   Yes, Tom has seen *The Godfather.*

3. _____

   No, Patty and Mark haven't seen *High Noon.*

4. _____

No, she didn't see it last weekend. She saw it on Tuesday.

5. _____

No, they didn't see _Psycho_. They saw _Casablanca_.

6. _____

Yes, he has. He saw it a couple of days ago.

7. _____

No, they haven't seen _Roman Holiday_, but they have seen _The Graduate_.

8. _____

No, he didn't. He saw it last weekend.

EXERCISE 3

Alice is on vacation in New York City. Complete her postcard home, choosing verbs from the list below (some of the verbs can be used more than once). Use either the simple past or present perfect form of the verb.

try	see	walk	eat
have	go	spend	take

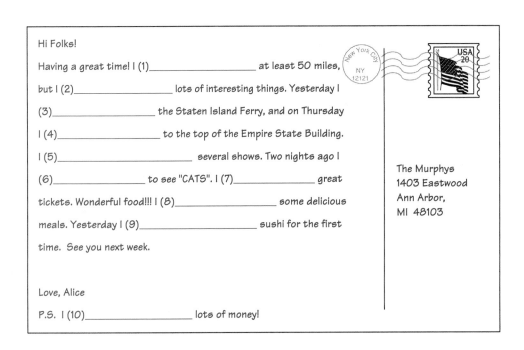

Hi Folks!

Having a great time! I (1)_____ at least 50 miles, but I (2)_____ lots of interesting things. Yesterday I (3)_____ the Staten Island Ferry, and on Thursday I (4)_____ to the top of the Empire State Building.

I (5)_____ several shows. Two nights ago I (6)_____ to see "CATS". I (7)_____ great tickets. Wonderful food!!! I (8)_____ some delicious meals. Yesterday I (9)_____ sushi for the first time. See you next week.

Love, Alice

P.S. I (10)_____ lots of money!

The Murphys
1403 Eastwood
Ann Arbor,
MI 48103

▶ *Ever* and *Never*
in Questions

EXAMPLES	EXPLANATIONS
(a) A: **Have** you **ever eaten** Mexican food?	Use *ever* in questions with the present perfect to mean "at any time before now."
(b) Yes, I **have eaten** it. **(c)** **NOT:** Yes, I have **ever** eaten it. **(d)** I **haven't ever eaten** it.	*Ever* is not usually used in affirmative statements (those that mean or use *yes*). *Ever* is used in negative statements.
(e) I **have never eaten** it.	Use *never* with the present perfect to mean "at no time before now."

EXERCISE 4

Read the conversation. Underline and correct any mistakes.

Mick: Have you ever <u>visit</u> Europe?
   visited

Dave: Yes. I've been there several times, in fact. Three years ago I've gone to
   France.

Mick: Really? Where did you go?

Dave: I went to Paris, of course. And then I rode my mountain bike in the
   Pyrenees. Last year I've ridden my bike in Germany and Switzerland.
   Have ever you been there?

Mick: I've never been to Germany, but I've ever been to Switzerland.

Dave: When was that?

Mick: I've taken an international business course there about eight years
   ago.

▶ **Present Perfect in Questions**

USE

EXAMPLES	EXPLANATIONS
(a) A: **Have** you **ever eaten** frogs' legs? B: No, I haven't.	Use the present perfect with *ever* when you want to know **if** something happened.
(b) A: **Have** you **ever been** to Sub-Saharan Africa? B: Yes, I have.	When you ask these questions, you usually expect the answer to be *Yes, I have* or *No, I haven't*.
(c) A: When **did** you **go** there? B: I went there **last year**.	Use the simple past in questions when you want to know **when** something happened.

EXERCISE 5

Complete the conversations, using the present perfect or the simple past of the verb in parentheses. The first one has been done for you.

1. A: Excuse me, sir, we're doing a survey. Can I ask you a few questions?

B: Sure, go ahead.

A: <u>Have you ever used</u> WonderWhite detergent? (you/use/ever)

B: No, _____ it. (I/try/never)

A: Why not?

B: _____ laundry in my life. (I/do/never) My wife always does it.

A: What about you, sir? _____ your clothes with WonderWhite? (you/wash/ever)

C: Yes, _____ it. (I/try)

A: When _____ it for the first time? (you/try)

C: _____ it for the first time about six months ago. (I/use)

2. A: _____ any books by Latin American writers? (you/read/ever)

B: Yes, I _____ . I _____ a great novel by a Colombian writer a few years ago. (read)

A: Which one?

B: I _____ his name. (forget) He _____ the Nobel Prize several years ago. (win)

A: Oh, you mean Gabriel Garcia Marquez.

3. A: My brother is coming to stay with us for a few days next week. Do you have any ideas about how we can entertain him?

B: _____ here before? (he/be/ever)

A: Yes. He _____ (come) once about three years ago.

B: _____ to Chinatown then? (he/go)

A: No, _____ to Chinatown (he/be/never), but _____ a lot in China and in the Far East. (he/travel)

B: Maybe you'd better not take him to Chinatown then! _____ him to the Greek restaurant when he was here three years ago? (you/take)

A: No, and _____ Greece (he/visit/never).

B: Great! Why don't you take him there?

4. A: _____ last night? (you/go out)

B: Yes. _____ to that new Italian restaurant. (we/go)

A: What's it like? _____ there. (I/be/never)

B: It's O.K., but _____ better Italian food in other restaurants. (I/eat)

A: _____ the one on Main Street? (you/try/ever)

B: Yes. _____ great meal there last weekend. (we/have)

FOCUS **4**

▶ *Already* and *Yet*

EXAMPLES	EXPLANATIONS
(a) I've **already** eaten. **(b)** I haven't eaten **yet.**	Use *already* to show that an event was completed earlier. Use *yet* when an event has **not** been completed before the time of speaking.
(c) Have you eaten **yet**? **(d)** Have you eaten **already**? OR **(e)** Have you **already** eaten?	*Yet* in questions is more neutral than *already*. The use of *already* in questions shows that the speaker expects that an event has happened before the time of speaking.

EXERCISE 6

Get information from your classmates about the following topics and add topics of your own. Use *already, yet, ever,* and *never* when appropriate.

1. study other languages (besides English)
2. receive an F in a class
3. receive an A in a class
4. give a speech
5. be a teacher/teach students
6. feel nervous about speaking another language
7. feel excited about studying/learning
8. earn a Bachelor's degree
9. forget about a test that was scheduled
10. finish studying this chapter
11. master the present perfect tense

EXERCISE 7

Sue and her roommate Betsy are discussing their evening plans. Fill in the missing parts of their conversation. Use *already, yet, ever,* and *never* when appropriate.

Sue: (1) _____ ?

Betsy: No, not yet. But I'm hungry. I didn't eat lunch.

Sue: Well, should we go out to eat? I'd love to try that new Mexican restaurant down the street. (2) _____ ?

Betsy: No, (3) _____ . I was going to go with Deb and Rebecca last week, but at the last minute they changed their minds. (4) _____ out to eat with them? They have a hard time making decisions!

Sue: No, (5) _____ . One time we made plans to, but at the last minute they canceled.

Betsy: I'd rather be invited to their house for dinner, anyway. Deb's a great cook. She went to a chef's school in Paris. (6) _____ ?

Sue: (7) _____ . She makes the best chicken curry. Yum! Which reminds me. . . . You're not the only one that's hungry! Do you need to stop at the cash machine on the way to the restaurant?

Betsy: No, (8) _____ .

Sue: Well, good, let's go then.

Use Your English

STEP 1 In this activity, you will be finding out about some of the things that your classmates have done. Look at the list below. Move around the class and ask questions to see if you can find anyone who has ever done any of these things.

First you need to find who has had the experience (name); then you need to get specific details about the experience (when) (where) (how/why). Take notes below; it is not necessary to write full sentences at this point. In the box marked ***, you can add an experience of your own if you want to.

Be ready to share your findings with the rest of the class.

HAVE YOU EVER . . . . . ?				
Experience	Name	When	Where	How/Why
met a famous person				
climbed a mountain				
seen a shark				
felt really frightened				
flown in a hot-air balloon				
***				

STEP 2 Now use the information you collected to write a report on your findings. Here is one way you can start your report:

A few days ago I interviewed some of my classmates about things they have done before now, and I learned some interesting things about their past experiences. For example, ...

ACTIVITY 2: SPEAKING/LISTENING

Move around the class and ask questions to find out if the following statements are true or false. If the statement is true, write T beside it; if it is false, write F.

1. Somebody in this room has appeared on TV. _____
2. Everybody here has eaten tacos. _____
3. At least three people have never ridden a motorcycle. _____
4. Somebody has swum in more than two oceans. _____
5. Several people have seen a ghost. _____
6. At least three people have been to Disneyland. _____
7. Nobody has been to Paris. _____
8. Somebody has run a marathon. _____
9. Half the class has never played soccer. _____
10. Somebody has never driven a car. _____

ACTIVITY 3: SPEAKING/LISTENING

The purpose of this activity is to confuse your classmates. You will tell the class about three things you have done in your life. Two of these things are true, but one is false. Your classmates will try to guess which one is false. For example:

I have ridden a bicycle from San Francisco to Los Angeles.

I have traveled by boat down the Nile.

I have broken my leg twice.

Which statement is false?

In order to decide which one is false, your classmates can ask you questions about the specific details of each experience. For example: "When did you ride your bike to Los Angeles?" "How long did it take?" "Which leg did you break?" and so on. After they have listened to your answers, the class will vote on which experience is false.

Take turns talking about your true and false experiences until everyone has taken part.

ACTIVITY 4: WRITING OR SPEAKING/LISTENING

STEP 1   Write down one of the true stories you told in Activity 3, this time providing lots of details. Read the story aloud and tape-record it.
OR If you want practice in telling the story without writing it down first, take a few minutes to think about the details you want to include. Then tell the story to a classmate and tape-record it.

STEP 2   Listen to your own or each other's tapes for verb tense usage. Was the present perfect used? If it wasn't, were there cases where it **should** have been used? Was the simple past used correctly? Did you use *already, yet, ever,* and *never* appropriately?

ACTIVITY 5: SPEAKING/LISTENING

You have probably had many different experiences since you came to this country, this city, or this school. In this activity you will be finding out the best and worst experiences your classmates have had since they came here. First go around the room and get as much information as you can from at least three different people. Use the chart to take notes on the information your classmates give you.

Name	Length of Stay	Best Experience	Worst Experience

ACTIVITY 6: WRITING

You have been asked to write a short article for your college newspaper on the experiences of international students.

Review the information you collected in Activity 5. Choose the two most interesting or surprising "best" experiences and the two most interesting or surprising "worst" experiences. Organize your article so that you talk first about the bad experiences and then about the good experiences. Start your article with a brief introduction to the topic and to the students you interviewed. For example:

> What is it like to be a international student? I will try to answer this question by describing both the good and bad experiences of my classmates. Recently I interviewed four students in my class, and they told me about some of their best and worst experiences since they came here. I would like to share with you some of the things I learned. . . .

ACTIVITY 7: WRITING/READING

Write a letter to a family member or a friend and tell him or her about the best and the worst experiences you have had since you left home. Review your letter for the use of the present perfect. If you feel comfortable sharing your letter with someone, you can review each other's letters. Was the present perfect used? If it wasn't, were there cases where it **should** have been used? Was the simple past used correctly? Did you use *already, yet, ever,* and *never* appropriately?

ACTIVITY 8: LISTENING

Listen to the tape of two people talking about their travels.

STEP 1 Take notes in the chart below, using information from their conversation.

	Speaker 1/the man	Speaker 2/the woman
WHERE? area of the world countries (list them)		
WHEN? what year(s)? length of stay		
HOW? transportation hotels/guesthouses		
WHY? reasons for traveling types of experiences		

STEP 2 Discuss these questions with a partner:

1. How would you describe each speaker's traveling style? In other words, what type of travel do they enjoy? What types of places do they stay in? Do they enjoy being tourists or residents?
2. How does your own style of traveling compare or contrast with these people's?

STEP 3 Now listen to the tape again for the way the speakers used verb tenses. List the phrases from the conversation where the speakers used the present perfect verb form in their questions or answers. Compare your list with your classmates' lists. Did the speakers use *yet, ever,* or *never* with the present perfect?

P R E S E N T   P E R F E C T
P R O G R E S S I V E

UNIT GOALS:

- To correctly use present progressive with *just*
- To form present progressive correctly
- To use present progressive to describe unfinished actions and new habits
- To correctly choose between present perfect and present perfect progressive

▶ O P E N I N G   T A S K
Recent Activities

STEP 1 Read the statements below. Why do you think they were said?

STATEMENT

1. A: Ugh . . . your hands are covered with oil and grease!
   B: Sorry.
2. A: Are you O.K.? Your eyes are all red.
3. A: You look terrible.
   B: I didn't get much sleep last night.
4. A: That's enough for tonight. Give me your car keys.
   B: Why?
   A: I'll take you home. You can't drive like this.
5. A: Why is your hair wet?
6. A: Hey, kids! Stop right there!
   B: What for?
   A: Take your shoes off! I don't want mud all over the carpet.

STEP 2 Now look at the activities in the list. Try to match each of the situations above to an activity below. Write the number of the situation beside the activity.

baking bread	_____	studying for a test	_____
swimming	_____	drinking	_____
chopping onions	_____	fixing a car	_____
eating garlic	_____	watching TV	_____
playing in the yard	_____		

▶ **P**resent Perfect Progressive and *Just*: Recent Activities

EXAMPLES	EXPLANATIONS
(a) A: Why are your hands green? B: I **have been painting** my room. *I've been painting my room.*	Use the present perfect progressive to talk about an activity that was happening (in progress) very recently in the past. In (a) the activity is so recent that you can still feel or see the effect or result.
(b) A: How come you're so thirsty? B: I've just been working out.	To emphasize that the activity is recent, use *just*.

EXERCISE 1

Look at the Opening Task on page 227. For statements 1–6, write sentences that give explanations for the situation. The first one has been done for you.

1. *She has been fixing a car.*
   _____

2. _____

3. _____

4. _____

5. _____

6. _____

▶ **Present Perfect Progressive**

Use *has/have* + *been* + verb + *-ing* to form the present perfect progressive.

STATEMENT	NEGATIVE	QUESTION
I You We They } **have been sleeping.** (**'ve**)	I You We They } **have not been sleeping.** (**haven't**)	**Have** { I you we they } **been sleeping?**
She He It } **has been sleeping.** (**'s**)	She He It } **has not been sleeping.** (**hasn't**)	**Has** { she he it } **been sleeping**

EXERCISE 2

You are riding the subway in a big city, late at night. There are several other people in the same car. You observe them carefully and try to figure out what they have been doing recently. You will probably be able to think of several possibilities for each one.

1. A young man with a black eye and ripped clothing:
   He's been fighting with somebody.
   _____

2. Two young men, wearing sweats and carrying tennis racquets:
   _____

3. Two young women with many bags and packages from well-known department stores:
   _____

4. A couple wearing shorts and walking shoes and backpacks. They seem very tired:
   _____

5. A young woman with a bookbag full of chemistry textbooks. She has a book open in her hands and she is asleep:
   _____

6. A woman with red stains on her hands:
   _____

7. A man with white hairs all over his clothes and scratches on his hands:
   _____

USE

► **Perfect Progressive: Unfinished Actions**

EXAMPLE	EXPLANATION
(a) He **has been waiting** for twenty minutes. (He's still waiting.) 20 Minutes Ago ———— Now →	Use the present perfect progressive to describe situations or actions that started in the past and are still going on.

EXERCISE 3

For each conversation, complete the following sentences. The first one has been done for you.

1. **Lee:** What are you doing?

   Mary Lou: I'm waiting to make a phone call. This woman <u>has been talking</u> on the phone for the last twenty minutes. (talk)

2. **Dan:** Haven't you finished writing that book yet?

   Heidi: No, we're still working on it.

   Dan: You _____ it for almost three years! (write)

3. **Steve:** What's up? You look miserable.

   Tom: I am. I want to go for a bike ride, but it _____ since eight o'clock this morning. (rain)

4. **George:** Excuse me, but is this your dog?

   Barbara: Yes. Is there a problem?

   George: I can't get to sleep because that dog _____ for hours! Please keep it under control, or I'll call the police. (bark)

5. **Martin:** Are these your glasses?

   Gin: Yes! Thank you so much. I _____ for them everywhere! (look)

6. **Sarita:** How are things going in New York?

Anastasia: We don't live there anymore.

Sarita: Really?

Anastasia: Yes. We _____ in Philadelphia since January. (live)

7. **Diane:** Why are Kemal and Cynthia so depressed?

Marianne: They _____ grammar for ages, but they still don't understand how to use the present perfect progressive. (study)

8. **Pam:** Aren't you ready yet?

Andrew: No. I've lost my keys and I _____ to find them for the last half hour. (try)

▶ Present Perfect Progressive for New Habits

EXAMPLES	EXPLANATIONS
(a) They**'ve been eating** out a lot recently.	Use the present perfect progressive to talk about a regular habit or activity that is still happening.
(b) He's been exercising a lot **lately**. (c) I've been walking to work **recently**.	Add a time phrase or word to show that the activity started recently.

EXERCISE 4

Pat is talking with her old friend Janet. They have not seen each other for several months, and Janet is surprised by some of the changes in Pat's appearance. Complete their conversation using the verbs from the list below.

happen	sail	cook	do
feel	take	go	study
eat	ride	date	ski
talk	think	see	spend

Janet: Pat, you look great! You've lost a lot of weight, too.

Pat: Well, I (1) <u>'ve been riding</u> my bike to school recently, and I

(2) _____ an aerobics class.

Janet: Is that all? No special diets or anything?

Pat: Not really. I (3) _____ (not) to any fast-food restaurants.

I (4) _____ at home instead—a lot of fresh vegetables

and salads and other healthy stuff like that. It really makes a

difference. I (5) _____ much better, with lots more

energy.

Janet: Well, you seem to be very busy these days. You're never home when I

call. What else (6) _____ you _____ ?

Pat: I (7) _____ somebody special. She's got a boat, so we

(8) _____ a lot, and she also has a cabin in the

mountains, so we (9) _____ time there, too. And

also, we (10) _____ about taking some longer trips

together. So it's all pretty exciting. But what about you? What

(11) _____ ?

Janet: Nothing. I (12) _____ for my final exams, but when

they're over, I'm going to start having fun!

FOCUS **5**

Present Perfect versus Present Perfect Progressive

EXAMPLES	EXPLANATIONS
(a) Jim **has worked** here for ten years. **(b)** Jim **has been working** here for ten years.	With certain verbs, there is no difference in use between the present perfect and present perfect progressive. Use both to describe something that started in the past and continues to now. These verbs include *work*, *live*, and *study*.

EXAMPLES	EXPLANATIONS
(c) They **have painted** their house. (d) They **have been painting** their house. (e) Jean **has visited** her grandmother. (f) Jean **has been visiting** her grandmother. (g) Geraldo **has exercised**. (h) Geraldo **has been exercising lately**.	In other cases the present perfect progressive: • shows that the action is incomplete (unfinished). In (c), the painting is complete. In (d), it is not complete (see Focus 3). OR: • emphasizes that the action was in progress recently. (e) tells us that the visit occurred earlier. (f) tells us that the visit occurred recently and perhaps is still in progress (see Focus 1). OR: • talks about a new habit. (g) tells us that Geraldo exercised at some time earlier. (h) suggests that he has started a new habit (see Focus 4).

EXERCISE 5

Read each situation and circle the statement that best describes the situation.

1. Sally ate frogs' legs in September, 1998, and again in December, 1999.
   (a) Sally has eaten frogs' legs.
   (b) Sally has been eating frogs' legs.

2. Bill started reading that book last week and he's not finished yet. He will probably finish it tonight.
   (a) Bill has read that book.
   (b) Bill has been reading that book.

3. I rode a motorcycle once when I was sixteen and once last year.
   (a) I've been riding a motorcycle.
   (b) I've ridden a motorcycle since I was a teenager.
   (c) I've ridden a motorcycle.

4. We first studied English grammar in school, ten years ago. This year we have grammar class for one hour a day, five days a week, and then there's all the homework—sometimes two or three hours every night.
   (a) We've been studying English grammar.
   (b) We've studied English grammar.
   (c) We've been studying English grammar for a long time.
   (d) We've studied English grammar for a long time.

5. My brother just can't quit smoking, even though he knows it's a bad habit. He started smoking when he was seventeen, and now he's almost thirty.
   (a) My brother has smoked.
   (b) My brother has been smoking.
   (c) My brother has been smoking for a long time.
   (d) My brother has smoked for a long time.

EXERCISE 6

What would Doug and Sandy say in each situation below? The words in parentheses will help you, but you will need to add some other words.

1. It's 4:00, and Doug's partner Sandy has been napping since 1:00. Doug is waiting for her to wake up. When she finally does, he says: (I/wait/three hours)

   _____

   _____

2. Sandy has promised to change the oil in Doug's car. While she is sleeping, Doug decides to try to do it himself, but he can't. When Sandy wakes up, he says: (I/try/forty-five minutes)

   _____

   _____

3. Sandy's mother calls to tell her that Sandy's sister has had another baby. Her mother asks, "When are you and Doug going to have kids?" Sandy tells her: (we/discuss/ten years)

   _____

   _____

4. After her nap, Sandy is hungry and she wants Doug to go out with her to eat pizza. Doug doesn't want to go because he bought fresh fish for dinner and wants to try out a new recipe. He tells Sandy, "I don't want to go out because (I/plan/dinner/all day)"

   _____

   _____

EXERCISE 7

Complete the dialogues below, using present perfect progressive, present perfect, or simple past. Be prepared to explain your choice.

Dialogue 1

Keven: What's the matter? You look frustrated.

Tsitsi: I am. I (1) _____ (try) to study all day, but the telephone never stops ringing. People (2) _____ (call) all day about the car.

Keven: That's great. I (3) _____ (hope) to sell that car for six months now. Maybe today's the day!

Dialogue 2

Maria: I'm sorry I'm so late. (4) _____ (you/wait) long?

Alex: Yes, I have! Where (5) _____ (you/be)?

Maria: I really am sorry. My watch is broken, and I didn't know what time it was.

Alex: Why didn't you ask somebody? I (6) _____ (stand) out here in the cold for at least forty minutes.

Maria: Oh, you poor thing! But we'd better hurry to get to the movie theater.

Alex: It's too late. The movie (7) _____ (start).

Maria: Really?

Alex: Yes. It (8) _____ (start) twenty minutes ago.

Use Your English

ACTIVITY 1: WRITING

You have just received a letter from the editor of your high school newspaper. She wants to include information about former students in the next edition of the paper. Write a letter to the editor, telling her what you have been doing recently. (Do not feel you have to use the present perfect progressive in every sentence! To make this a natural letter, think about all the other tenses you can use as well.)

ACTIVITY 2: SPEAKING

The purpose of this game is to guess recent activities from their current results. Work in teams. Each team should try to think of four different results of recent activities. An example of one of these could be:

Recent Activity	Present Result

You have been exercising and now you are exhausted.

When everyone is ready, each team takes turns acting out the results of the activities they have chosen. For example, Team A has chosen "being exhausted." Everybody in Team A gets up and acts out being exhausted. The rest of the class tries to guess what Team A has been doing. The first person to guess correctly, "You have been exercising and now you are exhausted," scores a point for his or her team.

ACTIVITY 3: SPEAKING

This is another team game. Each team presents a series of clues, and the rest of the class tries to guess what situation these clues refer to. For example, Team A chooses this situation: A woman has been reading a sad love story. The team tries to think of as many clues as possible that will help the other students guess the situation. When everyone is ready, Team A presents the first clue:

Team A: Her eyes are red.

The other teams make guesses based on this first clue:

Team B: She has been chopping onions.

Team A: No. She feels very sad.

Team C: She's been crying.

Team A: No. She's very romantic.

Team D: She's been fighting with her boyfriend.

Team A: No. She was alone while she was doing this.

Team C: She's been reading a sad love story.

You can choose one of the situations below or you can make up one of your own.

1. She or he has been crying.
2. She or he has been watching old movies.
3. She or he has been working late every night.
4. She or he's been training for the Olympics.
5. She or he has been chopping onions.
6. She or he has been feeling sick.
7. She or he has been gaining weight.

The person who guesses the correct situation scores a point for his or her team.

ACTIVITY 4: LISTENING

Listen to the tape of a conversation between two old friends. These people haven't seen each other for several years, so they have a lot to talk about.

STEP 1 Make a list of the things that each speaker has been doing or has recently done (or the things their family members and friends have done). Compare your list with a classmate's.

Speaker 1/man	Speaker 2/woman

STEP 2 Look at the lists that you and your partner made. Together, write a sentence about each thing on your lists using either the present perfect or the present perfect progressive.

ACTIVITY 5: SPEAKING/LISTENING

STEP 1 Interview a classmate about some of the things that she or he has been doing since coming to this country, this city, or this school that she or he has never done before. Tape-record your interview.

STEP 2 Think about your classmate's experiences. Choose three of them that you think are interesting, unusual, or important to your classmate. Write these down and then give this list to your teacher.

STEP 3 Your teacher will collect all of the lists from the class and then read them aloud. Can you guess who your teacher is talking about? No guesses are allowed if it is about you or the classmate you interviewed!

ACTIVITY 6: LISTENING/WRITING

Listen to the recording of your interview in Activity 5. Write down all the sentences which used the present perfect progressive (if there were any!). In each case, was it used correctly? Were there cases where the present perfect progressive could have been used but wasn't?

MAKING OFFERS WITH WOULD YOU LIKE

UNIT GOALS:

- To make offers with *would you like*
- To choose correctly between *would you like* and *do you want*
- To use correct forms when accepting and refusing offers

▶ OPENING TASK
A Noisy Party

Imagine that you are at a party. Your friend is on the other side of the room. You can see each other; but you cannot hear each other because the room is crowded and the music is very loud.

STEP 1 For this activity, work in pairs. Student A: Communicate the problem (listed on the chart below) to Student B **without speaking or writing.** Student B: **Do not** look at the list of problems. Your job is to offer a solution to Student A **without speaking or writing.** You will both need to act out your responses to each other. That is, you will need to use gestures, facial expressions, and other nonverbal ways of communicating.

STEP 2 When you have finished, check the list to see if Student B correctly understood Student A's problems. Then write down an appropriate **offer** using *Would you like . . . ?* on the Solutions side of the chart.

Problems	Solutions
Student A:	
1. You are thirsty.	
2. You have a headache.	
3. You are hot. The room is very stuffy. Your friend is standing by the window.	
4. You are hungry. Your friend is standing by a table with food on it.	
5. You have to sneeze but you don't have a tissue.	
6. You need a light for your cigarette and an ashtray.	
7. You are tired. You want your friend to give you a ride home.	
8. You are bored. The music is playing and you want to dance.	

▶ **O**ffers with *Would You Like*

EXAMPLES	EXPLANATIONS
(a) **Would you like** some coffee?	There are several ways to make offers.
(b) **Would you like** some help?	Use *Would you like* + noun phrase.
(c) **Would you like to** sit down?	Use *Would you like to* + verb phrase.
(d) **Would you like to** use the bathroom?	
(e) **Would you like me to** open the window?	Use *Would you like me to* + verb phrase to make an offer about yourself.
(f) **Would you like me to** take your coat?	
(g) **Would you like** Sally **to** open the window?	Use *Would you like* (person's name) *to* + verb phrase to make an offer about someone else.
(h) **Would you like** Auntie Bev **to** help you wash your hands?	

EXERCISE 1

Look back at the offers you wrote down in the Opening Task on page 239. Are your offers formed correctly? Change the ones that are not already correct.

▶ *Would You Like . . . ?* or *Do You Want . . . ?*

EXAMPLES	EXPLANATIONS
(a) **Would you like** a cup of tea?	Use *Would you like . . . ?* if you want to be polite. Offers with *Do you want . . . ?* are usually used with close friends and family. Example (a) is more polite or formal than (b).
(b) **Do you want** a cup of tea?	
(c) **Want** me to help you with your bags?	In informal situations *"Do you"* can be omitted from *Do you want . . . ?*
(d) **Would you like** me to help you with your bags?	Example (c) is less formal than (d).

EXERCISE 2

Your new friend is having her first party in North America. She has invited some of her classmates, her teachers and their partners, and her neighbors, two elderly women. She has asked you to help her because she is nervous and does not know English very well. Change her commands and questions into polite offers, using *Would you like . . .?* or *Do you want . . .?*

Make an offer to . . .

1. Come in . . . . everyone
2. Sit down . . . . the neighbors
3. Give me your coat . . . . the teachers and their partners
4. Want a chair? . . . . the classmates
5. Want something to drink?. . . everyone
6. Cream in your coffee? . . . . . . the classmates
7. Want the window open? . . . . the teachers and their partners
8. Give me your cup . . . . the neighbors
   I'll get more coffee.

EXERCISE 3

Look at the list below. Choose three things and make offers you hope your classmates and your teacher will accept. Go around the class and make offers with *Would you like . . .?* or *Do you want . . .?* to as many people as possible.

When you respond to an offer: (a) be as polite as possible, and (b) if you must refuse the offer, give a reason for refusing it.

1. borrow a book
2. eat something
3. drink something
4. read a magazine
5. use a Walkman
6. close the window
7. leave the room
8. erase the blackboard
9. _____ (make up your own offer)

▶ Accepting and Refusing Offers

EXAMPLES	EXPLANATIONS
	ACCEPTING OFFERS
(a) A: Would you like something to drink? B: **Yes, please.**	Use *please* along with yes to politely accept offers.
(b) A: Would you like me to help you? B: Yes, please. **That's very kind of you.**	To be **very** polite, use an extra phrase to show that you appreciate the offer. (This is not usually necessary in informal situations.)
(c) A: Do you want the rest of my hamburger? B: **Sure. Thanks.**	In informal situations, words such as *sure, yeah,* and *thanks* show that you accept the offer.
(d) A: Would you like some coffee? B: **No, thank you.** OR **No, thanks.**	**REFUSING OFFERS** Use *thank you/thanks* with *no* to politely refuse offers.
(e) A: Would you like some coffee? B: No, thank you. **I've had enough.**	For polite refusals, you can tell why the offer cannot be accepted.
(f) A: Would you like me to help you? B: No, thanks. **That's nice of you, but I can manage.**	

EXERCISE 4

Look at the following responses. What offer was probably made? Write it down in the blank.

1. Offer: _____

Response: No, thanks. I've had enough.

2. Offer: _____

Response: Yeah, sure. I haven't eaten a thing all day.

3. Offer: _____

Response: Oh, no, thank you. I've seen it already.

4. Offer: _____

Response: No, thanks. I'm warm enough.

5. Offer: _____

Response: Yeah, it's really heavy. Thanks.

6. Offer: _____

Response: Thanks, I'd love to. That sounds great.

7. Offer: _____

Response: Thanks, but I've already got one of my own.

EXERCISE 5

For each of the following situations, write a short dialogue in which one person makes a polite offer (using *Would you like . . .*) and the other person either politely accepts or politely refuses the offer. Then find a partner and read your dialogues aloud, taking parts.

1. The English instructor, at the front of the classroom, is ready to show a video in class today. The switch to turn on the video player is right by Stefan, at the back of the room.

Stefan says: _____?

The instructor says: _____ .

2. The dinner at Mrs. Zimunga's house is almost finished. Mrs. Zimunga notices that some of the guests ate their dessert—cherry pie—very quickly, and she thinks they might want another piece.

Mrs. Zimunga says: _____?

A guest says: _____ .

3. Alfredo has a seat at the front of the city bus. He notices that an elderly woman has just gotten on, but there are no more seats left.

Alfredo says: _____ ?

The elderly woman says: _____ .

4. As Mary is about to leave for the post office, she sees that there are several envelopes on the desk, stamped and addressed by her roommate Judith.

Mary says: _____ ?

Judith says: _____ .

5. Just as Thomas starts to drive away to work, he sees that his neighbor Rob is walking down the sidewalk to the bus stop. Thomas knows that Rob's office is not far from where he works.

Thomas says: _____ ?

Rob says: _____ .

6. Nyaradzo is jogging in the park, and she is about to cross a road. A stranger is waiting in his car, and he offers her a ride.

The stranger says: _____ ?

Nyaradzo says: _____ .

It's not always necessary to refuse offers **politely!** Check with your classmates to see their answers for Nyaradzo's response in item 6.

Use Your English

How do native speakers of English behave at parties? Is their behavior at formal parties different from their behavior at informal parties where the guests are all close friends or relatives?

Use the chart below to interview native speakers (or people who have spent a long time in an English-speaking country). There are blanks at the bottom for other topics you might want to find out about. Tape-record your interview.

What Does the Host Do or Say When He or She...	Formal Parties	Informal Parties
(a) invites the guests to sit down		
(b) offers the guests something to eat		
(c) encourages the guests to eat/drink more		
(d) invites the guests to start some activity (dancing/playing a game)		
(e)		
(f)		

ACTIVITY 2 : LISTENING

Listen to the interviews that you and your classmates tape-recorded in Activity 1. Did your classmates get any different information? Add to your chart as necessary.

ACTIVITY 3: LISTENING/ WRITING

Listen to the tape of two speakers talking about giving parties.

STEP 1 Listen to the tape of two people talking about giving parties. Write some of the problems the man talks about in the first column below. Write the suggestions the woman makes about each problem in the second column.

Party Problems	Suggestions
1.	
2.	
3.	

STEP 2 Discuss the problems and suggestions with a partner. How did the man respond to the woman's suggestions?

STEP 3 Listen again. What were the exact words the woman suggested using for the three problems you listed in Step 1? Write those words below.

Suggestions:

1. _____

2. _____

3. _____

STEP 4 What might the people at the party say in response to each of these suggestions? List three sentences they might use to accept the offers.

Accepting the Offers:

1. _____

2. _____

3. _____

STEP 5 List three sentences they might use to refuse the offers.

Refusing the Offers:

1. _____

2. _____

3. _____

ACTIVITY 4: SPEAKING/LISTENING

STEP 1 How can your classmate help you?

Think of two things that a classmate could do for you that would be helpful. Take two pieces of paper and write down one of those things on each piece. Do not write down your name.

Your teacher will collect the papers.

STEP 2 Your teacher will mix up the papers and give you two papers that other students wrote. (Make sure that you don't get your own!) Your job is to guess who wrote each request for help. Go around the room to find the person. Make an offer to help him or her using *Would you like . . . ?* or *Do you want . . . ?*

STEP 3 You must accept an offer if it is about the help you requested (the thing you wrote down on your piece of paper). You must refuse all other offers for help, even if they sound good.

ACTIVITY 5: SPEAKING/WRITING

STEP 1 Your good friend is at home in bed sick. You want to help out and make your friend feel better. Make a list of things that you might do to help. Then get together with a partner who will play the role of your friend. Make offers using *Would you like . . . ?* and *Do you want . . . ?* Your "friend" can accept or refuse your offers.

STEP 2 Write down responses to the offers you made in Step 1. If your friend accepted your offer, the response will go in the Accept column. If your friend refused your offer, the response will go in the Refuse column.

For each column, rank these responses in order of politeness. (Which responses seemed most polite? Which seemed least polite?)

Response to your offers	
ACCEPT	REFUSE

Compare your chart to other students' charts

REQUESTS AND PERMISSION

Can, Could, Will, Would, and May

UNIT GOALS:

- To make polite requests
- To politely agree to and refuse requests
- To ask for permission
- To give or politely refuse permission

▶ **O P E N I N G T A S K**

The Messy Note

You are going to take care of a friend's house while she is on vacation. Your friend has left you a note with instructions about what to do while she is gone. Unfortunately, someone has spilled coffee on the note, and now it is difficult to read.

STEP 1 Complete the missing parts of the note so that it makes sense. Example A has been done for you.

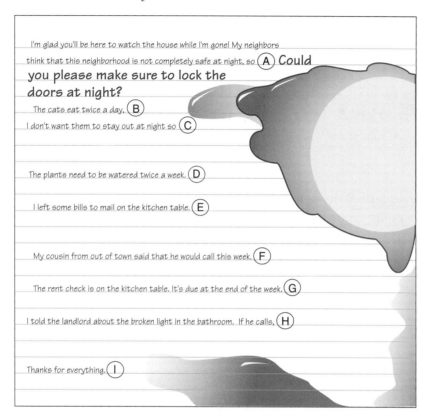

I'm glad you'll be here to watch the house while I'm gone! My neighbors
think that this neighborhood is not completely safe at night, so (A) **Could**
you please make sure to lock the
doors at night?
The cats eat twice a day. (B)
I don't want them to stay out at night so (C)

The plants need to be watered twice a week. (D)

I left some bills to mail on the kitchen table. (E)

My cousin from out of town said that he would call this week. (F)

The rent check is on the kitchen table. It's due at the end of the week. (G)

I told the landlord about the broken light in the bathroom. If he calls, (H)

Thanks for everything. (I)

STEP 2 Now look at the choices for the missing parts of the note above. Write the appropriate number in the spaces on the note.

1. . . . could you ask him to fix it as soon as possible?

2. . . . remember to lock the windows and doors when it gets dark. Thanks.

3. . . . so will you please give them water on Tuesday and Friday?

4. . . . See you next week!

5. . . . Would you mind mailing them for me tomorrow morning?

6. . . . please make sure they come in around 8:00.

7. . . . Would you take a message and tell him I'll be back on the twenty-ninth?

8. . . . so could you feed them in the morning and at night?

9. . . . Please mail it before Friday.

Were your "answers" to the missing parts similar to these?

▶ **Making Polite Requests**

USE

I left my notes at home.

(a)	**Would you mind** lending me your notes?
(b)	**Would** you (**please**) lend me your notes?
(c)	**Could** you lend me your notes (**please**)?
(d)	**Will** you lend me your notes (**please**)?
(e)	**Can** you (**please**) lend me your notes?
(f)	**Please** lend me your notes.

Most polite

↑

↓

Least polite

EXERCISE 1

Below are some situations in which requests are commonly made. For each situation, make a polite request.

1. You want to know what time it is. You find someone who is wearing a watch and you say: _____

_____

2. When you pay for your groceries at the supermarket, you remember that you need some change for the telephone. You hand the cashier a dollar and say: _____

_____

3. You have been waiting in line at the bank for fifteen minutes, but you need to get a drink of water. You turn to the friendly-looking person standing behind you in line, and you say: _____

_____

4. You are watching a videotape in class. Your classmate in front of you is in the way. You want him to move his chair. You say: _____

_____

5. Your class has just watched a videotape. It is finished; your classroom is still dark. Your instructor wants the student who is sitting near the light switch to turn on the lights, so she or he says: _____

_____

6. There is a lot of noise outside your classroom. Your teacher wants the student who is sitting near the door to close it, so she or he says: _____

_____

7. A classmate is giving a presentation, but she is speaking very quietly. You cannot hear her. You say: _____

_____

▶ **Politely Refusing Requests**

EXAMPLES	EXPLANATIONS
Can you lend me your notes? **(a) I'm sorry,** but I need them to study for the test. OR **(b) I'm afraid that** I didn't take any notes. OR **(c) I'd like to,** but I left mine at home, too.	If you have to refuse a request, it is polite to say **why** you are refusing. Phrases such as *I'm afraid that* or *I'm sorry* help to "soften" the *No*, and make it more polite.

EXERCISE 2

Make requests of all your classmates and find someone who will grant your request (say *yes*) for the following things. For each request, try to find at least one person who will say *yes*. If a classmate says *no*, write down the reason for refusing your request.

REQUEST	REASON FOR SAYING NO
1. lend you some money	
2. buy you a cup of coffee	
3. help you study for a test	
4. give you a ride home after class	
5. teach you how to dance	

▶ **R**esponding to Requests

EXAMPLES	EXPLANATIONS
Can you lend me your notes?	You can respond to requests with short answers.
(a) I'd be glad to.	Examples (b) and (c) are very informal.
(b) Sure, why not?	
(c) Yeah, no problem.	
(d) Yeah, I guess so.	Example (d) shows that the speaker is uncertain.
Could you loan me five dollars?	
(e) Yes, I can.	*Could* and *would* are **not** used in responses to requests.
(f) **NOT:** Yes, I could.	
Would you go to the store with me?	
(g) Yes, I will.	
(h) **NOT:** Yes, I would.	

EXERCISE 3

Make polite requests for the following situations. Use *can, could, will, would,* or *would you mind* in these requests.

What is the response? How is the request politely accepted or refused?

1. There's a place on your back that suddenly begins to itch. You ask your close friend to scratch it.

   You say: _____ ?

   What does your friend say? _____ .

   But your friend is not quite getting the right place. So you say:

   _____?

2. You are at a restaurant, and the people at the next table are smoking. You want them to stop, so you say: _____ ?

What do they say? _____ .

3. Your friend is helping you hang a picture on your wall. She is holding it up while you decide where it should go.

You say: _____ ?

What does your friend do or say? _____ .

4. You are visiting a famous tourist site, and a family wants you to take their photograph together.

One of the family members says: _____

_____

What do you do or say? _____

_____

5. You are trying to study for a test, and your neighbors are playing very loud music. You can't concentrate, so you say, _____ ?

EXERCISE 4

Write the number of the following questions in the appropriate box in the chart below. The first one has been done for you.

Something the Speaker Wants To Do (Request for Permission)	Something the Speaker Wants Somebody Else To Do (General Request)
1.	

1. Do you mind if I turn on the radio?
2. Can you open the window?
3. May I ask you a question?
4. Could you speak more slowly?
5. Would you mind lending me your dictionary?
6. Can I leave early?
7. Would you tell me the answer?
8. May we swim in your pool?
9. Could you show us how to do it?
10. Could I borrow your knife?
11. Would you mind if I handed in my assignment a day late?

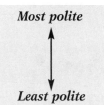

▶ **A**sking for Permission

(a) **Would you mind** if I left early?	*Most polite*
(b) **Do you mind** if I leave early?	↑
(c) **May** I leave early?	
(d) **Could** I leave early?	↓
(e) **Can** I leave early?	*Least polite*

EXERCISE 5

For each answer, what was probably the question?

1. Question: _____ ?

Teacher to student: No, I'd like you to hand it in on Friday. I announced the due date two weeks ago, so I'm afraid I won't be able to make any exceptions.

2. Question: _____ ?

Friend to friend: Sure, it is a little cold in here.

3. Question: _____ ?

Lecturer to member of the audience: Sorry, but I'm going to have to ask you to hold your questions until the end of my talk. We'll have 15 minutes for questions.

4. Question: _____ ?

Secretary (on phone): Yes, may I tell him who's calling?

5. Question: _____ ?

Twelve-year-old child (on phone): Yes, hold on and I'll go and get him.

6. Question: _____ ?

Mother (to child): OK, you can have one more. But only *one*, because we're going to eat soon and I don't want you to spoil your appetite.

7. Question: _____ ?

Hostess to guest: Oh, of course, please help yourself. I'm glad you like them.

8. Question: _____ ?

Customer to salesperson: Yes, I want to look at the sweaters that are on sale. The ones that were advertised in the newspaper?

▶ Responding to Requests for Permission

EXAMPLES	EXPLANATIONS
Would you mind if I left early?	
(a) No, not at all.	Use short phrases to answer requests for
(b) Sorry, but I need you to stay until 5:00.	permission. If you refuse a request, it is polite to give the reason.
May I leave early?	
(c) Yes, of course.	
(d) Sorry, but I'd rather have you stay until 5:00.	
Could I leave early?	
(e) Yes, you can.	*Could* is not usually used in responses to
(f) **NOT:** Yes, you could.	requests for permission.

EXERCISE 6

For each of the following situations, work with a classmate to make general requests or requests for permission, and then respond to these requests. Decide how polite you need to be in each situation and whether *can, could, will, would, may, would you mind,* or *do you mind* is the most appropriate to use. There is more than one way to ask and answer each question.

1. You are at a friend's house, and you want to use the phone.
2. Your teacher says something, but you do not understand, and you want her to repeat it.
3. Your friend has asked you to pick her up at the airport. You want to know if her flight, #255 from Denver, is on time, so you call the airline.
4. You want to borrow your roommate's car.
5. Your roommate is going to the store, and you remember that you need some film.
6. You are the first one to finish the reading test in class. You want to find out from your teacher if you are allowed to leave the room now.
7. It is very cold in class, and the window is open.
8. You see that your teacher is in her office with the door partly open. You want to go in to talk to her.
9. You are on the phone with the dentist's secretary because you want to change your appointment time.
10. You are at a close friend's house, and you would like a cup of tea.
11. You want to hold your friend's baby.

Use Your English

ACTIVITY 1: LISTENING/SPEAKING

STEP 1 Go to a restaurant or cafeteria and pay attention to the different kinds of requests that are used. Try to observe five different requests. Take notes on these, using the chart below.

Observation Sheet		
PLACE:		
TIME:		
DAY:		
REQUEST	WHO MADE IT	RESPONSE

STEP 2 Discuss the results of your observations with other classmates. Were their observations similar? What words were used most often in requests: *can, could, will, would,* or *would you mind*?

ACTIVITY 2: SPEAKING

Play this game in a group of five or six students or with the whole class.

STEP 1 Pick a letter from the alphabet. Ask a classmate to buy you something at the mall that begins with that letter.

STEP 2 Your classmate must think of something to buy that begins with the letter you chose and then he or she must tell you what it is.

STEP 3 Your classmate then chooses another student.

▶ **EXAMPLES:**

Sara: Bruno, would you please buy me something that begins with the letter S?

Bruno: Sure. I'll buy you some stamps. Sue, could you buy me something that begins with the letter M?

Sue: Ok. I'll buy you a magazine. Hartmut, would you mind buying me something that begins with the letter P?

ACTIVITY 3: LISTENING

How do people request permission to speak with someone on the telephone? Are these ways different depending on the situation?

Interview people about what they say in different situations. Some examples are speaking with a doctor, speaking with a teacher, speaking with a close friend, and speaking with a family member.

Setting	Relationship	What They Say

ACTIVITY 4: WRITING

Congratulations! You have just won a certificate for Easy-Does-It Housecleaning Services. This entitles you to four hours of housecleaning service for your home. First make a list of what you want the housecleaner to do in your home (clean the windows, do the laundry, mop the floor, etc.). Then write these requests in a polite note to your housecleaner.

ACTIVITY 5: READING/SPEAKING

STEP 1 What would you say in each of the situations below? Respond to each situation. Then compare your results with other students' results.

1. You are in the bookstore with a friend, standing in line to buy a textbook you need for class later that day. You realize you have left your wallet at home and you want your friend to lend you twenty dollars to pay for the book.

   You: ——————————————————————

   ——————————————————————
   Your friend: Sure. You can pay me back next week.

2. You have just heard about a new teaching assistantship in your field, and you feel that you are qualified. You need to ask your teacher for a letter of recommendation.

   You: ——————————————————————

   ——————————————————————
   Your teacher: I'd be happy to. When do you need it?

3. You are visiting a close friend at her house. You realize you are thirsty, but your friend hasn't offered you anything to drink.

   You: ——————————————————————

   ——————————————————————
   Your friend: Sure. Help yourself. You know where everything is, right?

4. You just made plans to study for a big test with your classmates, but suddenly you realize that you have a doctor's appointment at the same time—at 2:00 tomorrow. You decide that you want to change your doctor's appointment, so you call the doctor's secretary.

You: _____

_____

The secretary: I *think* it's possible. When would you be available?

5. It's time to leave the house to meet your friend for a dinner date. But you can't find your car keys anywhere, and your friend has already left her house to meet you. You want to borrow your roommate's car and look for your car keys later.

You: _____

_____

Your roommate: Yeah, no problem.

6. You are visiting a close friend's mother. She has made peach pie, and you'd love to have a second piece. Your friend has told you that her mother loves to feed people, so you know that it wouldn't be rude to ask for another piece.

You: _____

_____

Your friend's mother: Oh, of course! Let me get it for you.

STEP 2 Ask at least three native speakers of English or people who have spent a long time in an English-speaking country to respond to each situation. Tape-record their answers.

ACTIVITY 6: LISTENING/ WRITING

Now listen to the text tape to hear what other speakers said in response to some of the questions in Activity 5.

STEP 1 Compare the responses of the speakers on the tape with your responses in Activity 5, and also to the responses of the speakers you interviewed. What is your reaction to the speakers' responses? For example, were you surprised at anything they said? Do you consider these polite responses? Do you think any of their requests would be refused?

STEP 2 For each situation, write down the **exact** requests that the speaker made (if there were any). Then rate each request in terms of politeness on a 1 to 5 scale (1 = most polite; 5 = least polite/most informal). Are there any requests that are "off the scale" (not at all polite, or even rude)? Compare your ratings to other classmates' ratings, and discuss your results.

UNIT 18

USED TO WITH STILL AND ANYMORE

UNIT GOALS:

- To use *used to* to compare past and present situations
- To correctly form statements and questions with *used to*
- To use *still* and *anymore* correctly
- To know the correct sentence positions for adverbs of frequency

▶ OPENING TASK
Famous People Then and Now

STEP 1   Work with several other students. Look at the photographs of these well-known people as they look today. If you are not sure who all these people are or why they are famous, try to find someone in the class who is.

Look below at the photographs of the same people. These photographs all came from their high school yearbooks. Match the old photographs with the current ones.

STEP 3   In your opinion, who has changed a lot? Who hasn't changed much?

▶ **EXAMPLE:**   I think Tina Turner has changed a lot.

Why?

Because she used to _____ but now

_____.

▶ Comparing Past and Present with *Used To*

EXAMPLES	EXPLANATIONS
(a) Tina Turner **used to** have short, wavy hair (but now she doesn't).	***Used to*** can be used to show that something was true in the past, but now it isn't.
(b) Madonna **used to** wear ordinary clothes (but now she doesn't).	***Used to*** can also show that something happened regularly (often) in the past, but now it doesn't.

EXERCISE 1

Make statements with *used to* about the changes in Madonna and Bruce Springsteen. Use the words in parentheses. You can add other ideas of your own, and you can get information from other students if you need to know more.

1. Madonna
    (a) (go out every night) *She used to go out every night.*
    (b) (be a dancer) _____
    (c) (be poor) _____.
    (d) (live in Michigan) _____.

2. Bruce Springsteen
    (a) (have straight hair) _____
    (b) (play football in high school) _____
    (c) (live in New Jersey) _____
    (d) (sing about blue-collar life) _____

Now add statements with *used to* about the other people in the Opening Task.

▶ **U**sed To

STATEMENT	NEGATIVE	QUESTION
I You We They } **used to** work	I You We They } did not **use to** work (didn't)	Did { I you we they } **use to** work?
She He It } **used to** work	She He It } did not **use to** work (didn't)	Did { she he it } **use to** work?

FOCUS **3**

▶ **A**nymore

EXAMPLES	EXPLANATIONS
(a) Madonna used to live in Michigan, but she doesn't live there **anymore.**	Use *anymore* to show a change in a situation or activity.
(b) Madonna used to live in Michigan, but she doesn't **anymore.**	If the second verb phrase has the same verb, you can omit it.
(c) Madonna doesn't live in Michigan **anymore.**	You can use *anymore* without *used to*. In (c) we understand that she used to live there.
(d) We **don't** go there anymore. **(e)** They **never** talk to me anymore. **(f)** **No one** likes him anymore.	Use *anymore* only with a negative.

EXERCISE 2

Interview your classmates about the changes in their lives. Then write short statements about these changes, using *anymore* and *used to*. (The word *but* may be helpful.)

▶ **EXAMPLE:** Teresita used to live in Guam, but she doesn't anymore. She used to be single, but now she lives with a partner.

▶ *Still*

EXAMPLES	EXPLANATIONS
(a) She **still** lives in New Mexico. (She lived in New Mexico fifteen years ago; she lives there now.)	Use *still* to show that something or someone has NOT changed.
(b) He **still** runs five miles a day. (He ran five miles a day in the past; he runs five miles a day now.)	Use *still* to show that an activity or habit has NOT changed.
(c) He **still** lives in New Orleans.	Use *still* before the main verb.
(d) He is **still** crazy after all these years.	Use *still* after the verb *be*.
(e) She can **still** play the piano.	Use *still* after an auxiliary verb such as *can, may, should*, etc.

EXERCISE 3

Write statements using *still* about the people in the Opening Task on page 262 who have not changed very much. The following items will get you started, but you can add ideas of your own. Work with your classmates if you need more information.

1. Meryl Streep

    (a) (long, blond hair) _____.

    (b) (very slim) _____.

2. Bruce Springsteen

    (a) (house in New Jersey) _____.

    (b) (called "The Boss") _____.

EXERCISE 4

Now choose one of the people in the Opening Task, another famous person, or a classmate that you interviewed in Exercise 2. Write a short paragraph showing how that person has or has not changed. Use *still, anymore,* or *used to* in your description.

Share your paragraphs with each other and check to see if *still, anymore,* and *used to* were used appropriately.

EXERCISE 5

Complete the following sentences with *still* or *anymore.*

1. A: Where's Jeff?

    B: He doesn't live here _____.

2. A: Is Gary home yet?

B: No, he is _____ working.

3. A: Have you finished writing your book?

B: No, I'm _____ working on it.

4. A: Do you want a cigarette?

B: No, thanks, I don't smoke _____.

5. A: Where do you live?

B: I _____ live at home with my parents.

6. A: Hurry up! We're going to be late!

B: I'm _____ wrapping the gift.

7. A: How's your grandfather?

B: He's doing pretty well, even though he can't go out much _____ .

EXERCISE 6

Look at the maps of the island of Madalia. Work with a partner and use the information from the maps to complete the report below. Use *used to, didn't use to, still,* and *anymore* as appropriate. Use the verbs in parentheses. The first one has been done for you as an example.

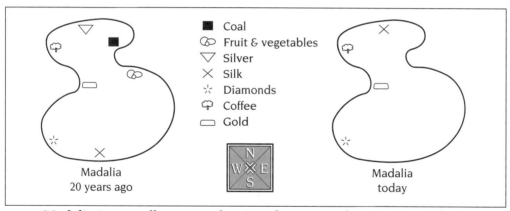

Madalia is a small country that is rich in natural resources, and Madalians have exploited those resources for many years. However, it is possible to note some changes in those resources in the last twenty years. For example, twenty years ago, Madalians (1) ___used to mine___ (mine) _coal_ _____ in the northeast. In addition, (2) they _____ (grow) _____ in the east. Also, they (3) _____ (mine) _____ , but today, they (4) _____ (not + mine) it _____ . Furthermore, in the past, they (5) _____ (not + produce) _____ in the north; they (6) _____ (produce) it in the _____ .

On the other hand, some things have not changed. They

(7) _____ (mine) _____ in the southwest, and

they (8) _____ (grow) _____ in the northwest.

Finally, they (9) _____ (mine) _____ in the west.

EXERCISE 7

The words below tell how often something happens. Arrange these words in a list with **most frequent** at the top and **least frequent** at the bottom. Add any other similar words you can think of and put them in the appropriate place on the list.

often	always	never	seldom
sometimes	hardly ever	usually	rarely

Check your answers with Unit 1, Focus 3.

FOCUS **5**

FORM

▶ Adverbs of Frequency

EXAMPLES	EXPLANATIONS
	Adverbs of frequency (**always,** etc.) can appear in different positions in a sentence:
(a) I **usually** get up at six.	• before the main verb.
(b) They were **rarely** happy.	• after the verb **be.**
(c) You will **sometimes** hear from them.	• after auxiliary verbs (**will, can, have,** etc.).
(d) I have **seldom** spoken to her.	
(e) They **never** used to dance.	• before **used to.**
(f) He **always** used to call her.	

EXERCISE 8

Write a short article for your old high school magazine, reporting on your life and habits and how they have changed (or not) over the years since you left high school. Also describe your present life and habits and compare these with your past.

Try to include the following:

• something you used to do but don't do anymore

• something you used to do and still do

• something you didn't use to do but do now

- something you never do
- something you seldom do
- something you sometimes do
- something you often do
- something you usually do

Don't forget to include changes (or not) in your physical appearance. We have begun the article for you:

I left high school in _____ (year). As I look back on my life since then, I realize that some things have changed, and some things have stayed the same. Let me start by telling you about some of the changes . . . .

Use Your English

ACTIVITY 1: WRITING

STEP 1 If possible, find an old photograph of yourself (as a baby, a child, or one taken several years ago). If you cannot find a photograph, draw a picture. Attach the photo or picture to a large piece of paper and write several statements about yourself, showing things you used to do and don't do now, things you didn't use to do, and things you still do. Do not write your name on the paper. Your teacher will display all the pictures and descriptions.

STEP 2 Work with a classmate and try to guess the identity of each person. Who in the class has changed the most and who has changed the least?

ACTIVITY 2: WRITING

Think of a place you know well—the place where you were born or where you grew up. Write about the ways it has changed and the ways it has not changed.

ACTIVITY 3: SPEAKING/LISTENING

Interview a senior citizen. Find out about changes in the world or in customs and habits during his or her lifetime. What does she or he think about these changes? Tape-record your interview, and then report on your findings to the class.

ACTIVITY 4: LISTENING

Listen to the tape-recorded interviews from Activity 3. Did the speakers use *used to, still,* or *anymore* when talking about changes? If not, what did they use instead?

ACTIVITY 5: LISTENING

Listen to the tape of two senior citizens talking about the changes during their lifetimes.

STEP 1   In your notebook, list each change that they discuss. Count the number of changes on your list and complete this statement:

The senior citizens talked about _____ (number) changes during their lifetimes.

Check with your classmates to see if they agree with your answers.

STEP 2   Listen closely to the **way** the senior citizens talked about changes. Choose five things on your list and answer these questions:

1. Did the speakers use *used to, still,* or *anymore* when talking about changes?

2. If not, what did they use instead?

Compare your findings with another student's.

ACTIVITY 6: SPEAKING/WRITING

The women's movement has helped change the lives of many women in different parts of the world. However, some people argue that things have not really changed and many things are still the same for most women. Think about women's lives and roles in your mother's generation and the lives of women today in your country. Make an oral or written report on what has changed and what has stayed the same.

ACTIVITY 7: SPEAKING

This activity gives you the opportunity to "become" a different person. Choose a new identity for yourself:

What is this person's name, age, sex, profession, habits, occupation, personality, and appearance? How does this new person differ from the "real" you?

Create a full description of this person and introduce the "new" you to the class, comparing him or her with the person you used to be. If you want to, make a mask or drawing to represent the "new" you.

▶ **EXAMPLE:** I want to introduce the new me. I used to be a college student, but now I am a secret agent. I never used to leave home, but now I often travel to distant and exotic places. I used to wear practical clothes that I always bought on sale. Now I usually wear black leather jumpsuits, dark glasses, and big hats, but sometimes I wear elegant evening dresses and expensive jewelry. . . .

ACTIVITY 8: SPEAKING/LISTENING/WRITING

Write a profile of one of your classmates.

STEP 1 Interview your partner and find out something that he or she

1. never does
2. seldom does
3. sometimes does
4. often does
5. usually does
6. always does

STEP 2 Write a report of your interview, **without using your classmate's name.** Begin with an introduction: for example, "I am going to tell you some things about one of our classmates." End your report with a question: "Can you guess who this is"?

STEP 3 Read your report out loud, or display it along with all the other reports written by your classmates. Can you identify the people described?

UNIT 19

PAST PERFECT

Before and After

UNIT GOALS:
- To correctly use past perfect and simple past in a single sentence
- To correctly form past perfect sentences
- To understand the meanings of *before, after, by the time*, and *by*
- To use past perfect and the present perfect in the right situations

▶ OPENING TASK
Family Changes

Family Tree A shows Tom's family when he left home in 1985 to travel around the world.

STEP 1 Work with a partner to study *Family Tree* A. (m) = married

Family Tree A

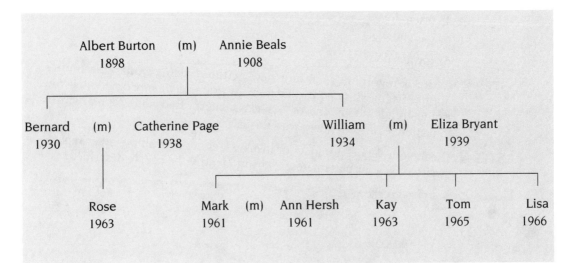

STEP 2   Now look at *Family Tree* B, which shows Tom's family after he returned home from his world travels in 1993.

Family Tree B

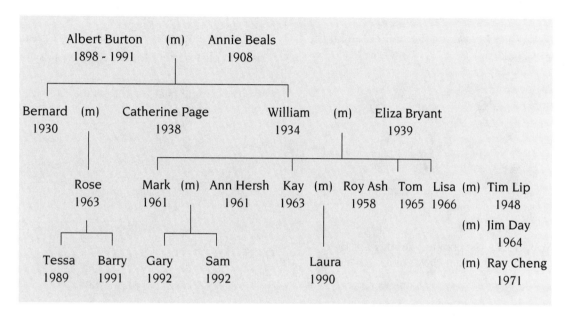

STEP 3   Make at least five statements about changes that had taken place when Tom returned from his travels. Start these statements with:

When Tom returned, ...
OR   *Tom returned after. . . .*
OR   *By the time Tom returned, ...*

▶ **P**ast Perfect and Simple Past

EXAMPLE	EXPLANATIONS
(a) When I got there, he **had eaten** all the cookies.  **First,** he ate the cookies; **then,** I got there. (I didn't see him eat the cookies.)	When two events both happened in the past: • use the past perfect for the first (earliest) event. • use the simple past for the second (most recent) event.

▶ **P**ast Perfect

To form the past pefect, use *had*+past participle (-*ed* for regular verbs; see Appendix 5, p. A-13 for forms of irregular verbs).

STATEMENT	NEGATIVE	QUESTION	SHORT ANSWER
I You We They } **had** arrived (**'d**)	I You We They } **had not** arrived (**hadn't**)	**Had** { I you we they } arrived?	Yes, we **had**.
She He It } **had** arrived (**'d**)	She He It } **had not** arrived (**hadn't**)	**Had** { he she it } arrived?	No, she **had not** (**hadn't**).

EXERCISE 1

Look at the family tree in the Opening Task on page 272 to complete the statements. If there is a verb in parentheses, use it; otherwise, use any appropriate verb. Example 1 has been done for you.

1. When he returned home, Tom found that his grandfather (die) <u>had died</u> .

2. When Tom returned, he learned that his cousin _____ .

3. Tom arrived home to find that his sister Lisa _____ .

4. When _____, his sister Kay _____ ; in addition, she and her husband _____.

5. On his return home, Tom found that his brother and sister-in-law _____ .

6. Tom learned that his grandmother had experienced both sorrow and joy. On the one hand, she (lose) _____ , but on the other hand, she (gain) _____ .

7. Sam and Gary have never met their grandfather, because he _____ when they _____ .

8. When Tom left home, he didn't have any _____ or nieces; when he got home, he had _____ and two _____.

9. By the time Tom got back home, his parents and his aunt and uncle (become) _____ .

10. Tom also found that Rose _____ children, but she (not) _____ . Lisa, on the other hand, _____ three times, but she (not) _____ any children.

EXERCISE 2

In the following pairs of statements, decide which event probably happened first. Write 1 beside the event you think happened first and 2 beside the one you think happened second. Then combine the statements to make one sentence using because. The first one has been done for you.

▶ **EXAMPLE:**   My legs ached.   2

   I played tennis.   1

   My legs ached because I had played tennis.

1. His car broke down.
   He took the bus.

   _____

2. Charlotte was depressed.
   She failed her English exam.

   _____

3. Tanya sat in the sun all afternoon.
   Her skin was very red.

   _____

4. We didn't eat all day.
   We were really hungry.

   _____

5. Brenda's clothes were too tight.
   She didn't exercise for several months.

   _____

6. Neville couldn't sleep.
   He drank several cups of very strong coffee.

   _____

7. We studied hard for three weeks.
   We thought the test was easy.

   _____

▶ **B**efore, After **B**y *the* **T**ime, **B**y

EXAMPLES		EXPLANATIONS
First Event	Second Event	
(a) She had left	**before** I arrived.	*Before, after,* and *by the time* show the order of events.
(b) She had left	**by the time** I arrived.	You can use the past perfect with *before* and *after,* but it is not necessary. You must use the past perfect in sentences with *by the time.*
(c) **After** she had left,	I arrived.	
(d) She left	**before** I arrived.	
(e) **After** she left,	I arrived.	*By* + a noun phrase can also show order of events.
(f) He had finished all his shopping	**by** Christmas.	

EXERCISE 3

Look at the following sentences; each one uses the past perfect. Check (✔) the sentences where it is necessary to use the past perfect to show the order of events.

1. My sister graduated from college after she had gotten married.
2. I didn't see Brad last night because he had left by the time I got there.
3. After I had finished my work, I took a long, hot bath.
4. Kozue had checked the gas before she started to drive to Houston.
5. By the time the party was over, they had drunk nine bottles of soda.
6. The teacher sent the student home before the class had ended.
7. The store had closed before I got there.
8. We didn't see the movie because it had started before we got to the theater.
9. Cathy never knew her grandparents because they had died before she was born.
10. By noon, when Shirley got to the library, she found that someone had borrowed the book she needed.

EXERCISE 4

Rewrite the following sentences. Omit the underlined words and use the word in parentheses. Use the past perfect where necessary.

▶ **EXAMPLE:** First Sue listened to the weather report <u>and then</u> she decided to go for a bike ride. (after)

After Sue listened to the weather report, she decided to go for a bike ride.

OR

After Sue had listened to the weather report, she decided to go for a bike ride.

1. Sue studied several maps, <u>and then</u> she decided on an interesting route for her bike ride. (before)
2. She changed her clothes, <u>and then</u> she checked the tires on her bike. (after)
3. She put fresh water in her water bottle, <u>and next</u> she left home. (before)
4. She rode for several miles, <u>then</u> she came to a very steep hill. (after)
5. She rode to the top of the hill, <u>and then</u> she stopped to drink some water and enjoy the view. (before)
6. She rode for ten more miles, <u>and then</u> she got a flat tire. (after)
7. She fixed the flat tire quickly, <u>and then</u> she continued her ride. (before)
8. It started to rain, <u>and then</u> she decided to go home. (after)
9. She rode 30 miles <u>before</u> she stopped. (by the time)
10. She took a long, hot shower, <u>and finally</u> she ate a huge plate of pasta. (after)

Were there any sentences where you **had to** use the past perfect?

FOCUS **4**

▶ **Past Perfect versus Present Perfect**

EXAMPLES	EXPLANATIONS
(a) She **was** tired yesterday because she **had taken** a long bike ride.	Use the past perfect to **contrast** two events in the past.
(b) She **is** tired (now) because she **has taken** a long bike ride.	Use the present perfect to **connect** the past with the present.

EXERCISE 5

Underline the mistakes in the following sentences and correct as necessary.

▶ **EXAMPLE:** I wasn't tired yesterday because I ~~have~~ ^{had} slept for ten hours the night
before.

1. Nigel wasn't hungry last night because he has eaten a large sandwich for
lunch.

2. Jan is really confused in class last Tuesday because she hadn't read the assignment.

3. Graham had gone home because he has a terrible headache today.

4. Howard is a lucky man because he had traveled all over the world.

5. Martha went to the hospital after she has broken a leg.

6. Before he has left the house, George locked all the doors and windows.

7. Professor Westerfield always returns our papers after she had graded
them.

8. I didn't see you at the airport last night because your plane has left before
I got there.

9. Matthew and James were late because they have missed the bus.

EXERCISE 6

In the story below, use the appropriate verb tense (simple past, past progressive,
past perfect, present perfect) for the verbs in parentheses.

Some people attend all their high school reunions, but Al (1)
_hasn't gone_____ (go + not) back to his high school since he

(2) _____ (graduate) ten years ago. Five years ago, he

(3) _____ (make) arrangements to go to his five-year high

school reunion, but two days before that reunion he

(4) _____ (break) his leg. He (5) _____ (paint) his

house on a tall ladder when he (6) _____ (lose) his balance. So

he (7) _____ (not + go) to his five-year reunion.

Al (8) _____ (not + visit) his hometown for ten years and

his new wife, Marta, (9) _____ (never + be) there. Al and Marta

(10) _____ (get) married about a year and a half ago and they

(11) _____ (not + be) married long when some of Al's high

school friends (12) _____ (come) to visit them last year. So at

least Marta (13) _____ (meet) a few of Al's old friends, even

though she (14) _____ (not + be) to his hometown.

Use Your English

ACTIVITY 1: SPEAKING/LISTENING WRITING

The purpose of this activity is to compare different events and achievements at different times in our lives. You will need to get information from five of your classmates to complete this activity.

STEP 1 The left-hand column in the chart below shows different ages; your job is to find one interesting or surprising thing each classmate had done by the time he or she reached those ages. If you don't want to talk about your life, feel free to invent things that you had done at those ages. Be ready to report on your findings.

	Name	Name	Name	Name	Name
By the time, she or he was five years old . . .					
By the time she or he was ten years old . . .					
By the time she or he was fifteen years old . . .					
By the time she or he was eighteen years old . . .					
By the time . . .*					
By the time . . .*					

*You choose an age.

STEP 2 Now choose **the three most surprising** pieces of information you found for **each age**.

STEP 3 Present this information as an oral or written report. Be sure to announce your purpose in an introductory sentence and to end with a concluding comment.

For example: *The age of fifteen is very interesting. By the time Roberto, Ali, and Tina were fifteen, they had done quite different things. Roberto had worked in his father's office, Ali had visited ten different countries, and Tina had won several prizes for swimming.*

ACTIVITY 2: SPEAKING

STEP 1 Use the information from Activity 1 for a poster presentation. Take a large poster-sized sheet of paper and use this to make a poster that communicates the information you found. You can use graphics, pictures, and diagrams to make your poster interesting and eye-catching.

STEP 2 Display your poster so that your classmates can enjoy it and be ready to answer any questions they might have about it.

ACTIVITY 3: SPEAKING /LISTENING

STEP 1 Find out about someone's family history, preferably someone sixty or older. You can help that person construct a family tree (as in the Opening Task), or you can use a chart like the one below to get information. Tape-record your information-gathering session.

STEP 2 Report your findings to the class, either in a written or an oral report. (Tape-record the report if it's done orally.) Be sure to use the past perfect and *before, after, by,* or *by the time* to contrast past events.

	Births, deaths, marriages, divorces
1980–present	
1960–1980	
1940–1960	
1920–1940	

ACTIVITY 4: LISTENING

Listen to the tapes of your oral reports from Activity 3 or from the actual information-gathering sessions. Was the past perfect used? Were the time words *before*, *after*, *by*, or *by the time* used? Were there occasions where the past perfect or time words could have been used, but weren't?

ACTIVITY 5: LISTENING

STEP 1 Listen to the tape of a senior citizen talking about her family history. Each time the speaker talks about an important family event—births, deaths, marriages, divorces—record the date (or the approximate date) on the chart below and write down who the event happened to. The first one is done for you.

Births	Deaths	Marriages	Divorces	Relationship to Speaker
	1940			mother

STEP 2 Work with a classmate to list the speaker's important family events in chronological order.

STEP 3 Listen to the tape for each usage of the past perfect. Write down the sentence. Were the time words *before*, *after*, *by* or *by the time* used?

Then complete these sentences.

1. The speaker used the past perfect _____ times.

2. The interviewer used the past perfect _____ times.

3. The time words *before*, *after*, *by* or *by the time* were used

   _____ times altogether (by both speakers).

Do your classmates agree with your answers?

ACTIVITY 6: WRITING/LISTENING

STEP 1 Work in teams. With your team, choose three famous people who are now dead. Make sure that you choose famous people everyone has heard of. For each person, write three statements about what she or he had done before they died.

STEP 2 Team A presents the first statement. The other teams have to try to guess the identity of the person from the statements. Each team can ask two yes/no questions after each statement. (The "trick" is to make your statements difficult, but not impossible!)

▶ **EXAMPLE:** Before he died, he had been a popular president.

People in America had admired him and his wife very much.

He had been born in Massachusetts and was killed in Texas.

(President Kennedy)

ACTIVITY 7: RESEARCH

The purpose of this activity is to compare and contrast important historical events in different countries. You might need to do a bit of research before you do this activity: Look in an encyclopedia or a history textbook to get information about your country or another country you know about.

STEP 1 Copy the chart below into your notebook. Use it to record three events that you think were important in the history of the country you have researched. (The **exact** date is not important, but just mark on the chart approximately when the event happened.)

1300s	1400s	1500s	1600s	1700s	1800s	1900s

STEP 2 Now go around the class comparing your chart with your classmates' charts. Add to your chart significant dates from at least three other students. Try to get information about other countries, if this is possible.

STEP 3 Use the information on your chart to compare and contrast important events in different countries. Present your findings as a written report; don't forget to include an introduction and a conclusion.

STEP 4 Exchange reports with a classmate. Check to see if she/he has chosen the most appropriate tense.

ARTICLES

The, A/An, Some, and Ø

UNIT GOALS:

- To understand the meaning of the articles *the, a, an,* and *some*
- To use articles correctly for first and second mentions of an item
- To know which articles to use with singular, plural, and noncount nouns
- To understand when to use no article

▶ **OPENING TASK**

Looking for the Perfect House

STEP 1 Put the following sentences in order so that they make a story. When you have finished, check to see if other students have the story in the same order.

a. _____ Esinam found a real-estate agent to help them.

b. _____ They finally decided to buy the little house and remodel the kitchen.

c. _____ The second place they saw was a pretty brick house by a lake, but the house was too expensive.

d. _____ Finally they saw a little one-bedroom house surrounded by trees at the end of a dead-end street.

e. _____ When I last talked to them, they had finished remodeling the kitchen, and they liked the house a lot.

f. _____ Esinam and Sunita decided to buy a house.

g. _____ The real-estate agent then showed them a house near some apartment buildings, but the house was too big, and the apartment buildings were too ugly.

h. _____ First they looked at a nice house in the suburbs, but there were no trees, and the house was too far away from work.

i. _____ They told the real-estate agent that they wanted to live in a quiet neighborhood. They also said that they preferred small houses.

STEP 2 Number the pictures below so that they match the order of the story.

▶ **Definite and Indefinite Articles:**
The, A/An, and *Some*

EXAMPLES	EXPLANATIONS
(a) Father to son: Where did you park **the** car? 	Use *the* to talk about a specific noun. In (a), the father and son are thinking about the same car—a car that they both can identify.
(b) Which car are they talking about? **The** family car.	With *the,* you can answer the question *Which . . . ?*
(c) Al needs **a** new notebook.	Use *a* or *an* to talk about one of a group of similar things, not about a specific thing. In (c), Al is thinking about notebooks in general. He's not thinking about a specific notebook that he can identify.
(d) What does Al need? **A** new notebook.	With *a/an,* you can answer the question *What . . . ?*
(e) Al needs **a** new computer, new software, and new instructional manuals.	Use *a* or *an* with singular count nouns; use Ø (no article) with noncount nouns or plural count nouns.
(f) Al needs **some** new software and **some** new instruction manuals.	Use *some* to talk about a nonspecific quantity (amount) with plural nouns or noncount nouns.

EXERCISE 1

Fill in the blanks in the story below with *the, a, an,* Ø (no article), or *some.*

1. Sarah wanted to buy _____ doll for her nephew Marty, who was going to turn nine at the end of the month.

2. Marty enjoyed playing with _____ dolls.

3. He had never been very interested in trucks, but he had been playing with _____ dolls since he was two years old.

4. Sarah went to three stores and saw _____ interesting dolls.

5. In the toy store, she finally chose _____ doll.

6. _____ doll that she bought was unusual, Sarah thought.

7. It was wearing _____ baseball player's uniform.

8. _____ uniform had "New York Yankees" written on it.

9. When Sarah gave Marty _____ doll, he was polite but not very impressed.

10. He already had _____ old doll that was similar to Sarah's birthday doll.

11. Sarah realized that she didn't know very much about _____ dolls.

12. She also realized that buying _____ presents for Marty was not an easy task!

FOCUS **2**

▶ **Using Articles: First and Second Mention**

EXAMPLES	EXPLANATIONS
(a) I read **a** great book yesterday. **(b)** Martha just bought **a** new backpack. **(c)** I found **an** old dress of my mother's in the attic.	*A/an* is generally used to talk about a noun for the first time (first mention). Since the noun is introduced for the first time, it is not yet identified as a specific thing.
(d) I found an old dress of my mother's in the attic in the trunk. **The** dress was beautiful, with pearl buttons and lace sleeves.	Use *the* when the noun has been introduced and is now identified (sometimes called "second mention").

EXERCISE 2

Now look back at Exercise 1 and tell why you used each article (*a/an, some, the* or Ø). Did you complete the exercise correctly? If not, go back and rewrite the sentences you missed.

EXERCISE 3

Read the following. For each underlined noun phrase, is the article usage correct? If the article usage is not correct, write the correct usage above the underlined words. These questions will help you:

- Is the writer talking about a noun for the first time?
- Is the writer talking about a specific noun?
- Is the writer talking about one of a group of similar things—**not** an identified/specific noun?

Since 1988, a herd of deer has come to Pedro's apple orchard each October
(1)
just after apple harvest. An orchard is bordered by a forest, and Pedro and his
(2)
family are able to watch the herd come out of a forest and walk directly to
(3)   (4)
the nearest apple trees. Within minutes after the deer enter the orchard,
(5)
the remaining apples are gone, and the deer return to the forest with their
(6)   (7)
cheeks still bulging. Watching the deer has become an annual event for Pedro
(8)
and his family. If Pedro could predict the annual apple-eating feast, he would
(9)
invite his friends and have the deer-watching party.
(10)

FORM

▶ Indefinite Articles with Singular, Plural, and Noncount Nouns

EXAMPLES	EXPLANATIONS
(a) I'd like to buy **a** piano and **an** organ. **(b)** **a** youngster **(c)** **a** university	Use *a* and *an* with singular count nouns. Use *a* before consonant sounds and *an* before vowel sounds. It is the **sound,** not the letter, which tells you whether to use *a* or *an*.
(d) **an** energetic woman **(e)** **an** unusual doll	If there is an adjective before the noun, then the first sound of the **adjective** tells you whether to use *a* or *an*, not the first sound of the noun.
(f) I'd like to buy **some** new CDs and tapes, and then I'd like to listen to **music** all day.	Use *some* or Ø (no article) with plural count nouns and noncount nouns.

EXERCISE 4

Fill in the blanks with *a, an,* or Ø (no article).

1. If I won the lottery, first I would buy _____ piece of land in the country.

2. Then I would build _____ unusual house and _____ huge barn.

3. Of course I would build _____ long fence, too.

4. Then I would buy _____ horses, _____ cows, and maybe _____ llama.

5. I would make sure to buy _____ hay for the winter, so that the animals would have plenty to eat.

6. I would probably hire _____ people to take care of the horses.

7. People say that you can't buy _____ happiness, but I think my ranch would certainly make me happy!

Some Instead of Ø (No Article)

EXAMPLES	EXPLANATIONS
(a) Al needs **some** new clothes. **(b)** I'd like to get **some** tickets to the concert on Friday.	Use *some* with plural count nouns and noncount nouns when you want to talk about quantity (amount).
(c) I'd like to listen to **some** jazz. (I'd like to listen to s'm jazz.) **(d)** Can we get **some** cookies at the bakery? (Can we get s'm cookies at the bakery?)	When *some* is used instead of Ø (no article) in conversation, it is not stressed.
(e) I'd like to listen to (some) jazz. **(f)** Al needs (some) new clothes.	Usually *some* is optional (you **can** use it, but it's not necessary).
(g) Cookies are called biscuits in England. **(h)** Spiders have eight legs.	Do not use *some* when you are talking about **all** members of a group of similar things.

EXERCISE 5

Look at your answers in Exercise 1. Mark with a check (✔) all the answers where Ø (no article) was used with either a plural count noun or a noncount noun. Could you use *some* instead? Explain your answers.

▶ *The* **with Singular, Plural, and Noncount Nouns**

EXAMPLES	EXPLANATIONS
(a) *Son to Father:* Where did you put **the** keys? 	Use *the* with all nouns that can be specifically identified: • plural count nouns: In (a) both speakers can identify which specific keys are being talked about.
(b) *Son to Friend:* Turn on **the** light, please.	• singular count nouns: In (b) they can both identify which specific light is being talked about.
(c) *Housemate to Housemate:* I can't find **the** sugar. Where did you put it?	• noncount (mass) nouns: In (c) they can both identify which sugar is being talked about.

EXERCISE 6
Fill in the blanks in the story below with *a/an, some,* or *the*.

1. Last fall Anita worked in _____ apple orchard, picking apples.

2. _____ work was not easy.

3. She had sore muscles _____ first week of work, and every night she slept very soundly.

4. _____ first orchard she worked in was considered small, with only fifty trees.

5. It was owned by _____ old, retired couple, who worked in the orchard as _____ hobby.

6. _____ next orchard Anita worked in was much larger, about twenty acres.

7. In this orchard, _____ trees had yellow apples, which were called "Golden Delicious."

8. Every day Anita ate _____ apples for breakfast and for lunch.

9. Even though _____ weather was beautiful, and _____ hard work made her feel very healthy, Anita was relieved when _____ apple-picking season was over.

Now work with a classmate and explain your choices.

FOCUS **6**

▶ Making General Statements with Ø (No Article)

EXAMPLES	EXPLANATIONS
(a) *Al:* I need **new clothes.**	Use Ø (no article) to make general statements.
	In (a), Al needs new clothes **in general.** He's not thinking about specific clothes that he and his listener can identify.
	Use Ø (no article) to talk about plural count nouns that are not specific.
(b) I'd like to get **flowers** for my birthday.	In (b), you can't identify **which** flowers; you and the listener are not thinking about specific flower.
(c) He is hoping to find **love.** **(d)** I like **jazz.**	Use Ø (no article) when you make a general statement using noncount (mass) nouns.
(e) Pencils are made with **lead.** **(f)** **Rice** is eaten in Asia.	Use Ø (no article) when you make a general statement about a whole group or category.
(g) **Medical care** is very expensive in the United States. **(h)** Most people like **vacations.** **(i)** The university offers excellent classes in **art** and **music.**	Statements that use Ø (no article) can usually be paraphrased with *in general.* In (g): *In general,* medical care in the United States is expensive. (There may be some exceptions.)

EXERCISE 7

Circle the errors in article usage in the sentences below. Specifically, should you use *the* or Ø (no article)?

1. The love is a very important thing in our lives.

2. Without the love, we would be lonely and confused.

3. I believe that the money is not as important as love, although some people don't feel this way.

4. If the money is too important, then we become greedy.

5. When we get old, the health becomes as important as love.

6. My grandmother says, "Just wait and see. Work you do and the money you earn are important now, but when you're old . . .

7. . . . love that you feel for your family and friends, health of your loved ones—these are the things that will be most important."

FOCUS **7**

MEANING

▶ *The* with Unique/Easily Identified Nouns

EXAMPLES	EXPLANATIONS
(a) In June, **the sun** doesn't set until 9:30.	The definite article *the* is used with nouns that are easily identified. Use *the* with nouns that are **universally** known (everyone in the world can identify it). In (a), everyone knows **which** sun they're talking about, since there's only one.
(b) Mary went to **the coast** on her vacation.	*The* is also used when the noun is **regionally** known (everyone in the region can identify it). In (b), everyone knows **which** coast they're talking about, since there's only one in the region.
(c) Did you feed **the cats**?	We can also use *the* when the noun is **locally** known (everyone in the immediate location can identify it). In (c), everyone in the immediate location knows **which** cats they're talking about, since they live together in the same house.

EXERCISE 8

For sentences 1–10 below, answer these three questions:

   (a)   Where would you hear this sentence spoken?

   (b)   Who do you think the speaker is?

   (c)   What do you think happened or what was the conversation about **before** or **after** the sentence was spoken?

   1. Please turn on *the* TV.

   2. Could you change *the* channel?

   3. We need some more chalk. Would you mind checking *the* blackboard in *the* back?

   4. *The* rosebushes are lovely.

   5. Could you pass *the* salt, please?

   6. Excuse me, where's *the* women's restroom?

   7. *The* sky is so blue today. I don't think you'll need *the* umbrella.

   8. Have you seen *the* dog?

   9. It's so romantic. See how bright *the* moon is?

   10. Let's go to *the* mountains for our vacation instead of to *the* beach.

Use your answers to the three questions above to discuss in class why *the* was used in each sentence.

EXERCISE 9

Tell why *the* is used in each of the sentences below. (Some of these you will recognize from Exercise 8.) In the space at the left, write down **where** you think this statement was made. Then, on the right:

   • If it is **universally** known, circle **U**.

   • If it is **regionally** known, circle **R**.

   • If it is **locally** known (because of the immediate location), circle **L**.

Setting

_____	1. Please turn on <u>the</u> TV.	U R L
_____	2. Could you change <u>the</u> channel?	U R L
_____	3. We need some more chalk. Would you mind checking <u>the</u> blackboard in <u>the</u> back?	U R L
_____	4. <u>The</u> rosebushes are lovely	U R L
_____	5. Could you pass <u>the</u> salt, please?	U R L
_____	6. Excuse me, please. Where's <u>the</u> women's restroom?	U R L
_____	7. <u>The</u> sky is so blue today. I don't think you'll need <u>the</u> umbrella.	U R L

	8. Have you seen <u>the</u> dog?	U R L
_____	9. It's so romantic. See how bright <u>the</u> moon is?	U R L
_____	10. Let's go to <u>the</u> mountains for our vacation, instead of to <u>the</u> beach.	U R L U R L
_____	11. *Son:* Hey Dad, can I borrow <u>the</u> car? *Dad:* Sure, if you can find <u>the</u> keys!	U R L U R L
_____	12. I like your dress. Did you buy it at <u>the</u> mall?	U R L

FOCUS **8**

▶ # **U**sing *The*: Second Mention, Related Mention, and Certain Adjectives

EXAMPLES	EXPLANATIONS
(a) She used to have a cat and a dog, but **the** cat died.	Sometimes we use *the* with a noun because the noun has been talked about before (second mention).
(b) Last year I bought a guitar and a banjo. I decided to sell **the** banjo since I rarely play it.	We can identify the cat in (a) and the banjo in (b) because they have been talked about before.
(c) He bought a suit but **the** jacket had a button missing, so he had to return it. **(d)** I had a lock but I lost **the** key for it.	In other situations we can identify a noun because it is *related* to something that has been talked about before (related mention). In (c), we know which jacket they're talking about, since *jacket* is part of *suit*.
(e) She had started to read a book when she noticed that **the** first chapter was missing. **(f)** She's **the** first person I met here and **the** only friend I have. **(g)** That's **the** hardest test I've ever taken. **(h)** You made **the** right choice.	Adjectives or phrases like *last, next, first, only,* and *right,* and superlatives like *best, hardest,* and *happiest* usually use the definite article *the* because they describe something that is "one of a kind." There's only one "first chapter" (in e), only one "first person" (in f), and only one "hardest test" (in g).
(i) It's **the** same old story. **(j)** We are taking **the** same class.	The definite article is always used with the adjective *same.*

EXERCISE 10

Decide why *the* is used each time it is underlined. If it is used because it has been talked about before, circle **S** (for **second mention**). If it is used because a **related** noun has been talked about before, circle **R** (for **related mention**).

1. Jerry was late for his appointment, so he went into a telephone booth near the bus stop to make a phone call. It looked like someone was living in the telephone booth.   S   R

2. There was a small blanket covering the window of the telephone booth like a curtain.   S   R

3. The floor of the telephone booth was swept clean with a broom.   S   R

4. The broom was hung on a hook in the corner of the telephone booth.   S   R

5. By the telephone, there was a pen and a notepad with a short list of names and telephone numbers.   S   R

6. Jerry also noticed that there was a coffee mug and a toothbrush sitting neatly by the telephone directory.   S   R

7. The coffee mug looked like it had recently been rinsed. There were still drops of water in it.   S   R

8. Jerry had such a strong feeling that he was in someone's living space that he decided to find another place to make the phone call.   S   R

EXERCISE 11

Look at the story in the Opening Task on pages 284–285, making sure that it is in the right order. How many times is *the* used? Underline each *the* and explain why it was used.

<u>Reason the is used</u>

▶ **EXAMPLE:** i. *the* real-estate agent   second mention

EXERCISE 12

Underline each use of *the* in the following story. Then tell why it is used. The possible reasons for the use of *the* with a noun are:

(a) It's universally known.

(b) It's regionally known.

(c) It's locally known—the immediate location makes it clear.

(d) Second mention.

(e) Related mention.

(f) The adjective or phrase makes it "one of a kind."

1   Nobody in eastern Washington, where I live, will forget the summer of
2 1994. My son Robin was only five weeks old when the fire came. Dan, my
3 husband, was a firefighter, and he had been away the whole week working
4 on what the reporters were calling "The Great Fires of 1994."

5   Dan could only come home three times that week, late at night. First he
6 got in the shower and washed off the soot and smoke, and then he looked
7 with wonder at little Robin while telling me the latest fire adventure. Then
8 we watched the fire coverage on the news, but before it was over, Dan was
9 sound asleep. Each morning the alarm went off at 4:00, and Dan was up
10 and out of the door just as the sky was getting light.

11   The fire started burning closer and we were finally forced to evacuate
12 our own home. The smoke was so heavy that we couldn't even see the
13 mountain right across the highway. And the fire seemed to have a mind of
14 its own.

EXERCISE 13

In the following newspaper article, circle each *the* and *a*. Then explain why those articles are used.

Vocabulary:

swath—a wide path

backburn/backfire—a fire started on purpose in order to control the direction that the fire takes next

scorched—burned black

evacuated—forced to leave

take for granted—to treat as fact; to accept without noticing or appreciating

---

Firefighting Takes a Personal Turn

By Rick Steigmeyer, World staff writer

PESHASTIN, WA- Dan Dittrich wanted to help save the forest and homes on familiar ground. He didn't realize that his toughest rescue mission would be his own home.

A contract logger by trade, Dittrich found a job working on the Tyee Creek Fire near Entiat after its start on July 24. When the Hatchery Creek Fire started getting out of hand, he came down to Leavenworth to help his friends defend their homes. Dittrich built his own house a few years ago on a densely wooded hillside on Mountain Home, above the Blewett Pass Highway.

Later, he went down to the Hatchery Fire base camp at the U.S. Fish Hatchery in Leavenworth to sign up for duty on the main fire.

"While I was at the camp signing in, the Rat Creek Fire took off," said Dittrich at the base camp Monday. Dittrich, smudged, unshaven, and weary after a 16-hour shift, said, "I told them, 'Sorry, I've gotta go protect my own house.'"

Dittrich and friends worked 27 straight hours clearing brush and trees and digging a fireline around his secluded house. The Rat Creek Fire, meanwhile, raged through Icicle Canyon across Wedge Mountain and onto the Leavenworth side of Mountain Home, devouring 14 homes and threatening countless others in the process.

Friends heard about Dittrich's problem and rushed to help him. Fellow firefighter Lance Wyman and later Mike King and Chris Fusare helped cut a swath around the structures. Joseph Roy and Phil and Joan Unterschuetz helped to water everything down and to disconnect the electricity.

"Just as we were finishing, the fire came rushing down over the hill," said Dittrich. "I went running down the hill, lighting fuses for a backfire as I ran. A helicopter above us was yelling out on a loudspeaker 'Negative on that backburn. Negative!' I just kept lighting and running.

Dittrich and friends made it safely to the bottom of the orchard-bordered property and watched the fire as it raced across the hill. The surrounding woods were scorched, but the house was left unharmed.

Dittrich's family had been evacuated soon after the fire started, but he went back to the house to get some sleep on Monday night.

He feels he's earned the right to sleep in his own bed. It's something he's not likely to ever again take for granted.

Use Your English

ACTIVITY 1: SPEAKING

TIC-TAC-TOE/Arranging Objects

Choose a small common object that can be moved around. It can be something that you are wearing (a ring, a watch) or carrying with you (a pencil, a book). It is all right if some people choose the same object. All of you will give your objects to one student. This student will draw a big tic-tac-toe chart on the blackboard.

   Form two teams. Each team will tell the student who has the objects to arrange them according to their directions, one sentence at a time. (For example, "Put a book under the ring. Put the red pencil next to the book.") If the article usage in the sentence is correct (and the person is able to follow the directions), then the team gets to put an X or O in any of the tic-tac-toe squares. If it is not correct, then the team must pass. The first team to get three X's or three O's in a row or diagonally wins the game.

ACTIVITY 2: SPEAKING/LISTENING

Find a photograph or drawing to bring to class. First describe the picture, and then work together to tell the class a story about it. This will be a "chain story." The first person says one thing about the picture, the second person repeats that and adds another sentence, etc., until each student has contributed at least one sentence to the story. Concentrate on using articles correctly.

ACTIVITY 3: WRITING

Now without the help of your classmates, write a short description of the picture that you described in Activity 2. It doesn't have to be exactly the same as the story you made, but again try to use the articles correctly.

ACTIVITY 4: SPEAKING/LISTENING/WRITING

Here are some things that people say contribute to their happiness: love, romance, success, wealth/money, fame, popularity, health, religion. Interview three people about what they think is most important for their happiness. (Tape-record people's answers, if possible.) Be sure to get information about the people you are interviewing, such as age group, gender and occupation.

In an oral or written summary, give the results of your interviews and see if there is agreement in people's answers.

ACTIVITY 5: READING

Find at least four headlines in a newspaper. Copy them down or cut them out and bring them to class. Put in articles (*the*, Ø article, *a/an*, or *some*) wherever you think they are appropriate in order to make the headlines into more complete statements. (Note: You might need to add main verbs or auxiliaries too, such as a form of *be* or *do*.)

With the headlines you have chosen, is it possible to use more than one of these articles? If so, does the meaning of the statement change?

▶ **EXAMPLE:**   BLIZZARD OF '96 PARALYZES EAST COAST

Adding articles: *The* blizzard of 1996 paralyzes *the* East Coast.

Explanation: *The* is used with *blizzard* because it is a specific blizzard (January 1996) that most North Americans have heard about.

The is used with East Coast because this is from a United States newspaper, so we know *which* East Coast is being talked about.

ACTIVITY 6: LISTENING

Listen to the tape of two people describing favorite children's toys.

STEP 1 Discuss these questions with a partner.

   1. What was the woman's favorite toy when she was young?

   2. What was the man's favorite toy when he was young?

STEP 2 Listen to the tape for each mention of (a) the specific toys that the speakers describe, or (b) toys in general. Write down these phrases in the order that you hear them.

Speaker 1/Woman	Speaker 2/Man

STEP 3 Compare your list with a classmate's list. Discuss the reasons for the speakers' choice of articles.

ACTIVITY 7: SPEAKING/LISTENING

Lots of people like to have nice possessions. What would you like? Describe your "wish list" to someone, and put your choices in order. (Some examples are: land, expensive jewelry, a vacation home, a swimming pool, a sports car, etc.) Tape-record your description.

   Listen carefully to your tape. Did you use articles correctly?

ACTIVITY 8: SPEAKING/LISTENING

Ask a native speaker of English and/or a classmate to describe their house, apartment, or other living space (for example, a dormitory) to someone who has never seen it. Tape-record their descriptions. How many rooms are there? Where are they located? How many doors and windows are there in each room? What kind of furniture is there? Are there curtains, or pictures on the wall?

   After you share these descriptions with the rest of the class, listen carefully to the tape for article usage.

UNIT 21

ARTICLES WITH NAMES OF PLACES

UNIT GOALS:

- To know how to use articles with names of places
- To know how to use articles with names of institutions

▶ **OPENING TASK**
Geography Quiz

STEP 1 Move around the classroom to collect information to complete the chart below. Write down all the different answers you get in each category.

WHAT IS. . . ?	
the largest continent in the world	
the longest river	
the largest country (in size, not population)	
the biggest island	
the highest mountain range	
the highest mountain	
the biggest desert	
the largest ocean	
the largest lake	
the largest planet	

STEP 2 When you have spoken to five other students, decide on the correct answers. Use a recent edition of an almanac to check your answers.

STEP 3 Take turns making complete statements based on the information in your chart. For example: *The Amazon is* _____.

▶ Articles with Names of Places

EXAMPLES	EXPLANATIONS
	Use Ø (no article) with names of:
South America	• continents
Zimbabwe	• countries
New York	• cities
First Avenue	• streets and highways
Interstate 90	
Mars	• planets
Jamaica	• islands
Mount Shasta	• single mountains
Lake Champlain	• lakes
Yosemite National Park	• parks
	Use *the* with names of:
the Yellow River	• rivers
the Gobi Desert	• deserts
the Arctic Ocean	• oceans
the Caspian Sea	• seas
the Andes	• mountain ranges
the Hawaiian Islands	• groups of islands
the Great Lakes	• groups of lakes
the Middle East	• most regions
the Bay of Bengal	• when *of* is in the name
	Note: These are regular patterns for using articles with place names. You will sometimes find exceptions. For example:
the United States	• countries that are collections take *the*
the United Kingdom	
the Earth or Earth	• certain places sometimes take *the* and sometimes do not
the Sudan or Sudan	

EXERCISE 1

Look at the categories below. For each category (1–10), put the correct answers from the Opening Task in either Column A or B. For example, the largest continent is Asia, which does not use *the*, so this would go in Column B for #1.

Category	(A) Use *the*	(B) Don't Use *the*
1. the largest continent in the world		Asia
2. the longest river		
3. the largest country (in size, not population)		
4. the biggest island		
5. the highest mountain range		
6. the highest mountain		
7. the biggest desert		
8. the largest ocean		
9. the largest lake		
10. the largest planet		

EXERCISE 2

Look at these conversations. Underline all the names of places, names of institutions (such as *the University of Washington*), and names of famous buildings or tourist attractions.

Dialogue 1
A: My brother is a freshman at the University of Washington.
B: Really? I thought he was at Louisiana State.
A: He was. He didn't like the climate in the South, so he decided to move to the Pacific Northwest.

Dialogue 2
A: How long did you stay in Washington, D.C.?
B: Not very long. We had just enough time to see the White House, the Capitol, and the Washington Monument.
A: Did you get to any museum or art galleries?
B: We wanted to go to the Smithsonian and the National Gallery, but we didn't have time.
A: Too bad!

In these examples, when is *the* used and when is it **not** used? List all the examples from the conversations if that is helpful.

EXERCISE 3

Fill in the blanks with *the* or Ø (no article).

(1) _____ Burma is sandwiched between (2) _____

India and (3) _____ Bangladesh on one side and

(4) _____ China, (5) _____ Laos, and

(6) _____ Thailand on the other. To the south is

(7) _____ Andaman Sea and (8) _____ Bay of

Bengal. Burma has several important river systems including

(9) _____ Irrawaddy, which runs almost the entire length of the

country and enters the sea in a vast delta region southwest of

(10) _____ Rangoon, the capital. (11) _____ Mekong

River forms the border between Burma and Laos. (12) _____

Himalayas rise in the north of Burma, and (13) _____ Hkakabo

Razi, on the border between Burma and Tibet, is the highest mountain in

southeast Asia, at 5881 meters (19,297 feet).

Adapted from *Burma, A Travel Survival Kit*, by Tony Wheeler. Lonely Planet Publications, 1982.

Now use the information from this exercise to complete labeling the map.

▶ # Articles with Names of Institutions

EXAMPLES	EXPLANATIONS
(a) Summit Elementary School (b) Children's Hospital and Medical Center (c) Boston College (d) Louisiana State (University)	**Use Ø (no article):** • for schools, hospitals, and prisons • when the place name comes **before** *College* or *University*
(e) **the** Eiffel Tower (f) **the** University of Northern Iowa	**Use *the*:** • for most tourist attractions • when *University of* comes before the place name

EXERCISE 4

The following conversation is between Sheryl Smith, a real estate agent, and the Joneses, who want to buy a house. Fill in the blanks with *the* or Ø (no article).

Sheryl Smith: I'm sure you'd like the area. It borders (1) _____ Discovery Park, which has free outdoor concerts at (2) _____ Rutherford Concert Hall, and also there's (3) _____ Whitehawk Native American Art Museum, which you've probably heard of. It's quite well known.

Mike Jones: Yes, yes.

Donna Jones: What about schools?

Sheryl Smith: Well, there's (4) _____ Smith College of Architecture, of course...

Donna Jones: I mean public schools for our children.

Sheryl Smith: Oh, well, (5) _____ Golden Oaks Elementary School is only a few blocks away, on (6) _____ First Avenue. And there's a high school about a mile north of the park.

Mike Jones: (pointing) Aren't those (7) _____ White Mountains?

Sheryl Smith: Yes. On clear days, you can even see (8) _____

Mt. Wildman, the tallest mountain in the range.

Mike Jones: Oh, yes. I heard about a good fishing spot there, on

(9) _____ Blue Lake.

Sheryl Smith: Yes, my husband goes there and to (10) _____

Nooksack River to fish. He could tell you all about it.

Mike Jones: Ms. Smith, I think you might have made a sale today.

EXERCISE 5

Fill in the blanks with *the* or Ø (no article). The first two have been done for you.

1. __Ø__ Hawaii
2. __the__ Hawaiian Islands
3. _____ Saudi Arabia
4. _____ Harvard University
5. _____ Himalayas
6. _____ Museum of Modern Art
7. _____ First Avenue
8. _____ Mississippi River

9. _____ University of Iowa
10. _____ Turkey
11. _____ United States
12. _____ Pyramids
13. _____ West
14. _____ Africa
15. _____ Lake Wenatchee
16. _____ Saturn

EXERCISE 6

For each underlined place name, check to see if the article is used correctly. If it is wrong, correct it: Add *the* or cross out *the*. The first one has been done for you.

SAN FRANCISCO MUST SEE'S FOR FIRST-TIMERS

Once considered impossible to build, (1) ^the^ Golden Gate Bridge, a 1.7 mile-long single-span suspension bridge, was opened in 1937. A walk across offers a fantastic view of the city, the Marin Headlands, and the East Bay. Experience a taste of (2) the Orient in (3) the Chinatown, the largest Chinese settlement outside (4) the Asia. Originally only sand dunes, (5) the Golden Gate Park owes its existence to Scottish landscape architect John McLaren. In addition to the beauty of its landscape, the park contains: a conservatory modeled after (6) Kew Gardens; (7) Asian Art Museum with its well-known Brundage collection; (8) the Strybing Arboretum with its worldwide plant collection; and (9) California Academy of Sciences, which includes a planetarium and aquarium.

Adapted from *San Francisco TESOL Convention* 1990, Leslie Reichert.

Use Your English

It is often said that Americans do not know very much about world geography, compared to people from other countries. The purpose of this activity is for people who grew up in other countries to conduct a small survey of Americans (or people educated in the United States) to find out to what extent this is true.

Use the information in the Opening Task on page 303 to draw up a chart of your own. Add other items to the chart if you want. Then use this chart to get information from as many Americans as you can—ideally from five different people. Compare the answers you receive with those that your classmates gave you, and share your findings with the rest of the class.

On the basis of the findings from everyone in the class, is it true that Americans know less about world geography than people from other countries? Are there any reasons to explain your results?

ACTIVITY 2: SPEAKING

With the help of your teacher, form teams. Each team will have five minutes to think of as many names of islands, mountains, and lakes as possible. Each name with correct article use will be worth one point. The team that has the most correct names + articles wins.

ACTIVITY 3: WRITING

Think of a city or region you know and like. What places are the "Must See's For First-Timers"? Write a short description of the tourist attractions and special features. If time allows, draw a map giving the relative locations of these places.

ACTIVITY 4: LISTENING 📼

STEP 1 Listen to the tape of a person talking about where she lives.

1. Work with a partner. Discuss the place the woman is talking about. Where is it? Why does she like it?

2. Listen again. Circle the names of the places the woman mentions.

——— Leblon Beach

——— Sugar Loaf Mountain

——— City Historic Museum

——— Museum of Brazil

——— North America

——— Santa Marinha Street

——— City Park

——— Ipanema Beach

——— Pacific Ocean

——— South America

——— Rio De Janeiro

3. In front of the names of the places you circled, write the word *the* or leave the space blank. Compare your answers with a classmate's. If you disagree on any answers, look back at Focus 1 and Focus 2 for help in deciding on the correct answer.

STEP 2 Work with a classmate to discuss why Ø (no article) or *the* was used with each place name.

ACTIVITY 5: SPEAKING/WRITING

You have been asked by the local chamber of commerce to design a poster to attract overseas visitors to the region where you are living. Or, if you prefer, you can make a poster about another place you know and like (See Activity 3), especially if there are other students interested in the same place.

Get together with a group of students to brainstorm local areas of interest. Your poster should have pictures and labels about the area and also short written descriptions.

Display and compare your posters.

ACTIVITY 6: READING

Rita and Ray were planning an overnight backpacking trip into the mountains, so they asked their friend Bill to give them directions to a nice camping spot where he had camped many times. Bill told Ray the directions over the phone. Below are the notes that Ray took:

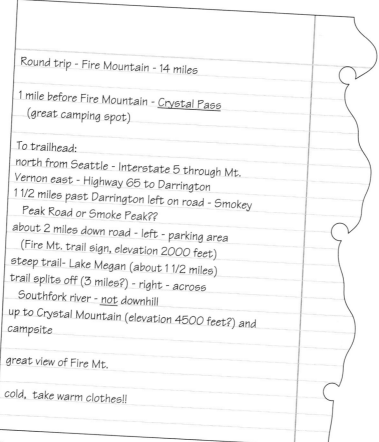

Round trip - Fire Mountain - 14 miles

1 mile before Fire Mountain - <u>Crystal Pass</u>
   (great camping spot)

To trailhead:
north from Seattle - Interstate 5 through Mt.
Vernon east - Highway 65 to Darrington
1 1/2 miles past Darrington left on road - Smokey
   Peak Road or Smoke Peak??
about 2 miles down road - left - parking area
   (Fire Mt. trail sign, elevation 2000 feet)
steep trail- Lake Megan (about 1 1/2 miles)
trail splits off (3 miles?) - right - across
   Southfork river - <u>not</u> downhill
up to Crystal Mountain (elevation 4500 feet?) and
campsite

great view of Fire Mt.

cold, take warm clothes!!

"Translate" this note into complete directions to Bill's special camping spot.

ACTIVITY 7: SPEAKING/LISTENING

The poster that you made in Activity 5 was so successful that you have been asked to talk about the region to a group of tourists and travel guides. Tape-record your short talk. Listen to the tape and check to see if you used *the* and Ø (no article) correctly.

THE PASSIVE

UNIT GOALS:

- To know when to use passives
- To correctly form *be* and *get* passives
- To know the difference between the *be* passive and the *get* passive
- To know when to include the agent in the sentence

▶ **OPENING TASK**
The Island of Campinilea

You are gathering information for a book on Campinilea, an island located off the coast of Peru. The first chapter will be called "The Products and Natural Resources of Campinilea."

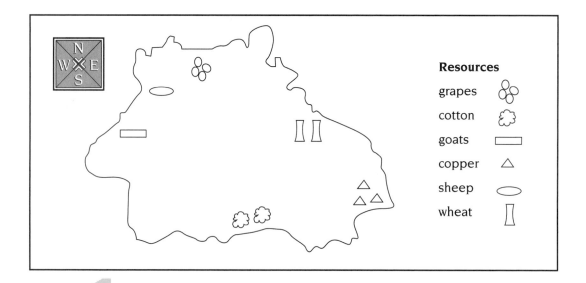

Resources

grapes

cotton

goats

copper

sheep

wheat

STEP 1   Use the information on the map on page 312 to discuss the island's resources.

▶ **EXAMPLE:**   Where are grapes cultivated? . . . in the north

Where is cotton grown?

STEP 2   Use the map to match the activities to the appropriate location. The first one has been done for you.

Activities	**Locations**
cultivate grapes	in the east
raise sheep	in the southeast
grow cotton	in the northwest
grow wheat	in the north
mine copper	in the west
raise goats	in the south

STEP 3   Using the same information, write five sentences about the products and natural resources of Campinilea for the first chapter of your book.

▶ **P**assive and Active

EXAMPLES	EXPLANATIONS
(a) Farmers **cultivate** grapes in the north.	Use the active to focus on the person who performs the action.
(b) Grapes **are cultivated** in the north.	Use the passive to focus on the result of the action, not the person who performs it.

EXERCISE 1

Look at each sentence you wrote in Step 3 of the Opening Task on page 313. Did you use the passive or the active? Write each statement both ways.

Which statement sounds better? Why?

▶ Forming the *Be* Passive

To form the passive, use the appropriate tense of *be*, followed by the past participle (pp):

EXAMPLES	TENSE	FORM	
(a) Wool **is produced** here.	Simple Present	*am/is/are*	+ pp
(b) Wool **is being produced** here right now.	Present Progressive	*am/is/are being*	+ pp
(c) Wool **was produced** here.	Simple Past	*was/were*	+ pp
(d) Wool **was being produced** here ten years ago.	Past Progressive	*was/were being*	+ pp
(e) Wool **has been produced** here since 1900.	Present Perfect	*have/has been*	+ pp
(f) Wool **had been produced** here when the island was discovered.	Past Perfect	*had been*	+ pp
(g) Wool **will be produced** here next year.	Future (*will*)	*will be*	+ pp
(h) Wool **is going to be produced** here.	Future (*be going to*)	*am/is/are going to be*	+ pp
(i) Wool **will have been produced** here by the year 2010.	Future Perfect	*will have been*	+ pp

EXERCISE 2

The second chapter of the book on Campinilea is called "The People of Campinilea and Their Customs." Look at the following statements about Campinilea; write 1 beside those you think belong to Chapter 1 (Products and Resources) and 2 beside those you think belong to Chapter 2 (People and Customs).

1. In the west, unmarried women leave their family homes at the age of twenty-five and raise goats in the mountains.
2. Miners mined silver throughout the island during the last century.
3. They will plant the first crop of rice in the south next year.
4. In the southeast, fathers take their oldest sons to the copper mines on their twelfth birthday in a special ceremony to teach them the legends and rituals associated with Campinilean copper.
5. Easterners are more traditional than southerners; for example, farmers in the east have harvested wheat in the same way for hundreds of years, while those in the south are constantly exploring new techniques for growing cotton.

6. They have produced grapes in Campinilea for only a few years.

Do you think it would be appropriate to use the passive in any of these statements? Why do you think so? Rewrite those statements here:

_____

_____

_____

_____

EXERCISE 3

Complete the following, using the verb tense that fits best.

Adventurous tourists are beginning to discover Campinilea, and the island is hard at work getting ready to welcome more visitors. A new airport

(1) _____ (build) last year, and at the moment, hotels

(2) _____ (construct) along the southern beaches. A new road

(3) _____ (finish) next year so visitors will be able to reach the

northern region. Five years ago, very little (4) _____ (know)

about Campinilea; but last year, three books (5) _____ (write)

about the island, and several guide books (6) _____ (publish).

At the moment, these books (7) _____ (translate) into different

languages. English (8) _____ (teach) in schools so many
Campinileans know a little English, but not many other foreign languages

(9) _____ (speak).

Tourism has brought many changes to this small island, and people are afraid that it will have a negative effect on the traditional customs and culture of the people. For example, last month in the capital, several young

Campinileans (10) _____ (arrest) for being drunk in public, and

some tourists (11) _____ (rob) near the beach. However, if you
leave the tourist areas and go up to the mountains, you will find that life is still the same as it was hundreds of years ago. For example, since the

sixteenth century, the same tribal dances (12) _____ (perform)
to celebrate the Campinilean new year, and the same type of food

(13) _____ (serve). For centuries, visitors

(14) _____ (invite) to join Campinileans in the celebration of
festivals, and you will find traditional Campinilean hospitality in these regions has not changed at all.

▶ **The Passive**

EXAMPLES	EXPLANATIONS
(a) All the cookies **were eaten** last night.	Use the passive when you don't know who performed the action.
(b) Wheat **is grown** in the East.	Use the passive when the person who performed the action is obvious. In example (b), it is obvious that farmers are the people who grow the wheat.
(c) A mistake was **made.**	Use the passive when you don't want to tell who performed the action.
(d) The computer **is protected** from electrical damage by a special grounding plug. **(e)** The proposal **was rejected** by the people of King County in last night's vote.	The passive is more formal than the active. It is more common in writing, especially in scientific and technical reports, and in newspaper articles. It is less common in conversation.

EXERCISE 4

With the growth of tourism, petty crime has unfortunately increased in Campinilea. The Campinilean police are currently investigating a robbery that took place in a hotel room a few nights ago.

Work with a partner. One of you should look at Picture A below; the other should look at Picture B on page A-17. One of you has a picture of the room **before** the robbery, and the other has a picture of the room **after** the robbery. Seven different things were done to the room. **Without looking at your partner's picture,** ask each other questions and find what these seven things were and complete the report below.

ROBBERY AT HOTEL PARAISO

Last night the police were called to investigate a robbery that took place at the Hotel Paraiso. The identity of the thief is still unknown. The police took note of several unusual occurrences. For example,

_____
_____
_____
_____

The public has been asked to contact the police with any information about the identity of the thief. Any information leading to an arrest will be rewarded.

Picture A

> ## Including the Agent in Passive Sentences

EXAMPLES	EXPLANATIONS
(a) Wheat is grown in the East. **(b)** **NOT:** Wheat is grown in the East by farmers.	In most situations where the passive is used, the *by*-phrase (the agent) is understood and therefore is *not* used.
(c) Wheat is grown in eastern Campinilea. It is planted **by men,** and it is harvested **by women and children.**	You can include the agent (the person who performs the action) with a *by*-phrase if that information is important. It is important to include the agent:
(d) *Hamlet* was written **by William Shakespeare.** **(e)** Several South American countries were liberated **by Simon Bolivar.** **(f)** I can't believe it! This novel was written **by a fourteen-year-old.**	• when new information is added, (Example c, second sentence) • with proper names or famous people (Examples d and e) • when the agent's identity is surprising or unexpected (Example f)

EXERCISE 5

Decide if each italicized phrase (*by* + agent) is necessary in the sentences below. Cross out the *by*-phrases that you think are unnecessary.

Passage 1

Campinilea was described (1) *by Jules Verne* in one of his early novels. It was seen (2) *by people* as an exotic yet stable society. Recently, it was rated (3) *by Travel Magazine* as one of the top ten tourists spots in the world. One of the reasons for the country's popularity is that the products produced (4) *by Campinileans* in Campinilea are excellent.

For example, rugs have been produced (5) *by Campinilean people* for centuries. They are woven (6) *by women from the mountain tribes* and are then transported to the capital (7) *by mule* and are sold in the markets (8) *by relatives of the weavers.*

Another excellent product is the mineral water of Campinilea. In restaurants in the capital city, bottled water is served (9) *by waiters.* It is interesting that this water is rarely drunk (10) *by Campinileans,* but it is much appreciated (11) *by foreign tourists.*

Passage 2

Dear Janette,

I've been working hard this whole week on my book. In some ways, I wish that I hadn't gotten paid an advance (1) *by the publishers,* since now I feel a lot of pressure to finish quickly. I guess that's the purpose of an advance! I really hope, though, that when the book is finally finished (2) *by me,* it will be appreciated (3) *by people.* I am hoping that I can finish soon, because it means that I will soon be paid in full (4) *by the publishers!* Even if it's done soon, the book won't actually be published (5) *by the publishers* until at least six months after the manuscript is received (6) *by them.*

Did I tell you that Scout got hurt (7) *by another dog?* She was playing with Patches, the neighbor's dog, like she always does, and her ear got bitten pretty severely (8) *by Patches.* I had to take her to the vet's and get it stitched up (9) *by the vet.* The vet asked me if Scout got attacked (10) *by Patches,* and I had to explain that no, she and Patches just like to play rough. Luckily, Scout's fine. And of course she and Patches are playing together again, just as hard as ever, so it's clear that their friendship hasn't been damaged (11) *by the experience.* Gotta run! Back to work on the book . . .

Love,

Dean

FOCUS **5**

▶ Forming the Get-Passive

To form the *get*-passive, use the appropriate tense of *get,* followed by the past participle (pp):

EXAMPLES		TENSE	FORM	
(a)	Her cookies always **get eaten.**	Present Simple	*get/gets*	+ pp
(b)	Her cookies **are getting eaten.**	Present Progressive	*am/is/are getting*	+ pp
(c)	Her cookies **got eaten.**	Past Simple	*got*	+ pp
(d)	Her cookies **were getting eaten.**	Past Progressive	*was/were getting*	+ pp
(e)	Her cookies **have gotten eaten.**	Present Perfect	*have/has gotten*	+ pp
(f)	Her cookies **had gotten eaten.**	Past Perfect	*had gotten*	+ pp
(g)	Her cookies **will get eaten.**	Future (*will*)	*will get*	+ pp
(h)	Her cookies are **going to get eaten.**	Future (*going to*)	*am/is/are going to get*	+ pp
(i)	Her cookies **will have gotten eaten** by the time we get home.	Future Perfect	*will have gotten*	+ pp

QUESTIONS: Simple present and past:

EXAMPLES	QUESTION FORM
(j) Do her cookies **get eaten**?	*Do/does* + subject + *get* + pp
(k) Did her cookies **get eaten**?	*Did* + subject + *get* + pp

NEGATIVE: Simple present and past:

EXAMPLES	NEGATIVE STATEMENT FORM
(l) Her cookies **do not get eaten.**	subject + *do/does* + *not* + *get* + pp (*don't/doesn't*)
(m) Her cookies **did not get eaten.**	subject + *did not* + *get* + pp (*didn't*)

EXERCISE 6

Read the following situations. What do you think probably happened before each one? Match the situation with one of the previous events in the box below.

SITUATION	PREVIOUS EVENT
1. Oh, no! Not my clean white shirt!	_____
2. We're finally able to pay our bills.	_____
3. It's so exciting to see my name in print.	_____
4. I told you not to leave it outside at night!	_____
5. When I came back to the parking lot, I found these dents on the side.	_____
6. They took him straight to the hospital by ambulance.	_____
7. Thank you for all your support. Now that I am mayor, I will work to improve our schools.	_____
8. The packet's empty, and there are only a few crumbs left!	_____

(a) They got paid.	**(b)** His car got hit.
(c) Someone got injured.	**(d)** Some coffee got spilled.
(e) All the cookies got eaten.	**(f)** She got elected.
(g) His book got published.	**(h)** Her bike got stolen.

EXERCISE 7

Complete the following with the *get*-passive and the appropriate tense.

1. A: I think I've prepared too much food for tomorrow's party.

  B: Don't worry. It _____ all _____ (eat).

2. A: Where's your car?

  B: It's _____ (fix).

3. A: How was your vacation last month?

  B: Terrible. We _____ (rob), and all our traveler's checks _____ (take).

4. A: Have you heard? Chuck _____ (invite) to dinner with the President at the White House!

  B: I don't believe it.

5. A: Please drive slowly.

  B: Why?

  A: If you don't, we _____ (stop) by the Highway Patrol.

6. A: Did you finish your assignments yet?

  B: Yeah. We turned them in, and now they _____ (grade).

7. A: Do you know if Sid has moved?

  B: No. Why?

  A: I sent him a letter last week, but it _____ (return) yesterday with no forwarding address.

  B: That's strange.

8. A: Al's writing a novel.

  B: Really?

  A: Yes. He hopes it _____ (publish) next year.

9. A: Rosa quit her job.

  B: Why?

  A: She _____ (not/pay).

10. A: There was a terrible accident here last night.

  B: _____ anyone _____ (arrest)?

▶ **Be-Passive versus *Get*-Passive**

EXAMPLES	EXPLANATIONS
(a) They **are married.** **(b)** They **got married** last year.	In most situations, the *be*-passive emphasizes a continuing state, while the *get*-passive emphasizes a change in the situation.
(c) The answer **was known.** **(d)** **NOT:** The answer **got known.** (***know =*** an unchanging state) **(e)** She **was wanted** by the police for shoplifting. **(f)** **NOT:** She **got wanted** by the police for shoplifting.	Because the *get*-passive emphasizes a change in a situation, it is only used with action or process verbs. It cannot be used with stative verbs (verbs that refer to situations, or "states," that do not change). Some common stative verbs: *own like hate see love* *know feel want*
(g) *To a friend:* Have you heard the news? Isao's car **got stolen!** **(h)** *In a police report:* A white Honda Civic **was stolen** last night.	*Get*-passives are often used in conversation and rarely in writing or formal speaking. *Be*-passives are more formal than *get*-passives.

EXERCISE 8
Where possible, change the underlined verbs to *get*-passives. If it is not possible to use the *get*-passive, explain why.

1. Last week, Marvin had a dinner party. He prepared lots of food, and everything <u>was eaten</u>.

got eaten

2. This ring is very valuable because it <u>was owned</u> by Napoleon.

3. We are very sorry that Mr. Gordon is leaving our company—he <u>was liked</u> and respected by us all.

4. What happened to your car?

It <u>was hit</u> by a truck.

5. Someone broke into her house, but surprisingly, nothing <u>was taken</u>.

6. At the time of his arrest, that man was armed and dangerous, and he <u>was wanted</u> by the police in three different states.

7. We really hope our book <u>will be published</u> some day.

8. I'm sorry I'm late; I had to go to the veterinarian's because my dog <u>was attacked</u> by a cat.

9. Many beautiful houses <u>were</u> badly <u>damaged</u> in last month's earthquake.

10. Marilyn Monroe <u>was admired</u> by many people.

EXERCISE 9

Tabloid newspapers present sensational, but usually untrue, stories. Look at the following tabloid newspaper headlines and in your notebook rewrite each one as a complete sentence. Use a *get*-passive wherever possible; use a *be*-passive where you cannot use a *get*-passive.

1. TEEN EATEN BY GIANT COCKROACHES
2. ELVIS SEEN IN SUPERMARKET LINE
3. VICE-PRESIDENT KIDNAPPED BY SPACE ALIENS
4. BILL AND HILLARY TO DIVORCE?
5. WORLD'S WORST HUSBAND MARRIED 36 TIMES
6. FALSE TEETH STUCK IN MAN'S THROAT FOR SIX MONTHS
7. (Add some that you find) _____
8. _____
9. _____
10. _____

What do you think each headline is about? Why?

Use Your English

ACTIVITY 1: READING/SPEAKING/LISTENING

Look at the following tabloid headlines and ask a native speaker of English to explain what she or he thinks the headline means. Tape the conversation and then listen to the recording to see if she or he uses any passive forms in his or her explanations. Share your findings with the rest of the class.

- WOMAN HYPNOTIZED BY ALIENS
- MAN'S LIFE SAVED BY HITCHHIKING GHOST
- SUITCASE DROPPED 5,000 FEET BY AIRLINE
- BIGFOOT FOUND IN NEW YORK CITY
- WOMAN PREGNANT WITH DAUGHTER'S BABY

ACTIVITY 2: SPEAKING/LISTENING

In this activity, you will make a chain story about somebody's bad day—a day when everything went wrong. One student will start the story and will continue until she or he uses a *get*-passive. When she or he uses a *get*-passive, the next person will continue. For example:

Student 1: *Andy had a really bad day. First, he overslept. When he got dressed, he forgot to put his pants on.*

Student 2: *He ran out of the house, but was embarrassed to realize he had forgotten his pants. Before he could get back inside, he got bitten by the neighbor's dog.*

Student 3: etc.

ACTIVITY 3: WRITING OR SPEAKING/LISTENING

Have **you** ever had a really bad day? A day when everything went wrong, through no fault of your own? Describe the day, either in an informal letter to a friend, or, if you prefer, out loud to a classmate. If you tell your story rather than write it, tape-record it. Listen to the tape for the use of the passive, especially the *get*-passive.

ACTIVITY 4: LISTENING

Ask someone (a native speaker of English, if possible) to tell you about a really frightening experience she or he has had. Find out what happened, and how it happened. Tape-record the conversation.

Listen to the recording. Was the passive used? If so, was it the *be*-passive or the *get*-passive? Was the agent (the *by*-phrase) used?

ACTIVITY 5: LISTENING

STEP 1 Listen to the tape of two people talking about bad experiences they have had. What experiences did the speakers have? What is similar and different about their experiences?

STEP 2 Listen to the tape again. Write down all the statements which use the passive. For each statement, was the *be*-passive or the *get*-passive used? Was the agent (the *by*-phrase) used?

ACTIVITY 6: READING

ACHIEVEMENT SNAP

STEP 1 Work in pairs. Try to think of twenty different achievements (discoveries, inventions, or works of art), as well as the name of the person(s) who created them. For example:

The telephone   Alexander Graham Bell

On the next page there are some more ideas to get you going, but you probably have better ideas of your own.

Write each name on an index card and then write each achievement on a **different** index card. You should have a total of forty cards:

William Shakespeare

Hamlet

Now you are ready to play Achievement Snap.

STEP 2
1. Get together with another pair. Put all your "People Cards" in one deck and all your "Achievement Cards" in another deck. Shuffle each deck carefully.
2. Put the deck of Achievement Cards face-down on a table.
3. Deal the People Cards to the players. Each player should have several cards. Do not look at your cards.
4. The dealer turns over the first Achievement Card and puts down his or her first People Card. The object of the game is to make a correct match between Achievement and Person.

5. Keep taking turns at putting down People Cards until a match is made. The first person to spot a match shouts "Snap" loudly and explains the match: "The telephone was invented by Alexander Graham Bell." If everyone agrees that the match is factually and grammatically correct, the player takes the pile of People Cards on the table.

6. The winner is the person who collects the most People Cards.

(Note: It is possible to continue playing after you lose your People Cards. If you correctly spot a "match," you can collect the cards on the table.)

Some ideas:

Mona Lisa	Leonardo da Vinci
hydrogen bomb	Edward Teller
"Yesterday"	John Lennon and Paul McCartney
Psycho	Alfred Hitchcock
Mount Everest	Tenzing

Remember to use an appropriate verb in matching the person and the achievement. Common verbs include: *compose, write, discover, invent, direct, sing, paint.*

ACTIVITY 7: SPEAKING OR WRITING

Make a presentation (oral or written) about your country or a place that you know well. Describe the resources and products, any changes over time, and any predictions for the future.

ACTIVITY 8: RESEARCH/SPEAKING

Walk around your neighborhood or city. In what ways do you think your neighborhood or city can become a better place to live? What is actually being done to make it a better place to live in?

Report your observation to your classmates: *While I was walking in the neighborhood, I noticed that . . . . (observations) . . . .* Use the passive in your report whenever it is appropriate.

PHRASAL VERBS

UNIT GOALS:

- To know when to use phrasal verbs
- To know which phrasal verbs take objects and which phrasal verbs do not take objects
- To correctly form sentences containing phrasal verbs and objects
- To know which phrasal verbs are separable and which are inseparable

▶ OPENING TASK
School Days

Calvin and Hobbes was a popular comic strip about a small boy called Calvin, who hates school.

STEP 1 Get together with a partner. Look at the comic strip about Calvin's day at school. How do you think he feels in each picture? What do you think he is saying? Discuss some possibilities with your partner.

1992 © Watterson. Distributed by Universal Press Syndicate.

STEP 2 Look at what Calvin said and match his words with their definitions below:

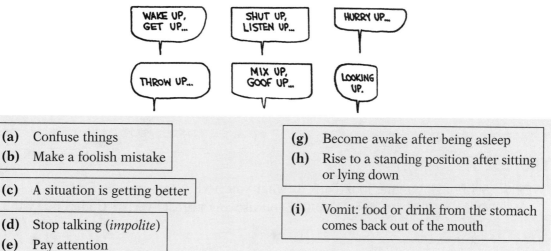

(a)	Confuse things	**(g)**	Become awake after being asleep
(b)	Make a foolish mistake	**(h)**	Rise to a standing position after sitting or lying down
(c)	A situation is getting better		
(d)	Stop talking (*impolite*)	**(i)**	Vomit: food or drink from the stomach comes back out of the mouth
(e)	Pay attention		
(f)	Make something happen more quickly		

STEP 3 Now match Calvin's words with the pictures in the comic strip. Write his words in the appropriate picture. When you finish, compare your version of the comic strip with the original on page A-18.

STEP 4 Why do you think Calvin uses words like *mix up* and *throw up* instead of *confuse things* and *vomit*?

STEP 5 When you and your classmate were Calvin's age, did you like going to school or did you hate it as much as Calvin does? Ask your classmate to describe a typical day at school when he or she was Calvin's age and make notes on the chart below.

BEFORE GOING TO SCHOOL IN THE MORNING, MY CLASSMATE . . .	AT SCHOOL, MY CLASSMATE . . .	AT SCHOOL, MY CLASSMATE'S TEACHER . . .

▶ **Phrasal Verbs**

EXAMPLES	EXPLANATION
Verb *Particle* (a) Calvin **gets** **up** at 7:00. (b) First, he **takes off** his pajamas. (c) Then he **puts on** his jeans.	Phrasal verbs have two parts: a **verb** and a **particle.** Common particles are *off, on, in, out, up.*

EXERCISE 1

STEP 1 With a classmate, look back at what you both wrote in Step 5 of the Opening Task on page 329. Did you use any phrasal verbs? Underline them.

STEP 2 How many **other** phrasal verbs can you think of to describe things you did in school as a child? Write them in the box below and then use each one in a sentence. (Remember that you are talking about the past in these sentences.)

> stand up
>
>
>
>
>
>
>
>
>
>
>
>
>
>   sit down

► # **When to Use Phrasal Verbs and How to Learn Them**

EXAMPLES	EXPLANATIONS
	Phrasal verbs are very common, especially in informal spoken English.
(a) **Look out!** There's a car coming!	It is often difficult to guess the meaning of a phrasal verb, even when you know the meaning of each part. In some situations, however, the context can help you make a guess.
(b) The movie starts at 8:00. Please don't **show up** late or we won't get good seats.	In (a), *look out* means be careful.
	In (b), *show up* means arrive.
	When you use the same verb with a different particle, the meaning usually changes.
(c) You should **look over** your homework before you give it to the teacher.	In (c), *look over* means to check or examine something.
(d) My friend David **looks after** my cats when I go on vacation.	In (d), *look after* means to take care of. To remember the meanings of phrasal verbs, learn the two parts together as one vocabulary item, in the same way that you learn new words.

EXERCISE 2

Get together with a classmate and match each verb with a particle from the box below to create a set of phrasal verbs to describe typical school activities. (Notice that some verbs can take different particles to express different meanings.) Check that you understand the meaning of the phrasal verbs you create (your teacher or a good English/English dictionary can help). Remember, in this exercise, we are only thinking about phrasal verbs that are often used to talk about "school."

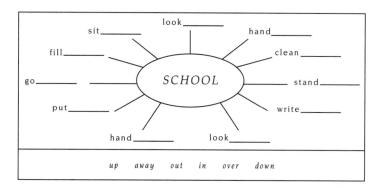

EXERCISE 3

Use the phrasal verbs from Exercise 2 to complete the text below.

French Lessons

I will never forget my first French lessons many years ago in high school. Our teacher was very strict and rather old-fashioned, even for that time. When she entered the classroom, we all had to (1) stand _____ and say "Bonjour, Madame Morel," and we couldn't (2) sit _____ until she gave us permission. Every class followed exactly the same routine, with absolutely no variation. First, we always had "dictée." The teacher read a passage, sentence by sentence, and we had to (3) write _____ exactly what she said, word for word. We weren't allowed to use dictionaries in class, so we couldn't (4) look _____ the meanings of any words we didn't know. Then, she always gave us precisely five minutes to (5) look _____ our papers to check the spelling and punctuation. This was very important because if we (6) handed _____ work that had more than one mistake in it, we had to stay behind after class. Next, she always (7) handed _____ a list of vocabulary words for us to memorize. Then after exactly ten minutes, she gave us a quiz that always told us to (8) "fill _____ the blanks with the appropriate vocabulary word." Finally, she (9) went _____ the vocabulary words from the previous day's lesson to make sure that we hadn't forgotten them. How I hated French lessons! Even when the bell rang at the end of the day, we couldn't leave until we (10) had cleaned _____ the classroom and (11) put _____ all our books.

EXERCISE 4

Use as many of the phrasal verbs from Exercises 1, 2, and 3 as you can to describe any classes you have taken or are taking now. Make a list and then describe the class to a classmate.

FOCUS **3**

▶ **P**hrasal Verbs that Take Objects

EXAMPLES	EXPLANATIONS
	Like other verbs, many phrasal verbs take objects.
(a) We had to **call off** the meeting because everyone was sick.	In (a), the object of the sentence is *the meeting*.
(b) We're trying to sleep. Please **turn down** that radio!	In (b), the object of the sentence is *that radio*.

Some common phrasal verbs that take objects:

PHRASAL VERB	EXAMPLE	MEANING*
Call off	We had to **call off** the meeting because everyone was sick.	Cancel
Put off	Let's **put off** our meeting until next week.	Change to a later time or date
Pick up	Please **pick up** your towel! Don't leave it on the bathroom floor.	Lift or take from a particular place
Set up	We need to **set up** a time to discuss this.	Arrange a meeting or appointment
Talk over	It's important for couples to **talk over** their problems and misunderstandings.	Discuss a problem

PHRASAL VERB	EXAMPLE	MEANING*
Throw out	I **threw out** all my old school books and papers when we moved.	Put in the garbage, get rid of
Turn down	We're trying to sleep. Please **turn down** that radio!	Lower the volume of radio, TV, etc.
Turn off	I'll **turn off** the TV as soon as this program ends.	Stop a machine, engine or electrical device
Turn on	She always **turns on** the radio to listen to the news.	Start a machine, engine or electrical device

Some of these phrasal verbs may have different meanings in different situations.

EXERCISE 5

Respond to the following situations using as many of the phrasal verbs discussed so far in this unit as possible. (Some of the language from Unit 10, *Giving Advice and Expressing Opinions,* and Unit 17, *Requests and Permission,* might also help you here.)

1. You are trying to talk on the phone but your roommate is listening to some very loud music. You say:

   Please turn down that radio!! _____

   _____

2. A friend is applying for a job and has just written a letter of application. He asks you to check the letter for grammatical errors. He says: _____

   _____

3. A family member is sick and you need to leave town for a few days to take care of her. You call a colleague and explain the situation. Then you ask him to telephone your clients and delay all the meetings you had arranged with them until the following week. You say:_____

   _____

   _____

4. It is the first class meeting of the school year. Your new teacher is explaining his policy about grading and homework. He expects students to give him their homework on time. He says: _____

   _____

5. You have helped organize a foreign film festival on campus. You ask some of your classmates to help you distribute fliers about the movies to students in the cafeteria during the lunch break. You say: _____

_____

6. A close friend is having problems with her boyfriend. He leaves his clothes all over the floor, has the TV on constantly, even when he isn't watching anything, and refuses to discuss their relationship. She asks for your advice, so you say: _____

_____

_____

FOCUS **4**

▶ **Separating Verbs and Particles**

EXAMPLES				EXPLANATIONS
subject	*verb*	*particle*	*object (noun)*	Many phrasal verbs are **separable**: When the object is a noun, you can:
(a) She	**turned**	**on**	the light.	Put the object **after** the particle.
OR				OR
subject	*verb*	*object (noun)*	*particle*	
(b) She	**turned**	the light	**on.**	Put the object **between** the verb and the particle.
subject	*verb*	*object (pronoun)*	*particle*	When the object of a separable phrasal verb is a pronoun, you must put the object **between** the verb and the particle.
(c) She	**turned**	**it**	**on.**	
(d) NOT: She **turned on** it.				
(e) He **cleaned** it **up.**				
(f) NOT: He **cleaned up** it.				

EXERCISE 6

Replace the underlined words with a phrasal verb from the list below. Separate
the verb and particle **where possible.**

try on	find out	take off	call up	throw out	set up	take back
	go over	put on	get off	put off		

taking your shoes off

Shirley: Why are you (1) removing your shoes? I thought you were going to go for a walk.

Julia: I decided to (2) wear my boots. It's raining outside.

Shirley: I thought those boots were too small. You said you wanted to (3) return them to
the store. Did you (4) discover if they have a larger size?

Julia: I guess I (5) delayed it too long. When I (6) phoned the store, the salesperson said I'd
have to wait at least a month for the next delivery, so I decided to keep these after all.

Shirley: That's crazy! Don't wear them if they're too small. Why don't you borrow my
hiking boots?

Julia: I thought you (7) put those in the garbage when we moved.

Shirley: No, they're somewhere in my closet if you want to (8) wear them to see if they fit
you.

Get together with a classmate. Compare your answers and then read the new dialogue
aloud to each other. Change roles and read the dialogue again.

FOCUS **5**

▶ **Inseparable Phrasal Verbs**

EXAMPLES	EXPLANATIONS
(a) Yesterday I **ran into** my friend Sal. OR	Not all phrasal verbs can be separated. Some phrasal verbs are **inseparable**: With these verbs you cannot put the object between the verb and the particle, even when the object is a pronoun.
(b) Yesterday I **ran into** her.	
(c) **NOT:** Yesterday I ran my friend into.	
(d) **NOT:** Yesterday I ran her into.	It is difficult to guess which phrasal verbs are separable and which are inseparable. It is a good idea to learn if a phrasal verb is separable or inseparable when you learn its meaning. A good dictionary will give you this information.

Some common inseparable phrasal verbs:

PHRASAL VERB	EXAMPLE	MEANING*
Come across	You never know what you'll find at a yard sale! Last week, I **came across** a valuable old Beatles record.	Find something or someone
Run into	Colleen was really surprised to **run into** her ex-boyfriend at the supermarket.	Meet someone unexpectedly
Get off	Don't **get off** the bus until it stops.	Leave a bus, train, or plane
Get on	You can't **get on** a plane without a boarding pass.	Enter a bus, train, or plane
Go over	Our teacher always **goes over** the main points in a unit before she gives us a test.	Review
Get over	Jeb has gone to bed early because he's still **getting over** the flu.	Recover from an illness

Some of these phrasal verbs may have different meanings in different situations.

EXERCISE 7

Replace the underlined words with phrasal verbs from the list below. Separate the verb and particle where it is possible or necessary.

pass away   find out   call up   cheer up   put off   run into   call on   get on

1. Sally tried to <u>phone</u> Marie yesterday, but Marie's line was busy. *call Marie up*
2. So, she decided to <u>visit</u> her <u>at home</u>.
3. Earlier that day, Sally <u>met</u> their friend Ron <u>unexpectedly</u> as he was leaving the apartment building.
4. He was ready to <u>enter</u> the bus to go to his sister's house.
5. He told Sally that his grandfather had <u>died</u>.
6. Of course, Sally was sorry to <u>hear</u> that.
7. She suggested to Marie that the three friends should <u>postpone</u> the dinner party they had been planning.
8. Marie agreed, and she also thought they should do something to <u>make</u> Ron <u>feel</u> <u>happier</u>.

EXERCISE 8

Where do you think the following were **probably** said?

STEP 1   Match the sentences in (A) with a context from the list below. Write the context in (B).

STEP 2   Underline the phrasal verbs. Rewrite each one, moving the particle **if it is possible to do so**.

STEP 3   In (C), write one more sentence, containing a phrasal verb that you might expect to hear in each context.

CONTEXTS:

In a library	At home	In an office	At school	At a concert
On the telephone	In a clothing store	On a bus	At a party	

A: Sentence and rewrite	B: Context	C: Another sentence same context
Please <u>hand in</u> your homework. (*Also possible:* <u>Hand</u> your homework in.)	At school	Let's <u>go over</u> last week's quiz. (*Cannot separate verb and particle.*)
1) Can I try this on in a larger size?		
2) We'd better sit down. I think they're about to begin playing.		
3) Sorry, but you can't check these out without a current ID.		
4) Turn it up!!!		
5) I want to get off at the next stop.		
6) All international lines are busy. Please hang up and try again later.		
7) Turn on the TV! I don't want to miss the news.		
8) Can we set up a meeting with the board of directors for sometime later in the month?		

FOCUS **6**

▶ **W**hen and When Not to Separate Phrasal Verbs

EXAMPLES	EXPLANATIONS
(a) Last week Sharifah organized her closet and **threw out** all her old clothes. OR **(b)** Last week Sharifah organized her closet and **threw** all her old clothes **out**.	You can separate the verb and the particle when the object consists of just a few words.
(c) Last week Sharifah organized her closet and **threw out** all the clothes that were several years old. **(d)** **NOT:** Last week Sharifah organized her closet and **threw** all the clothes that were several years old **out**.	Do not separate the verb and particle when the object is longer than three or four words.

EXERCISE 9

Are the underlined phrasal verbs correct in the following sentences? In sentences where the verb and the particle are incorrectly placed, circle the particle and draw an arrow to show its correct position.

▶ **EXAMPLE:** I have a meeting at 4:00 tomorrow, but I'm trying to *put* ⌐*off* ⟨it⟩ until the next day.

Put it off.   Correct

1. Cherie always <u>shows up</u> for work on time. She has to <u>get on</u> the bus at 7:00 a.m., but yesterday she overslept and didn't <u>get up</u> until 8:00. She was late for work!

2. Last month, Sunny went through her file cabinets and <u>threw</u> all the papers she had been keeping since her time in graduate school <u>out</u>.

3. When Nina <u>ran</u> Tim <u>into</u>, he <u>pointed out</u> that they had not been in touch for over a year. They promised to <u>call</u> each other <u>up</u> more often in the future.

4. When Sandra called, Graham was out. He tried to <u>call back</u> her, but he couldn't get through because the line was busy.

5. Eli's mother <u>passed</u> last year <u>away.</u> Since she died, he has <u>put</u> the decision about what to do with her house in Brooklyn <u>off</u> .

6. When Sally and the other children arrived at camp, the camp counselor <u>went</u> the rules <u>over</u> . The girls had to <u>clean up</u> after breakfast, and the boys had to <u>clean up</u> after lunch.

EXERCISE 10

Go over the sentences you wrote in Exercise 5 on pages 334 and 335. Underline the phrasal verbs you used and separate the particles where you think it is possible.

▶ Phrasal Verbs that Do Not Take Objects

EXAMPLES	EXPLANATION
(a) My roommate's gone on vacation and I have no idea when he's going to **come back**. **(b)** Cyril waited for his friends for over an hour but they didn't **show up**.	Some phrasal verbs do not take objects. Because they do not take objects, they are inseparable.

Some common phrasal verbs that do not take objects

PHRASAL VERB	EXAMPLE	MEANING*
Break down	My car **broke down**, so I walked.	Stop working (machine, engine etc.)
Catch on	Some fashions **catch on** right away.	Become popular
Come back	Goodbye, please **come back** soon.	Return
Come to	When I **came to,** I was in the hospital.	Regain consciousness
Eat out	Darlene is too busy to cook, so she usually **eats out**.	Eat in a restaurant
Get by	He doesn't earn much, but he seems to **get by**.	Survive satisfactorily, with limited money
Grow up	His mother **grew up** in Vancouver.	Become an adult
Pass out	When Pat broke her leg in a skiing accident, she **passed out**.	Faint, lose consciousness
Show up	It isn't a good idea to **show up** late for a job interview.	Arrive, appear at a place

Some of these phrasal verbs may have different meanings in different situations.

EXERCISE 11

Use phrasal verbs to complete the letter from Nancy to her housemate, Mary.

Replace the underlined words with phrasal verbs from the list below. You may need to change the form of the phrasal verb.

If the phrasal verb can or must be separated, put the particle in the appropriate position. (See the example.) You will need to use some of the phrasal verbs more than once; you may not need to use some of them at all.

run into	talk over	turn down	show up
come over	find out	pick up	get off
hang up	come back	grow up	put on
catch on	pass out	eat out	put off

Mary and Nancy have recently moved to a new city and have just bought a house together. Mary is currently overseas on a business trip, so Nancy has written her a letter, telling her all the news.

Dear Mary,

I miss you! Being alone in this new house is a good experience for me, but at the end of the day I wish you were here to (1) <u>discuss</u> talk over things with me. I've been very busy painting the kitchen—you won't recognize the place when you (2) <u>return</u> _____ ! However, at the moment it's a terrible mess and there's no way I can cook here yet, so I (3) <u>eat in restaurants</u> _____ every night. You'll be glad to know that there are several excellent Thai restaurants in our neighborhood. It's amazing how Thai food has (4) <u>become popular</u> _____ everywhere in the last few years, isn't it?

Guess what? The other day I (5) <u>met unexpectedly</u> _____ Ruth and Maureen. What a surprise! They 6) <u>were leaving/departing</u> _____ the bus at the bus stop right by our house. It turns out they were on their way to visit Ruth's grandmother, who lives just around the corner. Ruth's son, Sam, was with them. Actually it was a bit embarrassing because I didn't recognize him at first; you really won't believe how much he (7) <u>has matured/become an adult</u> _____ since we last saw him.

I (8) <u>am discovering</u> _____ lots of new things about our neighborhood . . . and our neighbors! We'll have to (9) <u>lower</u>

_____ the volume on our CD player by 7:30 each night. The neighbors in the green house (10) <u>arrived here/at this place</u> _____, to complain about the noise the other day. They have a three-month-old baby, so they need it to be quiet so the baby can sleep. We (11) <u>discussed</u> _____ it in a very "neighborly" way. I told them, though, that you're a night owl, and that night time is the time you like to listen to music. Loud! We decided you'll have to start (12) <u>wearing</u> _____ headphones!

There's a lot more I could say. I can't wait for you to (13) <u>return</u> _____ This time I promise (14) <u>I'll arrive</u> _____ on time at the airport. See you soon. . . .

Love,

Nancy

EXERCISE 12

STEP 1 Work with a classmate or a small group. Can you fill in the missing words in this word puzzle to create phrasal verbs? Sometimes the missing word is a particle that can combine with all the attached verbs to make different phrasal verbs; other times, the missing word is a verb that can combine with all the attached particles to make different phrasal verbs. (A good English/English dictionary may help you.)

STEP 2 Use each phrasal verb in a sentence, showing that you understand its meaning. State whether the phrasal verb is separable or inseparable.

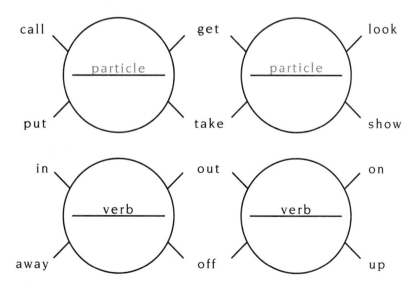

Use Your English

You can either play this game with a classmate or in teams. You need a die/dice to play.

STEP 1 Player (or team) 1 throws the die/dice and selects the verb from circle A that corresponds to the number thrown. For example, if she throws 3, then the verb is *turn*.

STEP 2 Player (or team) 2 throws the die/dice again and selects the particle from circle B that corresponds to the number thrown. For example, if she throws 1, the particle is *off*.

STEP 3 The first player (or team) to come up with a sentence containing the verb + particle, scores a point. For example, the player who comes up with a sentence using *turn off* correctly scores the point. If the combination of verb + particle does not create a meaningful phrasal verb, the first player to say "Impossible" scores the point.

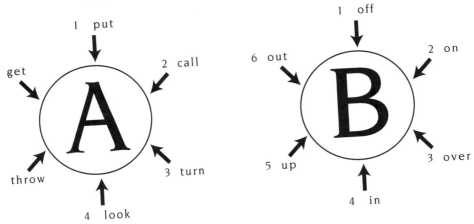

Variation: After you have played this game a few times, get together with some classmates to make your own version. Choose six verbs and six particles. Draw two circles and write the verbs and particles in each circle. Try your game out on your classmates.

If you are playing in a team, you could copy the two circles onto a big piece of paper and stick it on the wall so that everyone can see.

ACTIVITY 2: SPEAKING/LISTENING

STEP 1 Interview three different native speakers of English. Ask them to describe their typical routine every morning, from the moment they wake up until they leave the house to go to work or school. Tape-record their responses.

STEP 2 Listen to what they say. What differences and what similarities do you find? Write down any phrasal verbs that they use. Bring your tape to class and share your findings with your classmates and your teacher.

ACTIVITY 3: LISTENING

Listen to the tape of native speakers of English describing their early morning routines. What differences and similarities do you find among the speakers? Make a list of the phrasal verbs that the speakers used. Compare your list with a classmate's.

ACTIVITY 4: WRITING/READING

STEP 1 Choose one of the contexts below. What phrasal verbs do you associate with these contexts? Think of as many phrasal verbs as you can for each context and write them in the space around each one.

STEP 2 Exchange books with a classmate. Choose **one** of the contexts and write a dialogue. Include many of the phrasal verbs she or he has written down.

STEP 3 Exchange your paper with a different classmate. Read the dialogue. Can you guess the context she or he has chosen?

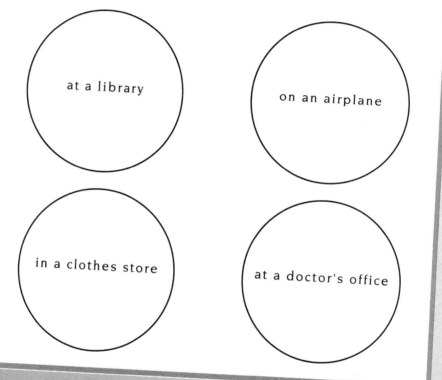

at a library

on an airplane

in a clothes store

at a doctor's office

ACTIVITY 5: LISTENING

Your teacher is going to give you a set of instructions. Listen to each instruction; if the instruction contains a phrasal verb, do what your teacher tells you to do. If the instruction does **not** contain a phrasal verb, do nothing. For example, if your teacher says "Stand up," you stand up because *stand up* is a phrasal verb. If your teacher says "Turn to your right," you do nothing at all because *turn* is not a phrasal verb. VARIATION: Anyone who follows a command that does not contain a phrasal verb drops out of the game. The last person to remain in the game is the "winner." After a while, give your teacher a rest and take turns giving the commands to the rest of the class.

ACTIVITY 6: WRITING/READING

The purpose of this activity is to write a set of instructions for somebody who doesn't know how to make a peanut butter and jelly sandwich. First, look at the bag of supplies that your teacher has brought to class. Then, work with your group to write your instructions, trying to use as many phrasal verbs as possible. When you are ready, read the instructions to your teacher, one step at a time, and he or she will try to follow your instructions exactly as you give them.

ACTIVITY 7: WRITING

With a group (or by yourself, if you prefer), think about everything you have done in the last week. Write a letter to your teacher, telling him or her about your week, **trying to use as many phrasal verbs as possible.** Before you hand your letter in, look it over carefully to find out how many phrasal verbs you were able to use. Write the number of phrasal verbs you used at the end of the letter.

A D J E C T I V E   C L A U S E S
A N D   P A R T I C I P L E S
A S   A D J E C T I V E S

UNIT GOALS:

- To form correct adjective clauses with *who* and *that* to describe people
- To use adjective clauses with *which* and *that* to describe things
- To understand how to use participles as adjectives
- To know the difference between *-ed* and *-ing* participles

► O P E N I N G   T A S K
Who Do They Love?

Lee, Tracy, Sid, and Kit are in love. Can you find who belongs together? Get together with a partner to read the clues, complete the chart, and solve the puzzle.

CLUES:

1. Lee loves the person who speaks Swahili.
2. Tracy loves the person who tells amusing stories.
3. The teacher loves the writer.
4. The pilot loves the person who is interested in history.
5. Sid loves the person that plays the piano.
6. The person who tells amusing stories is a pilot.
7. The person that runs three miles a day is a doctor.
8. The person who plays the piano is a teacher.
9. The person who is interested in history is a doctor.
10. The doctor loves the person who tells amusing stories.
11. The person who speaks Swahili is a writer.
12. The pilot loves the person who runs three miles a day.

Information about Lee:	Information about Tracy:
• _____	• _____
• _____	• _____
LEE *loves . . .*	**TRACY** *loves . . .*
• _____	• _____
• _____	• _____
Name:_____	Name:_____
Information about Kit:	Information about Sid:
• _____	• _____
• _____	• _____
KIT *loves . . .*	**SID** *loves . . .*
• _____	• _____
• _____	• _____
Name:_____	Name:_____

(The solution is on page A-18.)

Adjective Clauses: Using Who and That to Describe People

EXAMPLES	EXPLANATIONS
(a) The person **who speaks Swahili** is a writer. **(b)** The pilot loves the person **who runs three miles a day.**	Adjective clauses (also known as relative clauses) give information about a noun. They always follow the nouns they describe.
(c) The person **who** plays the piano is a teacher. OR **(d)** The person **that** plays the piano is a teacher.	Adjective clauses begin with a relative pronoun. To refer to people, you can use the relative pronouns *who* or *that*. *That* is more commonly used in informal conversation than in writing.
(e) Sid loves the person who **plays** the piano. OR **(f)** Sid loves the person that **plays** the piano.	Every adjective clause contains a verb.
subject **(g)** **The person** who tells amusing stories is a pilot. *object* **(h)** Lee loves **the person** who speaks Swahili.	An adjective clause can describe the subject or object of the main clause.

EXERCISE 1

Go back to the clues in the Opening Task on page 349.

  (a) Underline every adjective clause you find.

  (b) Circle every relative pronoun.

  (c) Draw a line to connect the relative pronoun with the noun it describes.

  (d) Write "S" if the adjective clause describes the subject of a sentence. Write "O" if it describes the object.

▶ **EXAMPLE:**   The pilot loves the person who runs three miles a day.

EXERCISE 2

Get together with a partner and look over the information in the chart below. The owners of the houses on this block of Upham Street are all women.

House	Habits	Likes	Dislikes	Place of birth	Occupation
1	swims three times a week	dogs	TV	Manchester	lawyer
2	eats out every night	fast cars	baseball	Madrid	marketing manager
3	lifts weights	music	politics	Miami	marketing manager
4	drinks five cups of coffee a day	cats	ballet	Mexico City	lawyer
5	sings in the shower	art	baseball	Montreal	marketing manager
6	walks to work	movies	basketball	Moscow	lawyer

Use the information in the chart to make as many true statements as you can about the owners of these houses, using adjective clauses. We have started the first ones for you.

1. The woman who <u>likes dogs</u> _____ lives next to the woman who _____ .

2. The lawyer that <u>dislikes ballet</u> _____ lives between the marketing manager who _____ and the marketing manager who _____ .

3. The marketing manager who _____ lives between the lawyer that _____ and the marketing manager who _____ .

4. The woman _____

_____

5. The lawyer _____

_____

6. The marketing manager _____

_____

7. _____

_____

8. _____

_____

9. _____

_____

10. _____

_____

Look back at the sentences you have written. Underline the adjective clauses, circle the relative pronouns, and draw arrows to the appropriate nouns (as you did in Exercise 1).

FOCUS **2**

▶ *Which* and *That*

EXAMPLES	EXPLANATIONS
(a) I bought a book **which** I really wanted to read. OR **(b)** I bought a book **that** I really wanted to read. **(c)** The book **which** he wrote is excellent. OR **(d)** The book **that** he wrote is excellent.	To refer to things in adjective clauses, you can use *which* or *that*. *That* is more common in informal conversation than in writing.

EXERCISE 3

Do this exercise with a group of five or six classmates. Make a chart like the one in Exercise 2, only instead of the "house" category, use "student." Decide on who will be Student #1, then use your positions in the group seating arrangement to finish writing your names in the chart.

Student	Habits	Likes	Dislikes	Place of Birth	Occupation or Desired Occupation
1					
2					
3					
4					
5					
6					

STEP 1 Interview each other to fill in the blanks on the chart. Ask each other questions using adjective clauses whenever possible. For example: *What does the student who comes from Beijing like to do?* Feel free to make up your answers, just for fun.

STEP 2 When you have filled in your charts, report to the class. Using adjective clauses in your statements, tell each other what you have found about your classmates.

EXERCISE 4

STEP 1 Complete the following to make true statements about yourself. Try to describe both people and things in your statements. Circle the appropriate relative pronouns. (More than one relative pronoun may be possible.)

which

1. I am bored by people that _____ .

who

which

2. I am interested in _____ that _____ .

who

which

3. I am frightened of _____ that _____ .

who

which

4. _____ that _____ are really annoying.

who

which

5. _____ that _____ is/are often interesting.

who

STEP 2 Get together with a partner and compare your statements. Be ready to share the most interesting or surprising statements with the rest of the class.

EXERCISE 5

Edit the following story. Use relative pronouns whenever possible to avoid repeating words, as in the example. After you have finished editing the passage, compare your suggestions for changes with a classmate's. (There is sometimes more than one way to make improvements and avoid repetition.)

1. It's interesting talking with women. ~~These women~~ *who* have had experiences. ~~Their~~ ~~experiences~~ *which* are similar to mine. There are a lot of things to talk about.

2. For example, *balance* is a topic. Most of my women friends are interested in this topic.

3. Achieving balance is a challenge for many women. Many women have jobs and family responsibilities.

4. Some women don't have jobs outside their homes. These women sometimes feel criticized. They feel criticized by other people.

5. These people think that women should have careers. This is an attitude. More and more people share this attitude.

6. Some women work at jobs and have young children. These women also feel criticized. They feel criticized by other people.

7. Other people think that all women should stay at home with their children. They should never be sent to a day care center. Day care is a business, not a loving home. This is a belief. This belief makes some women feel a lack of balance in their lives.

8. Some women never have children. These women may feel pressure from their own parents. Their own parents worry that their children won't provide them with grandchildren.

9. These are examples. These examples show how it can be difficult for women to feel sure they are doing the right thing for themselves and for their children.

FOCUS **3**

▶ Participles as Adjectives

EXAMPLES	EXPLANATIONS
(a) People who have traveled to many different countries are often very **interesting.** (b) We were very **amused** by the jokes that Bruce told us.	*Interesting* and *amused* are participles formed by adding *-ing/-ed* to a verb. These participles act like adjectives when they modify nouns.
(c) Professor Rand is very knowledgeable, but his lectures are **boring.** (d) Many students were **bored** during Professor Rand's lecture.	Adjectives that end with *-ing* usually describe the source (the thing or person that makes us feel a certain way). Adjectives that end with *-ed* usually describe the emotion (how we feel about something).

(Source/Boring)   (Emotion/Bored)

EXERCISE 6

STEP 1 In the pictures below, draw arrows that start at the source (the reason for the feeling) and that point to the emotion (the way the person feels).

STEP 2 Then use the word (on the right) to label the pictures with *-ing* adjectives (which describe the source) and *-ed* adjectives (which describe the emotion). The first one has been done for you.

excite

excited   exciting

embarrass

disgust

surprise

shock

confuse

stimulate

interest

amuse

inspire

EXERCISE 7

Choose the correct adjective for each of the following sentences.

1. Melanie likes the family in the apartment above her, but sometimes she feels that their teenage boy is annoying/annoyed, especially when he plays his stereo too loudly.

2. However, she usually finds their presence upstairs very comforting/comforted.

3. Once she heard a frightening/frightened noise outside. She thought it was a prowler, so she called up her neighbors.

4. They invited her to their apartment for a relaxing/relaxed cup of tea and a soothing/soothed conversation.

5. This helped her to calm down until she was no longer frightening/frightened.

6. Melanie especially likes Jane, the mother. Jane tells Melanie amusing/amused stories about herself and her family members' daily life.

7. Jane's husband Bob is a shoe salesperson. Even though this may sound like a boring/bored job, it's not.

8. Lots of surprising/surprised things happen to shoe salespeople. Just last week, for example, a real prince came into the store with his bodyguards and bought twenty pairs of Italian leather shoes.

9. The prince thought Bob was such a polite and amusing/amused person that he gave him a fifty-dollar tip.

10. Of course, Bob thought that this was very exciting/excited, and he took Jane and the family out to dinner that night.

11. Jane works part-time in a pet store as a dog groomer. She says that some of the customers never give their dogs baths. These dogs are sometimes so dirty and uncomfortable that it is shocking/shocked.

12. Jane's stories are so entertaining/entertained that Melanie usually doesn't mind the noise that Jane's teenage son makes.

13. In fact, Melanie was very disappointing/disappointed when she heard that Jane and her family might move.

EXERCISE 8

Circle all the *-ed* and *-ing* adjectives in the following passage. Then decide whether the correct form has been used. In other words, are there cases where the *-ing* adjective is used when the *-ed* adjective should be used (or vice versa)?

SHELLEY'S ANCESTORS

Shelley had an interested day yesterday. Three of her favorite cousins dropped in for an unexpected visit, and they had a very stimulating conversation. They told each other surprised stories about some of their relatives. Shelley was shocked by some of these stories. For example, when their great aunt—their grandmother's sister—was quite young, she traveled around the world, fell in love with a Dutch sailor, and had a baby but did not get married. Her embarrassing parents disowned her, but many years later they helped her raise the child. Another distant member of the family was a drug addict in New York in the thirties, and according to Shelley's cousins' mother, he was quite a rude and disgusting fellow. This man's brother was a horse of a different color, though. Apparently he was an inspired and talented artist, who also created amused illustrations for children's books. After hearing all of these stories, Shelley realized that her family history was certainly not bored!

Use Your English

CAN YOU TOP THAT?

STEP 1 Look at the list of adjectives below and choose one that describes an experience you have had (for example, an embarrassing moment, a boring day, an exciting date). Try to remember how you felt as a result.

embarrassing	disgusting	frightening	boring
horrifying	rewarding	exciting	entertaining
disappointing	surprising	relaxing	shocking
annoying	amusing	exhausting	inspring

STEP 2 Circulate for fifteen minutes and exchange experiences with classmates to find out if they have had an experience that "tops" yours—that is, an experience that is even more embarrassing, more boring, or more exciting than yours.

STEP 3 Report to the rest of the class on what you found. Vote on who has had the most embarrassing, boring, exciting (etc.) experience.

STEP 4 Choose two of the experiences that your classmates told you about and describe them in writing.

STEP 5 When you finish writing, read your work and circle any participles used as adjectives. Underline any adjective clauses that you used.

ACTIVITY 2: WRITING/READING

STEP 1 Think of a person that everyone in your class knows (someone famous **or** someone in your class!). Or think of a thing or object that is familiar to everyone. Write three statements using adjective clauses that describe this person or thing.

For example,
I'm thinking of something that I drink every day.
It's something that is more expensive now than it used to be.
It's something that helps me feel more awake.
(Answer: coffee)

STEP 2 Read your statements one at a time and have others guess what or who you are describing. Work in pairs or in teams if you prefer.

ACTIVITY 3: SPEAKING

Think of someone that you know. Choose someone who is quite a character. In other words, think of someone who stands out in some way or is easy to remember. Describe this person, using some adjectives clauses and some *-ed* or *-ing* adjectives to describe him or her.

ACTIVITY 4: LISTENING

STEP 1 Make a list of all the characteristics you would like to find in the ideal partner (spouse, girlfriend, boyfriend, companion).

STEP 2 Listen to the tape. You will hear three friends talking about their ideal partners. Take notes on the chart below.

PAT	LEE	CHRIS

STEP 3 Look at the list you made in Step 1 and compare it with the notes you made from the tape. How many differences and similarities can you find?

STEP 4 Listen to the tape again. Write down any examples of adjective clauses and participle adjectives that you hear.

ACTIVITY 5: LISTENING/SPEAKING

STEP 1 First think of as many *-ing* adjectives as possible. Your teacher will write each of these on a separate sheet of paper. As your game goes on, your group may add more to the list as needed.

STEP 2 You will use these words to play Password in teams or in pairs. In this game, one person (or team), the Clue-Giver, looks at the word on the piece of paper without letting the other person (or the other team) see it.

STEP 3 Then the Clue-Giver gives a one-word clue that describes this word to the other person (or the other team), the Clue-Guesser.

STEP 4 The Clue-Giver can continue to give as many clues as needed in order for the word to be guessed. The goal is to have the Clue-Guesser guess the word as soon as possible with as few clues as necessary.

ACTIVITY 6: SPEAKING

Think of as many *-ed* adjectives as possible. Then "mime" (act out) these words and phrases, which are written on separate sheets of paper. You can use gestures and facial expressions, or you can invent a silent story, but you cannot speak. The goal is to have the other person (or the other team) guess the word or phrase as quickly as possible.

UNIT 25

CONDITIONALS

UNIT GOALS:

- To know when to use hypothetical conditionals
- To form correct conditional sentences for present, past, and future situations
- To know the difference between future conditionals and hypothetical conditionals
- To understand the meaning of *would*, *might*, and *may* in conditionals

▶ OPENING TASK
Desert Island

Imagine you are on a desert island. You have nothing with you except these objects.

STEP 1 Get together with a partner and look at each object very carefully. What would you do with them on your desert island?

If we were on a desert island, we would use this [image: pocket knife] to

_____. We would _____ with this [image: sock] .

If we had this with us on the island, [image: fish hook] , we would use it to

_____. With this, [image: ball of yarn] , we

_____. And finally, we _____

with this [image: box of plastic bags] .

STEP 2 Share your ideas with the rest of the class. Vote on the most interesting and creative use for each object.

▶ **Hypothetical Conditionals**

EXAMPLES	EXPLANATIONS
(a) **Ty**: Have you ever thought about what **you would do if you were on a desert island by yourself?** (b) **Ann**: Yeah! **I would go** crazy. **Shin**: Really? **I'd try** and survive. **I'd look** for food and water, and then **I'd build** a shelter. **Kat**: Me too. **I'd try** to be very positive about the whole situation. **Tom**: Yeah? **I'd escape** as soon as possible. **Ray**: Not me. **I'd lie** in the sun and relax.	Use hypothetical conditionals to talk about an imaginary situation. This is not a real situation, but you are picturing it in your mind. To express these: use *were* for verbs with *be* and the simple past for other verbs in the *if* clause. Use would + base form of the verb in the main clause. Use an *if* clause to introduce the topic. After that, it is not necessary to repeat the *if* clause in every sentence. It sounds very unnatural to keep repeating the *if* clause. *Would* + base form of the verb shows that you are talking about a hypothetical situation that has already been introduced.

EXERCISE 1

STEP 1 Look back at the sentences that you wrote in the Opening Task. Check to see if you used *if* clauses and *would* correctly. If not, rewrite the sentences and check them with your teacher.

STEP 2 If you were on that desert island and you could choose three things (*any* three things—not just the ones in the picture) to bring with you, what three things would you choose and why?

_____

_____

_____

Share your ideas with a partner and then with the rest of the class.

EXERCISE 2

Get together with a partner and look at the pictures. What would you do if you were in these situations? Which situation would you prefer to be in and why? Share your ideas with the rest of the class.

EXERCISE 3

STEP 1 Choose one of your classmates to be the "leader" for this exercise.

STEP 2 The leader will finish this sentence:

If I were a millionaire, ...

For example: *If I were a millionaire, I would buy a big house in the country and retire.*

   (IF clause)   (Main clause)

STEP 3 The next person will change the main clause into an *if* clause and add a new main clause. For example: *If I bought a big house in the country and retired, I would write poetry all day long.*

STEP 4 Go around the room so that everyone has a chance to add to the "chain" of events.

▶ **Word Order in Conditionals**

EXAMPLES	EXPLANATIONS
(a) If we were on a desert island, we would use string to make a fishing line. OR We would use string to make a fishing line if we were on a desert island.	Differences in word order do not change the meaning.
(b) If we knew how to build a boat, we would escape. OR We would escape if we knew how to build a boat.	Use a comma after the *if* clause when it comes first.

EXERCISE 4

Read the following:

Ilene hates parties, so just over ten years ago, she was surprised to receive an invitation to a New Year's party from somebody that she didn't know very well. She didn't really want to go by herself, so she asked her friend Diana to go with her. Before the party, Ilene and Diana had a nice dinner together at Diana's house. It was a cold, snowy night and when it was time to leave for the party, all Ilene wanted to do was stay home and watch a video. Diana persuaded her to change her mind, however, and after they had driven all the way across town, Ilene realized that she had left the party invitation at home. Diana wanted to go back and get it, but Ilene thought she could remember the address. They found the right street, but Ilene wasn't sure about the number of the house, so they drove around until they came to a house where there was a party going on. They decided this was the right place. They didn't recognize anybody there and Ilene wanted to leave right away. However, Diana, who wasn't as shy as Ilene, persuaded her to stay. Feeling very uncomfortable, Ilene stood in a corner by herself, watching Diana have a good time. After about an hour, she decided to go home. As she was leaving, she tripped and fell down some icy steps outside the house. Luckily just at that moment, somebody was coming up the steps on his way to the party and he caught her in his arms. And that's how Ilene met her husband . . .

Ilene and Jeff have now been together for ten years, and they are still amazed at the way they met. For a start, Ilene had gone to the wrong party. The one she had been invited to was a couple of blocks away. And then it turned out that Jeff hadn't been invited to that party either. In fact, he was only in town because his sister was very sick and he had flown in from out of state to visit her. His sister lived next door, and when he ran into Ilene, he was on his way to ask the neighbors if they could turn the music down. Jeff, who is an anthropologist, was supposed to leave the next day to spend two years in West Africa, but that night, there was a terrible snowstorm and the airport was closed for three days. It was during those three days that Jeff and Ilene first got to know each other. But that's not all; when Jeff got to West Africa, there was a great deal of political unrest in the region where he was working. After two months, he was forced to abandon his research project. The first thing he did when he got back to the United States was call Ilene.

Now, every New Year's Eve, Jeff and Ilene laugh about how they almost never met. "What if. . . . ?" Jeff always asks. "Don't even think about it," Ilene always replies.

Get together with a partner and think about how Jeff and Ilene met (and how they almost didn't meet). How many statements containing hypothetical conditionals can you make about their story? For example: *If Ilene hadn't received a party invitation, she wouldn't have gone out on New Year's Eve. If Jeff had been gay, he wouldn't have been so interested in Ilene.*

Share your statements with the rest of the class. Who was able to make the most?

FOCUS **3**

▶ **Past Hypothetical Conditionals**

EXAMPLES	EXPLANATIONS
past perfect **(a)** **If you had called** me last night, I *would + have +* past participle **would have come** to see you. **(b)** If we **had known** it was Marianne's birthday, **we would have had** a surprise party for her. **(c)** If Bonnie **hadn't robbed** a bank, she **wouldn't have gone** to jail.	Past hypothetical conditionals talk about imagined situations in the past. It is not possible for these situations to happen because they refer to the past. To express these situations, use past perfect in the *if* clause and *would + have +* past participle in the main clause. We know that it is impossible to change the past, but we often think about how things might have been different in the past. In (a), I *didn't* come to see you because you *didn't* call me. In (c), Bonnie *did* go to jail because she *did* rob a bank.

EXAMPLES	EXPLANATIONS
past perfect **(d)** If John Kennedy **had lived,** he *would + base verb* **would be** an old man now. **(e)** If Pia **had been born** in Egypt, she **would speak** fluent Arabic by now. *past perfect* **(f)** If we **had won** last week's lottery, we *would + be + verb + -ing* **would be lying** on a beach in the South of France today.	Some hypothetical conditionals make a connection between the past and the present. They show an imagined change in a present situation, caused by an imagined change in a past situation. These are untrue situations because it is impossible to change the past. You usually use past perfect in the *if* clause and *would* + base form of the verb or *would + be* + verb + *-ing* in the main clause.

EXERCISE 5

How would **your** life be different now if things had been different in the past? Think of a topic and then make a list of as many differences as possible related to that topic. For example: TOPIC: *If I had been born in the United States, I wouldn't be studying English now. I would have gone to school in the United States so I would speak English perfectly, but I probably wouldn't be able to speak any other languages. . . .*

Some other ideas for topics: *If I had been born male/female, . . . If I had never gone to school, . . . If my parents had never met, ...*

When you have made your list, get together with another student and tell him or her about your topic and how your life would be different now. Then tell the rest of the class about your partner's topic and how his or her life would be different now.

EXERCISE 6

For each situation, complete the following hypothetical conditionals, using the given verb in your answers.

Situation A

▶ **EXAMPLE:** **1.** Eloise's husband has always been a thin man in good physical condition. If he suddenly _____ (become) fat, Eloise _____ (be) shocked.

This is a hypothetical situation which will probably **not** happen because Eloise's husband has always been a thin man.

Answer: Eloise's husband has always been a thin man in good physical condition. If he suddenly ___*became*___ (become) fat, Eloise ___*would be*___ (be) shocked.

2. Eloise started seeing a doctor about her cholesterol problem three years ago. If she _____ (knew) about her problem earlier, she _____ (change) her diet years earlier.

Situation B

3. Ali's doctor says that one of the reasons Ali has high blood pressure is that he never expresses his anger. His doctor says that it is not healthy to "bottle it up." He says that if Ali _____ (get) angry once in a while, his blood pressure _____ (not + be) so high.

4. Ali never gets angry with his family. His children _____ (run away) from him if he ever _____ (yell) at them.

Situation C

5. Dan, who doesn't earn very high wages, has been shopping at discount stores for years. Even if he _____ (have) a lot of money to shop with, he _____ (buy) from discount stores.

6. When Dan graduated from college, his father gave him a used truck. Together they worked on the truck until it was in excellent condition. If Dan _____ (not + learn) how to repair trucks, he _____ (be) more enthusiastic about new trucks.

Situation D

    7. People who live in this area have forgotten how to conserve water. If it
_____ (not + rain) so much last year, people _____
(remember) water conservation practices.

    8. People _____ (be able) to water their lawns every day if it
_____ (rain) more this summer. However, the forecast is
that this area is going to experience a drought this summer.

EXERCISE 7

STEP 1 On one sheet of paper, write the following words and complete the
hypothetical *if* clause.

    If I were _____ .

Now, on another sheet of paper complete the main clauses.

    I would _____ .

STEP 2 Your teacher will collect and scramble your *if* clauses and your main
clauses, and then you will take one of each. Read your sentence aloud
to the rest of the class. Does it make sense?

STEP 3 After hearing everyone read their sentences, find the person who has
the main clause that matches the *if* clause you have now.

STEP 4 Now find the person who has the *if* clause that matches your main
clause.

▶ Future Conditionals

EXAMPLES	EXPLANATIONS

simple present
               │   *will/be going to* + base verb
    │   │
(a) If you **study** hard, you **will get** a good grade.
(b) If it **rains** tomorrow, I'm **going to bring** my umbrella.
(c) Steve **will give** you a ride if you **ask** him.
	Future conditionals make predictions about what will happen in the future. You usually use simple present in the *if* clause and *will be* or *be going to* + base form of the verb in the main clause.

EXERCISE 8

Most countries have superstitions. Here's a common North American superstition: If a black cat crosses your path, you will have bad luck.

Match A and B below to create some other common North American superstitions. Check your answers with other students and with your teacher.

<table>
<tr><th>A</th><th>B</th></tr>
<tr><td>

1. If you break a mirror,

2. If you find a four-leaf clover,

3. You will have bad luck

4. You will prevent something bad from happening

5. If you open an umbrella indoors,

6. A rabbit's paw will bring good luck

7. If you catch the bride's bouquet at a wedding.

</td><td>

(a) if you knock on wood.

(b) you will bring bad luck to all the people in the house.

(c) you will have seven years of bad luck.

(d) if you carry one in your pocket.

(e) you will be the next person to get married.

(f) if you walk under a ladder.

(g) you will be vey lucky.

</td></tr>
</table>

Do you have any of these superstitions in your country? Do any of these superstitions have a different meaning in your country? (For example, in Great Britain, if a black cat crosses your path, you will have **good** luck.) Think of some common superstitions from your country and tell them to the rest of your class. How many people in your class believe in these superstitions?

EXERCISE 9

Go around the room and ask the other students the following questions. Change partners after every question. Write the answers you receive in the chart below.

When your chart is complete, compare your answers with your classmates'. In your opinion, what was the most interesting or surprising answer to each question? Write it in the chart.

▶ **EXAMPLE:** *Question:* What will you do if you get an A in this class?

Answer: I'll hug my teacher and say, "Thank you! Thank you!"

WHAT WILL YOU DO . . .

Question	Answer	Most interesting answer
1. . . . . . if you get an A in this class?		
2. . . . . . if your pants rip in tomorrow's class?		
3. . . . . . if I give you $10 right now?		
4. . . . . . if there is a fire drill?		
5. . . . . . if you don't see me tomorrow?		
6. . . . . . if our teacher is sick tomorrow?		
7. . . . . . if it's raining when class is over?		
8. . . . . . if you lose this book?		

▶ Future Conditionals or Hypothetical Conditions?

EXAMPLES	EXPLANATIONS
Future Conditional: **(a)** If Colin Powell **runs** for president of the United States one day, a lot of different people **will support** him.	Future conditionals talk about possible situations and show what you think will happen in those situations.
Hypothetical Conditionals: **(b)** If I **ran** for president, nobody **would vote** for me. **(c)** If Elvis **had run** for president, a lot of his fans **would have voted** for him. **(d)** If Ross Perot **had become** president in 1992, American politics **would be** quite different today.	Hypothetical conditionals talk about improbable situations: situations that probably will not happen (b), or impossible situations (c and d).

EXERCISE 10

Say whether the situations in the *if* clauses are future (possible) or hypothetical (improbable). Compare your answers with a partner's.

1. <u>If it rains</u>, I will not have to water the garden.
2. <u>If it rained</u>, I would be very happy.
3. Marcy would quit her job <u>if she got pregnant</u>.
4. <u>If I won the lottery</u>, I would travel around the world.
5. Aunt Shira will give us a wedding shower <u>if we decide on a wedding date</u>.
6. <u>If Laurel gets hurt again</u>, her father will make her quit the girl's soccer team.
7. <u>If the baby slept through the night without waking up</u>, his parents would finally get a good night's sleep.
8. Jasmine would buy a big house <u>if she were rich</u>.

EXERCISE 11

Work with a partner to complete the following. In each sentence, decide if the situation is possible or hypothetical and write an appropriate form of the verb.

Situation A

▶ **EXAMPLE:** Gao is a doctor, but if he _were_____ (be) a truck driver, he

_would have_____ (have) very different skills. (This situation is

hypothetical because Gao is not a truck driver.)

2. Gao's wife is a doctor, too, but she is planning to change her career. If

she _____ (change) her career, she _____

(study) to become a lawyer.

Situation B

3. Antonieta is Brazilian, but she has lived in the United States and New

Zealand, so she speaks excellent English. If she

(stay) in Brazil, her English _____ (not) (be) so good.

4. However, Antonieta _____ (speak) French too if she

_____ (move) to France next year.

Situation C

5. Mary's car is old. If it _____ (break down), she _____

(buy) a new one.

6. Because Mary has a car, she has driven to school every day this term.

But if she _____ (not) (have) a car, she _____

(take) the bus.

Situation D

7. Marcia has applied to graduate school. She _____ (start)

school next fall if she _____ (get) accepted.

8. When Marcia was twenty-one, she quit school for several years to get

married and raise a family. If she _____ (continue) her

studies instead of raising a family, she _____ (begin)

graduate school a long time ago.

▶ **F**actual Conditionals

EXAMPLES	EXPLANATIONS
simple present *simple present* **(a)** If you **leave** milk in the sun, it **turns** sour. **(b)** I **eat** yogurt and fruit for breakfast if I **have** time.	Factual conditionals talk about what usually happens in certain situations. You really expect these things to happen. Use simple present in the *if* clause and simple present in the main clause.
(c) **When** you leave milk in the sun, it turns sour. **(d)** I eat yogurt and fruit for breakfast **whenever** I have time.	Because you expect these situations to happen, you can use *when* or *whenever* (every time that) instead of *if*. The meaning does not change.

EXERCISE 12

Get together with a partner and complete the following statements to make factual conditionals with *if*, *when*, and *whenever*. Check your answers with your classmates and your teacher.

    1. Cats purr if _____.

    2. Water boils if you _____.

    3. An ice cube melts whenever _____.

    4. Red wine stains when _____.

    5. Rain changes to snow if _____.

    6. If you push the "Power" button on a computer, _____.

    7. Wool shrinks _____.

    8. In the theater, people applaud _____.

▶ *Would, Might, May,*
and *Will* **in Conditionals**

EXAMPLES	EXPLANATIONS
Hypothetical Conditions:	
(a) If I were on that desert island, I **would** definitely try to get away as soon as possible.	Use *would* in the main clause to show the most probable result of the *if* clause.
(b) If I were on that desert island, I **might** try to get away or I **might** wait for someone to rescue me.	Use *might* in the main clause to show other possible results of the *if* clause. When you use *might*, you are less certain of the result.
(c) If Americans got more exercise, they **might** be healthier.	
Past Hypothetical Conditionals:	
(d) If John Lennon hadn't died, the Beatles **might have** reunited. OR If John Lennon hadn't died, the Beatles **may have** reunited.	In past hypothetical conditionals, you can use *might have* + past participle or *may have* + past participle. The meaning does not change.
(e) If we had arrived at the airport ten minutes earlier, we **might have** caught the plane. OR If we had arrived at the airport ten minutes earlier, we **may have** caught the plane.	
Future Conditionals:	
(f) If it rains tomorrow, we **will** stay home.	In future conditionals, use *will* in the main clause to show that you strongly expect this result to happen.
(g) If it rains tomorrow, we **might** stay home or we **might** go to the movies. OR If it rains tomorrow, we **may** stay home or we **may** go to the movies.	Use *might* or *may* in the main clause to show that this result is possible, but you are not so certain that it will happen.

EXERCISE 13

Complete the following conversations with *will, would, may, might, would have, might have*, or *may have*.

Conversation A

Abel: Have you and Ken decided what you're going to do over Labor Day weekend?

Miles: Not really. It all depends on the weather. If it's nice, we
(1) _____ (go) camping, that's for sure. But if it rains, we
(2) _____ (visit) my folks in Oakland or we (3) _____ (stay)
here and catch up on our reading. I'm really not sure yet. I guess we'll just wait
and see.

Conversation B

Mother: Don't drop that glass!

Three-year-old Child: Why not?

Mother: If you drop something made of glass, it (4) _____ (break).

Child: Oh.

Mother: Watch out! Don't turn it upside down.

Child: Why not?

Mother: Because if you do that, it (5) _____ (spill).

Conversation C

Janette: Did you hear about the guy who found an old Lotto ticket in a trash
can?

Dean: Yeah, the guy who won eight million dollars? The guy with four grown
kids and a bunch of grandchildren?

Janette: Yeah. He bought the ticket six months ago and he found it just two
days before it was due to expire.

Dean: If he had found it two days later, he (6) _____ (not) (win)
the eight million dollars.

Janette: Yeah, and his children (7) _____ (not) (be) rich now.

Dean: And his grandchildren (8) _____ (not) (have) college funds.

Janette: And the eight million dollars (9) _____ (go back) into the
next Lotto!

Dean: And *we* (10) _____ (win) it!

Use Your English

STEP 1 Work in groups of four.

STEP 2 Read the following questions. Without showing anyone else your paper, write down what you think you would be and what each person in your group would be in the following situations:

(a) If you were an animal, what would you be?

(b) If you were a color, what would you be?

(c) If you were food, what would you be?

▶ **EXAMPLE:** *If I were an animal, I would be a cat. If Terri were an animal, she would be a deer. I also think that Rachel would be a mouse, and Peter would be a flamingo.*

STEP 3 When you have all finished, share your ideas and compare what **you** think your group members would be with what **they** think they would be.

	(a) Animal	(b) Color	(c) Food
You			
Name:			
Name:			
Name:			

Remember that it is not necessary to repeat the *if* clause in every sentence.

ACTIVITY 2: WRITING

In a paragraph or two, describe the most interesting results about **yourself** from Activity 1. First tell why you described yourself the way you did. Then tell why you think your group members described you the way they did.

For example, if you said "If I were a color, I would be purple," but everyone else said you would be yellow, give us the possible reasons for these opinions.

Remember that it isn't necessary to repeat the *if* clause in every sentence.

ACTIVITY 3: WRITING

Form teams. Together write an imaginary situation or a predicament on a piece of paper. For example, *What would happen if* . . . everyone in the world were ten feet taller? *What would you do if* . . . you found somebody's purse with two hundred dollars in it and no identification? *What would happen if* . . . there were suddenly a huge earthquake?

After you write down one predicament, work together to solve the problem or describe the results. Then your team will tell some of your solutions to the other teams. They will try to guess the situation and tell what the *if* clause is. The team that guesses the situation most often wins.

ACTIVITY 4: LISTENING

You have all heard of the Beatles. Find people who are familiar with the words to their songs and complete the following lyrics:

- If I fell in love with you, would you promise to be true . . . .
- What would you do if I sang out of tune, would you . . . .

Peter, Paul, and Mary were a popular folk-singing group in the sixties. Find people who are familiar with Peter, Paul, and Mary lyrics, and see if they can help you finish this sentence:

- If I had a hammer . . . .

What are the other *if* clauses in this song?

Carousel is a famous Rodgers and Hammerstein musical. Find people who can help you complete the *if* clause in the following song:

- If I loved you . . . .

ACTIVITY 5: LISTENING/SPEAKING

Your school is about to build a new library. The president of the student union wants to celebrate the event by placing a time capsule inside the walls of the new building. (A time capsule is a box containing a number of objects that represent the culture of a community at that point in time. You put into the time capsule objects that you feel reflect the ideas, culture, and values of the community. If people find the time capsule one hundred years from now, they will have an idea of what life was like in the past.)

If the president asked you about what to put in the time capsule, what would you say? Get together with two or three other students and decide on a list of five objects that you would put in the time capsule because you believe they represent American culture now. Share your ideas with the rest of the class and explain why you chose these objects. When you have heard everybody's ideas, vote on the five objects that you, as a class, would put in a time capsule to represent current American culture.

ACTIVITY 6: RESEARCH/LISTENING

The purpose of this activity is to find out what Americans would put in a time capsule like the one in Activity 5.

STEP 1 Interview three different native speakers of English by asking the question: If you had to put three things in a time capsule to reflect American culture right now, what would you choose and why? Tape your interviews.

STEP 2 Lisen to your tape and report your findings to the rest of your class. As a class, make a list of the objects that everyone interviewed would put in the time capsule. What does this tell you about American culture today? Compare this list with the one that your class made in Activity 5. How many differences and similarities are there in these lists? Do your ideas about what represents American culture differ from Americans' ideas?

STEP 3 Listen to your tape again. How many times do the speakers use would/'d? Write down any sentences conaining would/'d. How many times do the speakers use full *if* clauses? Why do you think this is so? Write down any sentences containing *if* clauses. What does this tell you about the use of *if* clauses in real conversations?

ACTIVITY 7: LISTENING

Listen to the tape of three different Americans talking about what they would put in a time capsule.

STEP 1 What would they put in the capsule? List the objects.

STEP 2 Listen to your tape again. How many times do the speakers use *would/'d*? Write down any sentences containing *would/'d*. How many times do the speakers use full *if* clauses? Why do you think this so? Write down any sentences containing *if* clauses. What does this tell you about the use of *if* clauses in real conversations?

ACTIVITY 8: SPEAKING/LISTENING OR WRITING/READING

If you had to put five objects representing **your** culure into a time capsule, what would you choose and why? Make a report (eihter written or oral) on your choices. If you make a written report, read your or another student's work carefully and check to see if you or s/he were able to use any of the language from this unit. If you choose an oral report, tape yourself as you make the report. Listen to your tape and write down any sentences containing language from this unit.

Appendices

Appendix 1A   Simple Present (verb/verb + –s)

Statement	Negative	Question	Short Answers
I You We They } work. He She It } works.	I You We They } do not/ don't work. He She It } does not/ doesn't work.	Do } I you we they } work? Does } he she it } work?	Yes, } I you we they } do. Yes, } he she it } does. No, } I you we they } don't. No, } he she it } doesn't.

Appendix 1B   PRESENT PROGRESSIVE (*am/is/are* + *verb* + *–ing*)

Statement	Negative	Question	Short Answers
I am (I'm) working.	I am not (I'm not) working.	Am I working?	Yes, I am. No, I'm not.
You are (you're) working	You are not (aren't) working.	Are you working?	Yes, you are. No, you aren't. **OR** You're not.
She/He/It is (She's/He's/It's) working.	She/He/It is not (isn't) working.	Is she/he/it working?	Yes, she/he/it is. No, she/he/it isn't. **OR** She's/He's/It's not.
We are (We're) working.	We are not (aren't) working.	Are we working?	Yes, we are. No, we aren't. **OR** We're not.
They are (They're) working.	They are not (aren't) working.	Are they working?	Yes, they are. No, they aren't. **OR** They're not.

Appendix 1C   Simple Past (verb + –ed or irregular form)

Statement	Negative	Question	Short Answers
I You We They He She It } worked.	I You We They He She It } did not/ didn't work.	Did { I you we they he she it } work?	Yes, { I you we they did. he she it } No, { I you we they didn't he she it }

Appendix 1D   Past Progressive (was/were + verb + –ing)

Statement	Negative	Question	Short Answers
I She } was He } sleeping. It	I She } was not He } sleeping. It } (wasn't)	Was { I she he sleeping? it	Yes, { I she } was. he it
We You } were They } sleeping.	We You } were not They } sleeping. (weren't)	Were { we You sleeping? they	No, { we you } weren't. they

Appendix 1E   Present Perfect (*has/have* + verb + past participle)

Statement	Negative	Question	Short Answers
I You We They } have gone. ('ve) She He It } has gone. ('s)	I You We They } have not gone. (haven't) She He It } has not gone. (hasn't)	Have { I you we they } gone? Has { she he it } gone?	Yes, { you we they } have. Yes, { he she it } has. No, { I you we they } haven't. No, { he she it } hasn't.

Appendix 1F   Present Perfect Progressive (*has/have* + *been* + verb + *–ing*)

Statement	Negative	Question	Short Answers
I You We They } have been ('ve) sleeping. She He It } has been ('s) sleeping	I You We They } have not been (haven't) sleeping. She He It } has not been (hasn't) sleeping.	Have { I you we they } been sleeping? Has { she he it } been sleeping?	Yes, { you we they } have been. Yes, { he she it } has been. No, { I you we they } haven't been. No, { he she it } hasn't been.

Appendix 1G Past Perfect (*had + verb + past participle*)

Statement	Negative	Question	Short Answers
I You We They She He It } had ('d) arrived.	I You We They She He It } had not (hadn't) arrived.	Had { I you we they she he it } arrived?	Yes, { I you we they he she it } had. No, { I you we they he she it } hadn't.

Appendix 1H Future: *will* (*will + verb*)

Statement	Negative	Question	Short Answers
I You We They She He It } will leave. ('ll)	I You We They She He It } will not/ (won't) leave.	Will { I you we they she he it } leave?	Yes, { I you we they he she it } will. No, { I you we they he she it } won't.

Statement	Negative	Question	Short Answers
I am going to leave. ('m)	I am not going to leave. ('m)	Am I going to leave?	Yes, I am.
You	You		Yes, you
We } are going ('re) to leave.	We } are not going (aren't) to leave.	Are you we they } going to leave?	Yes, you we they } are.
They	They		
She	She	she	he
He } is going ('s) to leave.	He } is not going (isn't) to leave.	Is he it	Yes, she is. it
It	It		
			No, I am not. ('m not.)
			No, you we they } are not. (aren't)
			No, he she is not. it } (isn't)

Appendix 2A   The *Be* Passive

To form the passive, use the appropriate tense of *be*, followed by the past participle (pp).

	Tense	Form of *Be*
(a) Wool **is produced** here.	Simple Present	*am/is/are* +pp
(b) Wool **is being produced** here right now.	Present Progressive	*am/is/are being* +pp
(c) Wool **was produced** here.	Simple Past	*was/were* +pp
(d) Wool **was being produced** here ten years ago.	Past Progressive	*was/were being* +pp
(e) Wool **has been produced** here since 1900.	Present Perfect	*have/has been* +pp
(f) Wool **had been produced** here when the island was discovered.	Past Perfect	*had been* +pp
(g) Wool **will be produced** here next year.	Future *(will)*	*will be* +pp
(h) Wool **is going to be produced** here.	Future *(be going to)*	*am/is/are* +pp *going to be*
(i) Wool **will have been produced** here by the year 2010.	Future Perfect	*will have been* +pp

Appendix 2B   The *Get* Passive

	Tense	Form of *Get*
(a) Her cookies always **get eaten.**	Simple Present	*get/gets* +pp
(b) Her cookies **are getting eaten.**	Present Progressive	*am/is/are getting* +pp
(c) Her cookies **got eaten.**	Simple Past	*got* +pp
(d) Her cookies **were getting eaten.**	Past Progressive	*was/were getting* +pp
(e) Her cookies **have gotten eaten.**	Present Perfect	*have/has gotten* +pp
(f) Her cookies **had gotten eaten.**	Past Perfect	*had gotten* +pp
(g) Her cookies **will be eaten.**	Future *(will)*	*will get* +pp
(h) Her cookies **are going to get eaten.**	Future *(be going to)*	*am/is/are* +pp *going to get*
(i) Her cookies **will have gotten eaten** by the time we get home.	Future Perfect	*will have gotten* +pp

Appendix 3A   Factual Conditionals

If Clause [*If* + simple present]	Main Clause [simple present]
If you heat water,	it boils.

Appendix 3B   Future Conditionals

If Clause [*If* + simple present]	Main Clause [*will/be going to* + base verb]
If you study hard,	you will get a good grade.

Appendix 3C   Hypothetical Conditionals

If Clause [*If* + simple past]	Main Clause [*would* (*'d*) + base verb]
(a) If we had lots of money,	we'd travel around the world.
[*If* + B*e* verb → subjunctive *were*]	[*would* + base verb]
(b) If I were rich,	I'd travel around the world.

Appendix 3D   Past Hypothetical Conditionals

If Clause [*If* + past perfect]	Main Clause [*would* + *have* (*'ve*) + *verb* + past participle]
If you had called me,	I would have come to see you.

Appendix 4A   Probability and Possibility (Unit 5)

	Possible (less than 50% certain)	Probable (about 90% certain)	Certain (100% certain)
Present Forms	less certain ⬆ He *could* play golf. He *might* play golf. ⬇ He *may* play golf. more certain	He *must* play golf.	He plays golf.
	less certain ⬆ She *could* be a doctor. She *might* be a doctor. ⬇ She *may* be a doctor. more certain	She *must* be a doctor.	She is a doctor.
Question Forms	less certain ⬆ *Could* he play golf? ⬇ *Might* he play golf? more certain	—	*Does* he play golf?
	less certain ⬆ *Could* she be a doctor? ⬇ *Might* she be a doctor? more certain	—	*Is* she a doctor?
Negative Forms	less certain ⬆ He *might* not play golf. He *may not* play golf. ⬇ He *couldn't* play golf. more certain	He *must not* play golf.	He *does not/doesn't* play golf.
	less certain ⬆ She *might not* be a doctor. She *may not* be a doctor. ⬇ She *couldn't/can't* be a doctor. more certain	She *must not* be a doctor.	She *is not/isn't* a doctor.

	Possible (less than 50% certain)	Probable (about 90% certain)	Certain (100% certain)
less certain ↑ He *could have* played golf. He *might have* played golf. ↓ He *may have* played golf. **more certain**		He *must have* played golf.	He played golf.
less certain ↑ She *could have* been a doctor. She *might have* been a doctor. ↓ She *may have* been a doctor. **more certain**		She *must have* been a doctor.	She *was* a doctor.
less certain ↑ *Could* he *have* played golf? ↓ *Might* he *have* played golf? **more certain**		—	*Did* he play golf?
less certain ↑ *Could* she *have* been a doctor? ↓ *Might* she *have* been a doctor? **more certain**		—	*Was* she a doctor?
less certain ↑ He *could be* playing golf. He *might be* playing golf. ↓ He *may be* playing golf. **more certain**		He *must be* playing golf.	He *is* playing golf.
less certain ↑ He *could have been* playing golf. He *might have been* playing golf. ↓ He *may have been* playing golf. **more certain**		He *must have been* playing golf.	He *was* playing golf./ He *has been* playing golf.

Past Forms (rows 1–4)
Progressive Forms (rows 5–6)

Possible (less than 50% certain)	Probable (about 90% certain)	Certain (100% certain)
less certain It *could* rain tomorrow. It *may (not)* rain tomorrow. It *might (not)* rain tomorrow. **more certain**	It *will probably* rain tomorrow. It *probably won't* rain tomorrow.	It *will/will/not/won't* rain tomorrow.

Future Forms

Appendix 4B   Giving Advice and Expressing Opinions (Unit 10)

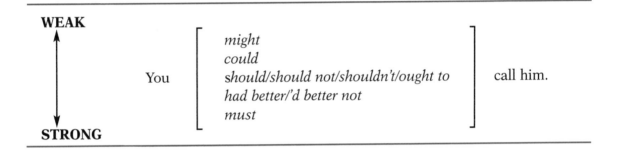

WEAK

You [*might* / *could* / *should/should not/shouldn't/ought to* / *had better/'d better not* / *must*] call him.

STRONG

Appendix 4C   Necessity and Obligation (Unit 11)

Present	Past	Future
Necessary and Obligatory		
She *must* go.	—	She *must* go.
She's/*has got to* go.	—	She's/*has got to* go.
She *has to* go.	She *had to* go.	She *has to* go./
		She'll/*will have to* go.
Not Necessary and not Obligatory		
She *doesn't/does not have to* go.	She *didn't/did not have to* go.	She *doesn't/does not have to* go.
		She *won't/will not have to* go.

Appendix 4D   Prohibition and Permission (Unit 11)

Present	Past	Future
Prohibited and not Permitted		
We *can't/cannot* smoke in here.	We *couldn't/could not* smoke in here.	We *will not/won't be able to* smoke in here.
We *mustn't/must not* smoke in here.	—	
Permitted.		
We *can* smoke in here.	We *could* smoke in here.	We *will be able to* smoke in here.

Base Form	Past-Tense Form	Past Participle	Base Form	Past-Tense Form	Past Participle
be	was	been	leave	left	left
become	became	become	lend	lent	lent
begin	began	begun	let	let	let
bend	bent	bent	lose	lost	lost
bite	bit	bitten	make	made	made
blow	blew	blown	meet	met	met
break	broke	broken	pay	paid	paid
bring	brought	brought	put	put	put
build	built	built	quit	quit	quit
buy	bought	bought	read	read*	read
catch	caught	caught	ride	rode	ridden
choose	chose	chosen	ring	rang	rung
come	came	come	run	ran	run
cost	cost	cost	say	said	said
cut	cut	cut	see	saw	seen
dig	dug	dug	sell	sold	sold
do	did	done	send	sent	sent
draw	drew	drawn	shake	shook	shaken
drink	drank	drunk	shoot	shot	shot
drive	drove	driven	shut	shut	shut
eat	ate	eaten	sing	sang	sung
fall	fell	fallen	sit	sat	sat
feed	fed	fed	sleep	slept	slept
feel	felt	felt	speak	spoke	spoken
fight	fought	fought	spend	spent	spent
find	found	found	stand	stood	stood
fly	flew	flown	steal	stole	stolen
forget	forgot	forgotten	swim	swam	swum
get	got	gotten	take	took	taken
give	gave	given	teach	taught	taught
go	went	gone	tear	tore	torn
grow	grew	grown	tell	told	told
hang	hung	hung	think	thought	thought
have	had	had	throw	threw	thrown
hear	heard	heard	understand	understood	understood
hide	hid	hidden	wake	woke	woken
hit	hit	hit	wear	wore	worn
hold	held	held	win	won	won
hurt	hurt	hurt	write	wrote	written
keep	kept	kept			
know	knew	known			
lead	led	led			

* Pronounce the base form: /rid/; pronounce the past-tense form: /red/.

Answer Key (for puzzles and problems only)

Answers to Exercise 8 (page 11)

- Horses sleep standing up.
- Bats use their ears to "see."
- Scorpions have twelve eyes.
- Elephants sometimes go for four days without water.
- Swans stay with the same mates all their lives.
- Antelopes run at 70 miles per hour.
- Bears sleep during the winter months.
- Spiders live for about two years.

Answer to Opening Task (page 19)

Answers to Exercise 5 (page 25)

1. I love you.
2. I see you.
3. I hate you.
4. I hear you.
5. He knows you.
6. Are you 21?
7. I see you are too wise for me.
8. I think you are great.

UNIT 4

Answers to Exercise 10 (page 62)

1. A	5. M	9. E	13. O	17. K
2. P	6. R	10. B	14. F	18. D
3. G	7. Q	11. I	15. C	19. S
4. J	8. N	12. L	16. H	

UNIT 5

"Official" Answers to Activity 1 (page 84)

1. A giraffe passing a window.
2. A pencil seen from the end.
3. A cat climbing a tree.

UNIT 6

Solution to the Opening Task (pages 88–89)

Mrs. Meyer killed her husband. She entered the bathroom while he was brushing his teeth, and she hit him over the head with the bathroom scale. Then she turned on the shower and put the soap on the floor.
How do we know this?

• From the toothbrush: He was brushing his teeth, not walking out of the shower.
• From the soap: It was not possible to slip in this position.
• From the bathroom scale: The scale does not indicate zero.

UNIT 7

Solution to the Opening Task (pages 104–105)

LINDA	BOB	GEORGE
SUSAN	DIANA	FRANK
	CARLA	

Solution to Exercise 7 (page 159)

First, the woman should take the mouse to the car, leaving the cat with the cheese. Next, she should return and pick up the cat and take it to the car. As soon as she gets to the car with the cat, she should remove the mouse and take it with her, leaving the cat in the car. When she gets back to the shopping area, she should pick up the cheese and leave the mouse. Then she should take the cheese to the car and leave it there with the cat. Finally, she should return to collect the mouse and bring it with her to the car.

UNIT 22

Solution to Exercise 4 (page 317)

Picture B

Solution to Opening Task (pages 328–329)

Solution to the Opening Task (page 349)

Lee loves Sid.
Kit loves Tracy.

Credits

Text Credits

p. 88: From *Crime and Puzzlement* by Lawrence Treat, Illustrations by Leslie Cabarga Reprinted by permission of David R. Godine, Publisher, Inc.
Copyright © 1981 by Lawrence Treat, Illustrations by Leslie Cabarga.

p. 146: Idea from Wendy Asplin, University of Washington.

p. 176: "How not to collide with local road laws." Adapted from The European (Magazine Section), June 9, 1985.

pp. 286, 287, 291–293: Focus Boxes 1, 2, 5, 6, and 7: Ideas from *Systems in English Grammar* by Peter Master. Reprinted by permission of Prentice Hall, 1995. Ideas also from Master, P. (1990). "Teaching the English articles as a binary system." TESOL *Quarterly,* 3, pp. 461–478. Copyright © 1990 by Teachers of English to Speakers of Other Languages, Inc. Excerpt used with permission.

p. 295: Focus Box 8: Idea from "Rearticulating the articles" by Roger Berry, from ELT Journal 45, 3, 1990. Reprinted by permission of Oxford University Press: pages 252–299.

p. 306: Adapted from *Burma; A Travel Survival Kit,* by Tony Wheeler. Lonely Planet Publications, 1982.

p. 308: Adapted from *San Francisco TESOL Convention* 1990, Leslie Reichert.

p. 328: "Calvin and Hobbes." Copyright Universal Press Syndicate. Reprinted with permission.

p. 365: Idea from Betsy Branch, Melissa Anne Povey Rowden, and Gabrielle Nicas, English

Photo Credits

Page 1: The Stock Market/Tom & Deeann McCarthy. Page 5: Upper left, © Corbis/Kevin R. Morris; lower left, © Corbis/Michael Pole; lower right, © Corbis/Bob Rowan.

Page 10: Photo by Jonathan Stark, property of Heinle & Heinle.

Page 29: Photo by Jonathan Stark, property of Heinle & Heinle.

Page 48: Photo by Jonathan Stark, property of Heinle & Heinle.

Page 59: Photo by Jonathan Stark, property of Heinle & Heinle.

Page 70: © Corbis/Gail Mooney.

Page 71: Photo by Jonathan Stark, property of Heinle & Heinle.

Page 85: Photos by Jonathan Stark, property of Heinle & Heinle.

Page 96: © Corbis/Bettmann.

Page 120: © Corbis/Todd Gipstein. Page 136 © Corbis/Ellen Frank; middle left, © Corbis/Carl Corey; middle right, © Corbis/Michelle Garrett, far right, © Corbis/Richard Fukuhara.

Page 196: © Corbis/Warren Moran.

Page 226: Photo by Jonathan Stark, property of Heinle & Heinle.

Page 248: Photo by Jonathan Stark, property of Heinle & Heinle.

Page 262: Upper left, © Corbis/AFP; upper middle, © Corbis/Neal Preston; upper right, © Corbis/Neal Preston; lower left, © Corbis; lower middle, © Corbis/Neal Preston; lower right, © Corbis/Neal Preston.

Page 263: Michael Jackson, UPI/Bettmann. All other photos on this page are from *Yearbook, The Most Star-studded Graduating Class* by the Editors of *Memories Magazine*, © 1990 by Diamandix Communications, Inc. Used by permission of Doubleday, a division of Bantam Doubleday Dell Publishing Group, Inc.

Page 284: © Corbis/Joel W. Rogers.

Page 297: © Corbis/Raymond Gehman.

Page 314: Photo by Jonathan Stark, property of Heinle & Heinle.

Page 340: Photo by Jonathan Stark, property of Heinle & Heinle.

Page 348: Photo by Jonathan Stark, property of Heinle & Heinle.

Index

Use the Entire Grammar Dimensions Series

Grammar Dimensions Book 1, Platinum Edition
High Beginning
Student Text: 0-8384-0260-7
Workbook: 0-8384-0266-6
Audiocassette: 0-8384-0261-5
Teacher's Edition: 0-8384-0267-4

Grammar Dimensions Book 2, Platinum Edition
Intermediate
Student Text: 0-8384-0268-2
Workbook: 0-8384-0274-7
Audiocassette: 0-8384-0269-0
Teacher's Edition: 0-8384-0275-5

Grammar Dimensions Book 3, Platinum Edition
High Intermediate
Student Text: 0-8384-0277-1
Workbook: 0-8384-0284-4
Audiocassette: 0-8384-0278-X
Teacher's Edition: 0-8384-0285-2

Grammar Dimensions Book 4, Platinum Edition
Advanced
Student Text: 0-8384-0286-0
Workbook: 0-8384-0291-7
Audiocassette: 0-8384-0287-9
Teacher's Edition: 0-8384-0292-5

Read the Definitive Source for Grammar Reference and Teaching Guidance
The Grammar Book: An ESL/EFL Teacher's Course, Second Edition
Marianne Celce-Murcia and Diane Larsen-Freeman ISBN:0-8384-4725-2

For more information about ***Grammar Dimensions, Platinum Edition*** and
The Grammar Book, please contact your Heinle/Thomson Learning
representative or call (toll-free in the U.S.) 1-877-NEED-ESL